THE LIST

"a hero is always a hero"

MEHMET DAGCI

1st Print
May 2023

ISBN: 979-8-9883708-0-2

Design Director:
Hakan Dagci

Editor:
Levent Erkan Basegmez

I dedicate this book to my wife and children, who have supported me in all circumstances, and to all the people who did not bow down in the face of the oppressor...

I dedicate this book to my wife and children, who have supported me in all circumstances, and to all the people who did not bow down in the face of the oppressor...

PREFACE

There have been many tragedies throughout the history of humanity; many influential individuals have resorted to despotic methods to fortify their power. They have slaughtered thousands or millions without hesitation, aiming at the lives of innocent people. Millions of people who became imprisoned in their homeland had to take refuge in foreign lands to be protected from the persecution of these despotic regimes. Thus, it is appropriate to say that history has been written with the blood, tears, and lives of the communities that have been tyrants' victims.

However, the masses – dragged into poverty, misery, nothingness, and death – have become the actors of a resurrection saga each time, rising from their ashes like a phoenix. Every society that built a civilization has always had a story written with pain. But many of these stories were the beginning of happy endings or the harbinger of great births.

In the Republic of Turkey's hundred-year history, rulers who turned to despotism have focused on polarization and witch hunts. They tagged and segregated the society based on people's religious and ethnic affiliations, such as secular, atheist, Alevi, minority, Kurdish, leftist, rightist, or socialist. These innocent people were oppressed, had their freedoms stolen, and were ostracized because of their beliefs, identities, and dissident views.

The modern version of this persecution tradition occurred when the coup attempt happened on July 15, 2016. People whose hearts were full of patriotism and who would not hesitate to sacrifice their lives were declared traitors overnight. Hundreds of thousands of innocent people who had nothing to do with the coup were purged from public service; their property was confiscated, and they were imprisoned and subjected to severe torture. A modern witch hunt began with the rule of law was put aside. Many innocent people, including pregnant women, newborn babies, thousands of children, and seniors with disabilities, were targeted without any grounds. All the while, the institutions of the state collapsed, its resources were plundered, and the people were condemned to poverty.

This book will express the author's steadfast support and sympathy for all innocent people who fell victim to these acts of discrimination. The author firmly believes they will rise from their ashes, and his story will serve as a harbinger of the dawn of a new era. This book will, hopefully, also shed some light on how the ties of the heart run more profound than the ties of blood, with great examples of human solidarity among nations of different languages, colors, and religions.

The author, who has suffered the same fate as many of the persecuted citizens of Turkey – his homeland- believes this empathy and solidarity is one of the best ways to end these acts of discrimination and segregation. It will also turn all human differences into a new kind of wealth to reach better days under peace, tranquility, democracy, and law.

As a soldier who has served his country and the cause of world peace for twenty-four years, the author hopes that this book, based on his life and the events he has witnessed, will be the voice of millions of people who have been wronged. Hopefully, one day, this dark period will dissipate with the first light of the expected dawn, and the sun of truth will rise with all its brightness... one day.

THE LIST

Virginia Beach, USA, November 22, 2016

I woke up at around 3 am to hear my phone ringing. When the thought of "I must be dreaming" subsided, the phone rang incessantly and stubbornly. I got out of bed and answered the phone. It was my brother-in-law, Ahmet.

Although an in-law, we were like brothers for nearly 20 years. He was with us in our difficult times and comforted me with his mindset to not make any struggle into a larger problem by saying, "We'll overcome this, brother."

For the first time, there was concern in Ahmet's voice.

"Is everything all right? Are you okay?" I asked.

He ignored my question.

I asked again, "Ahmet, are you okay? Is everything ok?"

He was finally able to speak.

"It was published in the Official Gazette, and you are on the list!"

Then I understood why Ahmet's voice was different and the mood he was in.

The list…

This short four-letter word was the keyword of very tough encryption.

It embodied many changes that were about to happen in our lives. Now I would not have a job, a passport, insurance, a hometown to go to, friends who were so close, my uniform, identity card, career, or dreams. In short, the life I had worked and built for a lifetime would not be there anymore… because of the list.

7

That night, thousands of miles from home my homeland, I was purged from public service in Turkey with a Decree-Law. This simple phrase "on the list," which had 15,600 other names, was equivalent to a death sentence for my family and me at the time, and it is still valid for many innocent people in Turkey. I was declared a traitor by an ad-hoc court established without a lawyer, prosecutor, or judge. There was no formal accusation against me, and I was even deprived of the fundamental human right to defend myself. The worst part was that the whole of Turkish and international society kept silent in the face of this injustice.

How could they think that I betrayed my country after I protected it for 24 years, two months, and 22 days, and for which I made all kinds of sacrifices without hesitation?

Just 15 months earlier, I was selected among thousands of officers and appointed to the NATO ACT headquarters in Norfolk, Virginia, representing the Republic of Turkey and the Turkish Armed Forces (TAF). I entered the United States with a diplomatic passport and started my next tour of duty.

I was startled by Ahmet's voice. After a short silence, I unconsciously said, "Don't worry, let's hope for the best," and hung up.

I hadn't turned on any lights in the house. My wife, Hatice, slept in the bedroom with our daughter, Nilgun. Our sons, Hakan and Fatih, were downstairs, unaware of the unfolding events, perhaps breathing softly in an innocent dream. I went back to the bedroom with silent steps and woke up Hatice. "We are on the list," I said as she opened her eyes to the darkness of the night.

That one word was enough for her to understand everything. For five months, we witnessed thousands of teachers, lawyers, doctors, police, nurses, and officers being dismissed daily. Thousands of dreams and decades of effort were being suppressed and destroyed by a single line on a "list." The regime declared anyone it saw as their opposition traitors and purged them from public service. The supporters of the regime and its lawless acts were rubbing their hands with the greedy expectations of filling positions.

This apocalypse in state institutions continued exponentially in every part of society. Many companies and private enterprises were seized and plundered. The five months after that fated night in November 2016 were the most challenging period of my life.

In the meantime, I was trying to represent my country at NATO Allied Command Transformation (ACT) headquarters. On the other hand, I was saying goodbye to my friends who were discharged like those whose plugs were pulled in the movie "The Matrix." My temples throbbed as I wondered how my country could escape this terrible situation. With each list and each plug pulled, there was dead silence in the headquarters. My colleagues from other countries were asking questions, one after another, to try to understand the situation.

What was the regime's intention? What kind of connection could the personnel, each at the top of their profession working thousands of miles away, have to the coup?

Was Turkey considering leaving NATO?

What happened on July 15?

Who attempted the coup?

Was the coup real?

What did all this mean?

The List

DECEPTION

Taurus Mountains, Turkey, July 15, 2016

These moments were my favorite times of the day. I am at the summit of the Taurus Mountains in southern Turkey, about three hours from the Mediterranean coast. Here at night, there is no light except for the stars and the reflections from a few houses in the distance, and at a time when everyone is asleep, I enjoy the magical moment of peace when a glass of Turkish tea accompanies me.

I have found this peace at the summit of the Taurus Mountains and the vast waters of the Indian Ocean. At the summit of the Taurus, the stars are amazing. After taking another sip of tea and listening to the sweet tunes of the night for the last time, I made eye contact with my favorite star, the Pole Star. And then I finished my tea and went inside.

It had gotten late, and everyone was already asleep.

Not only were the stars of the Taurus beautiful, but the sleep there was also extraordinary. If you were tired from spending time in the garden all day, a sweet heaviness would settle in with the dusk. As soon as I walked inside, the smell of pine was replaced by the smell of new furniture and paint.

We built our first house at the summit of the Taurus Mountains. It was a special place where we came every summer, where I met my wife for the first time. My mother-in-law would greet us with tears of joy each time we visited and prepare our room in a cheerful rush.

In their two-bedroom house, they would give us their bedroom, move themselves into the smallest room where a bed could barely fit, and make beds for the children in the living room. In every conversation, they would say, "I wish we could build a house here and be neighbors." We all dreamt of a future where this was a reality.

My father-in-law would tell me, "Mehmet, the house is your home, but you need to find a place you like. Let's be neighbors with you." He continued to fan his dreams.

Since my money was barely enough to support my family, we did not dare lay a foundation. Every year, we would be guests in the modest house of my in-laws, where they opened their hearts to us as permanent guests, and we would visit where we were engaged.

When I learned I would be appointed to a NATO post, we decided to build a house, relying on the salary we would receive there. It was a bittersweet joy for us. We lost my mother-in-law to cancer a few years ago. These lands, where our love sprouted, seemed to have lost its mystery with her absence. We had considered my mother-in-law's wish to be a neighbor as a testament and planned to build our house right next to her house, her precious memory. Since this house would be our first home, we would dream until the morning, and one night we decided on its plan. We were able to buy the starting material with installments on our credit cards, and we were able to finish the rough construction before going to the USA. This house would reconcile us with the Taurus, and we could raise our children here, just like my mother-in-law.

We brought household goods to this house while it was under construction since our NATO assignment was only for two years. We were so excited. I remember dreaming that this assignment would end in two years and that I could start living here.

My father-in-law was even more enthusiastic than we were. During our absence, he coordinated the construction work and started to complete the other missing parts of the house. In the United States, we had a one-time hometown visit leave, and the Armed Forces covered the plane tickets. We decided to keep the tradition and come to the Taurus Mountains for a summer vacation.

With this vacation, we would satisfy our longing for our homeland, visit family, friends, and relatives, and sit in our new home for the first time. With this in mind, we again loaded our credit cards, completed the rest of the house, and bought furniture to meet our needs. After all, one year later, our overseas assignment was over, and we would be moving in permanently.

We planned to pay off the debts in the second year of the NATO deployment and save a little money. With the sweet excitement of our dreams, it was just two weeks before the surprising July 15 coup attempt that we spent our first night in our new home in the Taurus Mountains. We were so excited to host guests in our house from the first evening, and we opened our home to those who opened their doors to us. We devoted most of our days to housework, but Hatice and I took peaceful walks to our private places. And we hosted guests almost every evening. Neither of us had the slightest sign of fatigue. Our children liked their rooms very much, especially Hakan. He had an extreme dislike of insects, and he enjoyed our new insect-protected house. As always, we put the children to sleep, and Hatice and I chatted for a while under the stars. But tonight, Hatice went to sleep early, exhausted from the day. I thought I'd watch TV before going to bed. But I could not understand the images before me when I turned on the TV.

A few tanks and some soldiers blocked one side of the Bosphorus Bridge, which spans the Bosphorus Strait and connects Europe and Asia.

The speaker on the TV was trying to convey this situation that she could not understand. Bridge traffic continued to flow in the other direction as usual, and the soldiers stood there, unsure of what to do. "It must be a military drill," I thought.

Just as I was about to turn off the TV, the announcer connected to Ankara, the region where the Turkish General Staff Headquarters and other Military Service Headquarters were located. The images were stranger this time because the announcer reported that the

Turkish Armed Forces was attempting a coup. Military buildings were surrounded by police vehicles and ambulances. The announcer stated that there were low-flying military jets and helicopters in the skies of Ankara. Gradually, all channels began to broadcast news of the coup by cutting off their broadcast streams. With the TV remote in my hand, I was stunned. The summit of the Taurus Mountains was frozen. The thoughts in my mind had begun to scatter like snowflakes brought by the strong winds.

These lands were accustomed to coups. The military coups of 1960 and 1980 and the postmodern coup of February 28 were examples of the direct involvement of the military in politics in our recent history. For this reason, almost every adult in Turkey, depending on age, has witnessed one or more military interventions.

I was a child during the 1980 coup, and during the February 28 coup, I was already an ensign in the Navy. In both cases, the absolute power and dominance of the military could be felt from the very first moment.

In the images on the screen, it was clear that the control was not in the military but with the police, the politicians who appeared on the screens one after the other, and finally, President Erdogan.

There needed to be more clarity in the WhatsApp group I was a member of, which included my classmates from the Naval Academy class of 1996. Everyone was asking who the coup plotters were and trying to understand the situation. The situation was so complicated that one of my classmates, the Turkish Warship Sokullu Mehmet Pasha's Commander, asked what he should do in the group chat because he could not get any orders from his regular chain of command. His ship was in transit to Russia to participate in an exercise in the Black Sea, and he could not reach anyone in authority to get final orders.

Hatice woke up to the sound of the television and came to the living room. After staring at the screen for a while, worrying, she asked me, "Is this a military coup?" I hugged her tenderly and anxiously muttered, "A coup is being staged against the military."

In the new images transmitted from different parts of the country, we saw that the military units were surrounded by police vehicles, garbage trucks, ambulances, and construction equipment. The military personnel was so unaware of the situation that an acquaintance of mine, who was on duty in eastern Turkey then, called me and asked, "What's going on? The televisions say it's a coup. We did not receive an order. What should I do?" He was trying desperately to get an idea from me.

While the chaos in the Class of 1996 WhatsApp group continued, some officers, to benefit from the coup and who later became favorites of the regime, dared to say, "Ours!"

I sent the following message to the group: "Friends! Anyone who aims their guns at their people can never be right. This coup is against our nation. So never be a part of this process." A few friends expressed, "Mehmet is telling the truth." They supported my statement. And later that night, the unfolding events proved me right, "This coup was being staged against the military and the Turkish nation."

Meanwhile, we were startled by the call to prayer echoing from the mosque's loudspeaker. The call for the night prayer had already been recited, and there was still much time until the morning call to prayer, but there was a call to prayer being recited from the mosque; chants and salutations followed. I have never seen something like this in my entire life since there is no scheduled prayer.

How could it be that the mosque imam of a quiet village on the top of the Taurus Mountains was calling the people to the streets by chanting the call to prayer and salutations simultaneously with all the other imams in Turkey? There was no military unit or military activity here. The people being invited out on the streets would protect who against whom? I checked the door's locks because I was the only soldier in the neighborhood who had come to his hometown to take his annual leave. Suddenly, I felt a chill and wanted to hug Hatice and my children tightly. The night I had already become one of the longest nights of my life. Just a few hours ago, I was looking at the clear light of the stars, thinking about how relative the concept of time can be.

As the events unfolded, the concept of time got heavier and heavier; every news report increased the pitch blackness of the night, and after a while, time had almost stopped. President Erdogan urged people to gather in the streets; millions were out that evening. In the morning, televisions showed admirals and generals who were tortured, their heads covered in blood and their throats cut, and half-naked soldiers lying on the ground. There were strangely dressed, bearded people who trampled on their heads like hyenas swarming with their prey and lowering their belts and sticks onto the soldiers' backs, shouting victory on top of the tanks.

I was also shocked to hear that there were thousands of arrest warrants for judges and prosecutors, and the police were storming their homes to arrest them. These arrest warrants could not be prepared overnight, and why were these people targeted? How could it be proven so quickly that they had anything to do with the coup? With each piece of news, our level of sadness and desperation increased. The number of civilians who lost their lives grew every minute, and more than two hundred deaths were reported. There was complete chaos and confusion, and every image that fell on the screens reinforced the pain in my heart and the questions in my mind.

I thought of the moment in the 1980 military coup when the Chief of General Staff, Kenan Evren, announced the coup. That morning, there was not a single person on the streets except for the military. Even at a time when communication was much more limited, the military took control of everywhere within hours. Everyone, more or less, knew how a coup was done and the aftermath that followed.

How could a group of less than 2000, mostly low-ranking privates and Military Academy students, attempt a coup that was likely unsuccessful in the evening hours when influential politicians were outside Ankara and the people were on the streets?

This event, which caused turmoil and plunged the country into abysmal darkness, was described by Erdogan as a "gift from God." A witch hunt of a magnitude that the Republic of Turkey had never seen before began. I couldn't take my eyes off the screen for even a minute and was devastated by the images of my fellow soldiers in arms being tortured. I couldn't hold back my tears any longer and started to cry.

The day had already dawned, and the famous winds of the Taurus Mountains had begun to blow through the branches of the great pine trees. I started every day by going out early in the morning and rushing to get the first hot pita out of the local brick oven bread store amid the smell of resin and the sharp winds; this morning, I hadn't even opened my window. I felt like I was in a scene from the movie Bird Box as if the whole town was covered with an indescribable black power that would destroy me when I looked into its eyes.

This feeling, accompanied by indescribable anxiety, anger, and uncertainty, was gnawing at my brain. No one called me. My first job was to call my unit in America. I reached Colonel Huseyin Seslikaya, the senior Turkish officer at the NATO Allied Transformation Command Headquarters and asked him what was happening. He was more surprised than me. He said he had no information and worried about my safety when he saw the tortured soldiers.

What kind of feeling was this? A soldier serving at NATO to represent the Republic of Turkey, who devoted his life to serving his country, had become worried about the safety of his life in his own country.

I thought of a song by a famous Turkish folk singer, Ahmet Kaya, "What a grave contradiction, mother!" Ahmet Kaya was the first singer I adored at the age of 13. I bought his albums and admired his voice and commentary. He sang about injustice and oppression in his songs and expressed them without fear. His courage connected him to me, and even though I was an officer, I did not hesitate to listen to his songs even when he was considered an outcast. I would share with my friends my beliefs that the country could only come to light with peace, tolerance, respect, and justice. The songs of the hero singer of my youth, Ahmet Kaya, came to my rescue and translated my feelings that I had difficulty putting into words. I found myself in a dark whirlpool, full of contradictions, with no end in sight. I would never have thought I would experience these feelings on our first days at home, which we had dreamt about for years. We had such beautiful dreams about our little house. Now our house was surrounded by haze, suspicion, and hatred; we had entered a dark tunnel where time traveled slower than an oxcart.

DANCE WITH THE FIRE

Taurus Mountains, Turkey, July 16, 2016

The first person I came across in the morning was a relative of my wife. Whenever he saw me, he would ask me how I was doing and always address me with a "sir" beside my name.

He would always tell me how sacred my duty as a soldier was. That morning, there was neither affection in his eyes nor the word "sir" beside my name. He commented, "Captain, we have praised the Armed Forces for years, but they have harbored many traitors." He stared at me suspiciously, searching for something, wondering what I would say.

"We don't know what's going on; there is no mobilization in the military other than a few reports on television. I'm still trying to understand the situation," I replied.

As soon as I finished my words, "All these traitors must be hanged!" he continued.

How did everything change overnight? Those who just yesterday put their soldiers in the highest positions and praised them were eager to put a noose on the soldier's head today the morning of the previous night, which was already full of contradictions, had turned even darker than the night.

The people continued to be called to the streets, and images of tortured commanders, who had served their country and world peace for years, were being shown on screens and social media. The houses and lodgings of officers and non-commissioned officers were stormed, and hundreds of military officers trained in the Military Academy were loaded into buses and detained. The little chaos unfolding in Ankara and

Istanbul was now spreading to every corner of the country by Erdogan and his supporters. When the public saw a person who seemed to have a military haircut, they would attempt to lynch him without question. The situation had become so brutal that a high-ranking clergyman, a fervent supporter of the regime, could issue a 'fatwa' saying, "These soldiers' wives and daughters are now halal (permissible) for us." He tried to compromise the honor of the families of his own country's soldiers.

I was calling my friends one by one, hoping to get some news. However, the WhatsApp group was silent, and all my calls went unanswered. The Taurus Mountains, which have always been peaceful, started to cover me, and all its weight fell on my shoulders like a scepter. "I have to do something," I was saying to myself. There had to be something to stop this chaos, to end this apocalypse. Every minute, the bad news continued incessantly. President Erdogan declared that Fethullah Gulen, a cleric in exile in the US, and his supporters in the military had planned and carried out the coup. For this reason, hundreds of schools, dormitories, stationeries, and hospitals affiliated with the Gulen movement were looted throughout the day. Those who worked in these places were arrested on a whim. The fact that those who participated in the apparent coup attempt were detained pending trial was understandable as a first reaction. However, what kind of crime could a teacher, doctor, lawyer, journalist, bureaucrat, and tens of thousands of civilians working at almost all levels of the state have committed deserve to be subjected to this persecution?

The why and how questions kept increasingly gnawing in my mind, so much so that I felt like a traveler in the desert longing for a drop of water. I needed just the slightest answer to keep my sanity intact. I couldn't reach anyone and didn't know what to do. I felt my soul-crushing under the weight of these feelings that invaded my mind.

I was startled by my father-in-law's voice. He was asking Hatice about me. I looked at myself in the mirror before walking from the bedroom to the living room. It looked like I aged overnight, just like in the movies. My eyes were sunken from lack of sleep and crying; the whites of my eyes were bloodshot, and the white hair on my temples seemed to have become prominent. There was anger and anxiety on my face that I couldn't hide even if I tried. I wore the same clothes for two days. That was the only thing that felt familiar at this point. When I met my father-in-law's eyes, I saw a similar anxiety and panic on his face. He asked, "Mehmet, what is going on, my dear? How will these things end?" He asked. Without waiting for an answer, he mentioned that he went to the mosque for the morning prayer and that many people asked about me. The government-controlled media and prominent political figures were fueling hostility towards military personnel. I was next to them, a high-ranking naval officer who happened to be posted at a NATO Headquarters during the coup. I was sure they wanted to say many things about me or even harm my family and me. Millions all over the country were captivated by the images they had seen on TV, and angry crowds filled the streets. They had become capable of committing any crime the regime instructed without question. The people in this small remote village were no different. My father-in-law felt this too, and even though he didn't speak it out loud, I could feel that he began to worry that something might happen to us.

Meanwhile, the regime revoked all official leaves for government employees, and all members of the Turkish Armed Forces were ordered to report to their institutions at once and start working. This step was plausible as a natural reflex in such an extraordinary situation. However, as we would witness in the coming days, tens of thousands of people returning to their duties were arrested one by one as if they were being lured into a trap and tortured for days in gymnasiums that had turned into prisoner concentration camps.

My situation remained uncertain. Since I was serving at NATO, I had to change my plane ticket. After the coup attempt, the United States suspended all commercial and military flights from Turkey. Although I wanted to return to my post immediately, this option seemed impossible under these conditions. I had finally made my decision. At any cost, I would go to Ankara, where all military service headquarters were located, and try to reach my friends there. At least I could find out from the headquarters if they had any instructions.

While explaining this decision to Hatice, I asked her to give me her blessing and take care of our children and herself if anything happened to me. She looked me in the eyes like a mother sending her child to the front line in a battle and said, "If you can do even the slightest thing to fix this situation, go and don't worry about us."

Although we didn't say it, we knew this might be the last time we saw each other. Hatice once again proved herself as a great military spouse; she was able to control her feelings and agreed to let me go with the hope that we could do something to stop this unfortunate course. I left without wasting any time. It did not take too long before I arrived in Yahyali, a small town on the foothills of the Taurus Mountains. I was born and raised in this beautiful town and had great memories and friends here, but now I floored the gas pedal as if I was passing through enemy territory. I didn't want anyone to see me; I didn't know what people I knew as friends would think of me now as an officer. I had no minute to waste; I wanted to reach Ankara immediately.

Every time I saw police officers or military police on the road, I had a rush of adrenaline with the thought of being stopped and detained. I felt like an outlaw, I slowed down for a while so they wouldn't feel suspicious, and then I accelerated again.

I was hoping to find something that could calm the storm inside me. As soon as I entered Ankara, I went to military housing in Oran, which was on my way. I couldn't reach any friends by phone, so I could go to a friend's house and talk about the unfolding events before I went to the Naval Headquarters. Although Oran military housings were built on one of the highest points of Ankara, it was a favorite housing for many military personnel due to its proximity and access to many public spaces. Thousands of officers and non-commissioned officers working in the service headquarters and the General Staff lived in these housings. I lived there for a year in 2005. Amid all the confusion and chaos, my memory took me back to those days, and even if it was for the slightest moment, I was relieved of the tremendous weight of this moment and returned to my years spent here. However, this little dream of mine was over very quickly.

When I approached the entrance gate, there was no sound except sirens. The gate was full of police cars, and instead of the regular military guards, there were heavily armed police forces. Their faces and looks were reminiscent of the police officers I had seen on television since the morning of July 16, next to the tortured soldiers.

Suddenly, like a patient awakened by electroshock, I came to my senses and began to rethink my plan. I realized, again, that this was not a military coup against the regime but a coup against the military personnel and their families.

I had rushed into Ankara under these conditions, and here I was at the center of the witch hunt. What was I thinking?

What a mistake this was!

All my friends in the military could have been arrested already or were dealing with the same ordeal in the midst of chaos and uncertainty.

I brought myself here, and it felt like I was offering a golden opportunity to the regime. I saw the news headlines: "A high-ranking naval officer serving in NATO was arrested trying to escape." Under these conditions, they could accuse me of anything.

Even though I was in the Taurus Mountains the day before and had nothing to do with the coup, they could portray me as someone who organized a coup in Ankara on behalf of NATO. Prime Minister Binali Yildirim and President Recep Tayyip Erdogan had already made a veiled accusation against the United States and NATO for setting up this coup. I could be used as proof of these false and baseless statements and be subject to various forms of torture. The pictures and videos of tortured military personnel were on all TV news channels, and this very threat was also genuine and imminent to me.

I felt like my brain was processing the events just like in the movie

Limitless, looking for a way out of the situation I had fallen into.

I steered the car away from the gate and continued to drive away. It felt like all eyes were on me. I wasn't even changing lanes to avoid attracting attention. I knew how futile this was. I was driving in a car that had an out-of-state license plate. Tragically, a bitter smile appeared on my face for the first time. I was trying not to attract attention while driving a car with an unusual "01(Adana)" out-of-state license plate in Ankara, where almost every car had the standard "06 (Ankara)" license plate.

Those who plotted the coup attempted to put their plans into action and arrested valuable military leaders and personnel who could have improved the situation. The number of those detained at the end of the first day had exceeded tens of thousands because there was little resistance against them.

Leaving Ankara was the best decision. Before sunset, I looked around one last time. It may be the last time I see Ankara. Like fulfilling a prisoner's last wish, I engraved Ankara in all its splendor in my tired eyes.

On my way back, I called Hatice. She said that no one came and that people were in awkward silence. I wanted to know if anyone had asked about me. She said that neighbors asked and that she told them that I was going to buy something from the city.

While debating in my mind how I could manage this process, I saw the lights of the police cars. I had just left Ankara and had not even reached Kirikkale. The police officer standing in the middle of the road with a strong flashlight was signaling me to pull the car to the right.

They had received warrants to stop every vehicle leaving Ankara and search for the cars. Five or six other cars were pulled over in front of me. I started to floor the gas pedal with all my power and tried to escape. I couldn't believe what I was going through or thinking.

In my homeland, where I came to have a little rest on my annual leave, I had become a fugitive overnight and was trying to fight my crazy thoughts, each one different from the other. At that time, the news started on the radio, and it was reported that several thousand military personnel were arrested.

Being a high-ranking staff officer was a sufficient criterion for being arrested at the time. Here I was, also trying to leave Ankara with a car with a "City of Adana" license plate. While the police officer was walking towards the car, the last couple of days flashed through my mind: Hatice's face, eyes, and words when she bid farewell to me.

In ordinary police patrols, the first question is usually "Where did you come from" and "Where you are going," followed by whether you have a driver's license or why you were speeding. This time it was different. The police officer said they "stopped and interrogated all vehicles leaving Ankara per direct instructions." The first question was, "What is your job?" I was content with the direction my destiny would take me, and I said, "I am a naval officer," despite the thoughts running through my mind. When the police officer asked where I served, I said I was on duty at the NATO HQ in USA and was still on vacation. When he asked why all the soldiers were called to duty and why I was still here, I said I had come to Ankara to receive a final order and would return when my vacation was over. He was unsatisfied with my response, "Do you have a permit?" He asked. I took out my permit from my wallet and handed it over. He took the document and told me to wait in the vehicle. With my permit in hand, he headed toward the other police officers.

Even though minutes passed, they continued to talk amongst themselves while I was now waiting as the only vehicle left. Perhaps they had been satisfied with the size of the prey that had fallen into their hands and did not bother stopping other cars passing by. Once again, I could see the headlines in the newspapers; "US-linked high-ranking officer was caught fleeing Ankara." Once again, the thought of flooring the gas pedal and breaking through the police barricade crossed my mind. However, my permit was in the hands of the police, and in such a case, I would give them more reasons to be declared a traitor. Again, I decided to wait for the end that fate had prepared for me. After long minutes that felt like years, the police officer came to the car, and at that moment, something I never expected happened. "Commander, as you know, the whole country and public are very confused due to the coup. It can be dangerous to travel alone in this way, be careful," he said, allowing me to go on my way by handing me my permit.

The night was full of surprises. I slowly drove away, trying not to reflect the confusion going through my mind. I still couldn't believe it. From feeling like I was drowning at the bottom of a blind well, within an hour, I was on my way to the Taurus Mountains to be reunited with my wife and children. This joy did not last long. I still had more than 400 km to go, and if there was a police check at every city entrance and exit, it was inevitable that I would reencounter the same situation, either in Kirsehir or Kayseri. I thought, "I wish I could teleport myself or be a bird and fly." After driving a little further, I thought traveling at night would be much riskier, so I decided to wait for the morning in my car at a gas station. With the effect of what I had experienced, I was now exhausted, and I could not keep my eyelids open. When I opened my eyes after a restless sleep, the sun was beginning to rise.

Even in the middle of July, the nights were frosty in Anatolia, but the first light of the day in the morning gradually reduced the severity of the frost, and the smell of soil wrapped the air. For a moment, I forgot everything. The morning was so calm despite all the stress I endured. "I must be on my way as soon as possible," I thought because I had disappeared for a day, and I was sure that this would not go unnoticed by the villagers. Contrary to the previous day, I arrived in Kayseri without encountering a police or military police vehicle. I had never turned on the radio. I was afraid of hearing bad news. I was trying to get away from the situation I was in. With these feelings eating me up, I arrived at the Yahyali sign. I was in the place where I was born and grew up, where I spent the difficult years of my childhood. I never thought that one day I would experience days harder than those days. At that moment, I felt like driving the car to my childhood home, to my father's house. However, the people had already filled the square and taken to the streets under the name of a so-called democracy watch. I was a child of this land. I knew almost everyone and would chat briefly with the people I saw and met whenever I came. However, at the moment, I was unsure what my friends or relatives thought of me. I continued to drive on the highway without taking a last glance at my childhood home. With every mile, I moved away from Yahyali, a feeling I couldn't resist within me was taking me back to my youth, to the years when I struggled with poverty, loneliness, and destiny.

The List

UNLIVED CHILDHOOD
Yahyali, Turkey, 1970s

The first thing that came to mind was the endless fights between my mother and father. They were forced into an arranged marriage when they were still only children, and when they were at an age where they could not even manage their feelings, they had to work with each other.

My mother was only 17 when I was born. I spent my childhood in a room used as a kitchen, bedroom, and living room under my grandparents' two-story house. Although my grandfather had many grandchildren, he loved me very much. I remember, though vaguely, that he always brought me candy or a snack every time he came from the store. When my grandfather was alive, he would get involved in my parents' fights before they got bigger and somehow take control of the situation. My grandfather died when I was five years old. I remember that the front of our house was filled with a vast crowd, and I watched from the room's window on the second floor while his body was being washed. It would be my last goodbye. Everything in my life began to change rapidly after my grandfather's death. The first change was that we moved upstairs. My grandmother said, "I'm all alone anyway. One room is enough for me," and went downstairs. We had a two-bedroom house for the first time. Then my brother Ramazan was born. He was named after my grandfather. One Ramazan left the two-story house, and a new Ramazan joined us the following year. I realized at a young age that life is just a journey. Even though the house remained in its place, the passengers were changing, and no one stayed in their room forever.

The fights between my parents started to become more frequent and lasted longer. My father started being treated for chronic schizophrenia, which worsened at certain times of the year. His condition did not improve because he did not take his medications regularly or keep track of his doctor's appointments. I saw school as an escape from home. After the bell rang at the end of the school day, I would spend my day playing soccer outside until late in the evening. The scale of the fights between my parents had reached violence. Thinking that I was now a grown man, I would try to interfere in those fights even though I was seven years old and trying to protect my mother in my tiny mind. I failed each time, and I was also beaten and would wait in the corner of the house for my father to calm down. My mother's family took over the situation and asked us to move to Adana. They thought we would be better off with them. Thus, in the third grade of primary school, I found myself in a completely different place, Kozan, where the sour smell of lemon blossoms surrounded the air during winter. This change was initially suitable for all of us. My father had started working at a job, and my mother had a refreshed hope to live with the comfort of being close to her relatives. My brother, Emrah, was born during this period. Emrah did not take his name from anyone. However, when my father went to Yahyali to get his newborn baby's identity card, he forgot what he would name the baby. Thinking head-to-head with the civil registration officer, they had my brother's name registered on the identity card as Serdal. Thus, from that day on, my brother would be known as Emrah at home and Serdal at school and all other official business.

As our lives were getting in order, my father's illness recurred, and the fights started again. This time, the intensity of the arguments had changed a little. My mother would run upstairs to my grandparents each time, and we, the three brothers, were waiting for my father to calm down like ships in the middle of a storm. In the following days, my father decided that coming to Adana was not a good idea and moved back to Yahyali. Since schools were closed, I would stay at my aunt's house in Adana. The school was the only thing that kept me alive. No matter how severe the storms at home were, I somehow found peace at school. Despite what I went through in my personal life, I managed to be a very successful student. When I was in school, I became a different person, and even though I started school two years early, I could take the lead against my older classmates. After completing third grade, one summer evening, I said goodbye to my aunt and returned to our home in Yahyali.

My grandfather had brought me home, and we had breakfast with the whole family in the morning. Surprisingly, everything seemed calm. However, I was unaware that this day would be one of the darkest days of my life. After breakfast, my mother and father would go to the courthouse, the judge would decide on their divorce in a hearing, and this family gathered around the same breakfast table in the morning, would disperse, never to come together again.

It was a coincidence that a large crowd gathered in our street for the funeral of our neighbor's daughter, who was in a traffic accident on the same day. As always, I watched this uproar from the window of the upper floor, trying to observe and understand people's reactions to death. At that moment, a police car stopped in front of our house. It was my grandfather and my mother. The crowd forgot about the funeral, and curious eyes turned to the police car. Our eyes met when my mother came upstairs and took the suitcase she had prepared earlier. "Take care of your brother Ramazan," she said to me.. Since Emrah was still a baby, she took him in her arms. We hugged for the last time. My mother's tears wet my cheeks, and after I had experienced the same thing with my grandfather, I sent my mother off from the window of that small room. I was entering a period where I had to sail through rough seas alone. With Ramazan, we were dropped in the middle of an ocean, with no island in sight. Ramazan was only three years old, and it had been a few weeks since I turned nine. I can't remember anything about that evening or the following few weeks. My mind had erased that period to get over the trauma. All I remember is that we moved from the upper to the lower floor again and tried to start a new life with my grandmother in the one-room house.

In my mother's absence, my father abandoned life entirely and could not accept the reality of divorce. Most of the time, he did not come home or communicate with us. My 70-year-old grandmother became both a mother and a father to us. She was trying to make a living in the house by weaving rugs with her trembling hands, but it was not enough. So, I started a shoeshine business at just nine years old. Life didn't care about my age, and it expected me to carry a load that was even too heavy for an adult. Shining shoes after school and on the weekends made enough money to buy a few loaves of bread from the grocery store. But there was a problem. The money I earned ran out the day I earned it, and I had no pennies to set aside. One day, I ran inside a bank in the middle of the bazaar and asked the teller, "Can I hide my money here?" The middle-aged banker, smiling with a mother's affection, said, "If you become a big man in the future, you will make money, and you can save it here. But now is your time to play with your friends and have fun." These words came out of her mouth because she could not see the shoeshine box on my shoulder from behind the counter.

"No, I'm making money. I shine shoes, but when I buy bread at the grocery store on the way home, it just goes away," I said. The banker understood the situation. "I will open an account for you now. Bring some money you earn here, and we will save it for you. If you want to withdraw your money, you must come with your mom or dad. Deal?" she said. I opened my first bank account at nine and saved a few cents a day.

An indescribable sadness covered the house in the evenings, but my grandmother was telling tales to Ramazan and me every night. In a way, she wanted to tackle this sadness in the air and disperse it. Every fairy tale takes us to distant lands from our life, and we somehow forget the situation we were in, adopt the identity of a fairy tale hero, and fall asleep. When the sun came up, the struggle for survival rose with it. Although the school was heaven for me to escape reality, having no parents always haunted me: I had to wear the same un-ironed trousers and school shirt every day, and I had messy hair.

The winters in Central Anatolia were very harsh, and everything got even more difficult at home when winter came. Some days, we could not find any firewood or coal at home, and I would go to the foothills of the Taurus Mountains to collect wood. My cousins would come with me some days, but mostly I would go alone. How could I have spent a whole day alone in the mountains covered with snow that reached my height? I need help understanding even today. At the end of every hard day, when I entered the house with a shekel of wood, my grandmother greeted me like a hero. I'd need to remember my cold hands, wet shoes, and snow-covered hair. "I am a grown man now," I would say to myself. This must have been a grain of truth because I would listen to and often interrupt the elders' conversations. They would joke around with me, saying, 'This child has an old head on young shoulders; he has an idea about everything."

What I went through really matured me. Unlike other children, I had become responsible and aware of everything. I would read any book I could find and follow the national agenda, including the news of the day that I would listen to from the old radio in our house. Since we couldn't turn on the lights after my grandmother went to sleep, I used to put the radio next to my bed, listen to the radio theater known as "Back to Tomorrow" on low volume, and dream of being the hero in this theater. I used to dream of being on this radio one day. When I thought of my mother's absence, I would try to make sense of her departure. Why did she leave us? I was not able to accept the situation.

Two years passed with these questions, hectic days, and deep dreams, and I finished primary school as class valedictorian. This result, which deserves wonderful celebrations in a typical environment, meant little in Yahyali. Most low-income families sent their children to work as apprentices, and only a few of my relatives went to middle school. The mine extracted from the Taurus Mountains was the main livelihood of almost the entire town, and families sent their children to work as apprentices in this industry. Those who were relatively well-off worked as chauffeurs in their father's trucks. As the child of a low-income family, it was my turn to start as an assistant in the mining industry, and the option of continuing to middle school had not even occurred to me. However, the school was everything to me. It was my hope, my dream, the only place where I could escape the harsh realities of life and enjoy every minute of my time. I wanted to go to school and change my destiny. My father was firmly against me going to middle school. "Who will pay for all the books and notebooks?" he would say. The registration period was about to expire, and no one around me saw, felt, or shared the desire to go to school that was burning like a fire in me. Only my grandmother supported me as she always has. "I will do my best. Finish your registration in the school, and the rest is God's grace," she said. I felt so helpless. It occurred to me to report the situation to my primary school teacher. I left the house and rushed to Mr. Dervis' room. I said, "Teacher, I want to attend school, but everyone is against it. They say, 'Are you going to go to school and become unemployed?' My father does not want to be my guardian for the school." I sounded tearful, but it was loud enough to show my determination. Mr. Dervis looked at me and said calmly and lovingly, "How could that be? If you don't go to school, then who will? Don't worry; I will be your guardian, but you will promise me you will succeed."

Mr. Dervis enrolled me in Yahya Gazi High School and said, "Mehmet, my son, never lose your determination and desire to study! Because I am sure you will be a great man in the future". I felt like a victor who had won a big field battle against a mighty army. When I returned from school, I gave my grandmother excellent news. I was able to register. I needed school supplies, jackets, shirts, and ties, but I was in full of joy that I didn't worry about these for a second. I bought used clothes from the market. On the other hand, my grandmother sold the last rug in our house and bought my school supplies. I planned to go to school from morning to noon and contribute to the house's livelihood by continuing to shine shoes after class. Even though my brother Ramazan was young, he understood my excitement and helped in his way while preparing my school materials. When school started, it became clear that everything would be more challenging than I had planned. The school was a mile away. I walked to school every morning and returned home for lunch because I didn't have pocket money. When the school day was over, it would be late afternoon when I returned home. In autumn, these commutes were not very difficult; however, when the winter came, it was tough to repeat this journey with my shoes that had holes in them, without gloves or a beanie, and significantly more challenging to shine shoes upon all of this. The people around me were waiting for me to accept this idea as foolish behavior and vain enthusiasm, and they accused me of being stubborn for my "careless" actions.

No matter how tired I was, I would do my homework every day, finish a few books a week, and get up early to review the topics we would learn at school. This persistence and determination soon began to bear fruit. I had become one of the most successful and one of the students that all teachers knew by name and asked about. Meeting with our school principal, Mr. Vahit, was one of the crucial events that constituted a turning point in my life, but I will mention this later. Our class had chosen English as a foreign language, and it had been a few weeks since foreign language classes had started. I was told that one day, ten students would be transferred to the German department due to capacity, and I was one of them. This also meant that I had to change my class. "This is unfair!" I thought. They were changing my class and foreign language without even asking my opinion. Our literature teacher, Mr. Mikail, taught us how to write a petition in his beautiful writing and speaking class. I thought it was time to put what I had learned into practice, and I wrote a petition to the school principal demanding that this decision be revoked. I stood at the principal's door. Students were not allowed into the school principal's office unless there was an extraordinary situation. Students referred to the disciplinary committee or suspended from school could enter this room, and the principal would explain this decision to their face in his room. I knocked on the door with the petition in hand. A deep voice from inside yelled, "Come in!" Even though I was afraid then, I started something and had to finish it. I walked in, buttoned up my shirt, and headed toward his desk. Mr. Vahit lifted his head from his desk and looked at me under his glasses. When he said in a father-like tone, "Come, my son, what is the matter?" My fear subsided, and I put the petition in my hand on his desk.

Mr. Vahit said, "Let me take a look," and read the petition in one go. He looked at me, then the petition, then back at me again. "Who wrote this? Where are your parents?" he said.

"Sir, I wrote it. I came to your room alone because my father was against me going to school," I replied. He looked at the petition once again. He obviously couldn't believe I had written this by myself and came to his office. He picked up the phone and called the vice principal Mr. Mustafa to his room. "Mr. Mustafa let's re-register Dagci in his old class. If he wants to learn English, let's see his talent," he instructed. Seeking my rights, fighting for them, and then getting what I wanted was the feeling I felt at just ten years old. This feeling would shape my character throughout my life and enable me to defend what I believed to be correct, whatever the circumstances. I returned to my old class and started learning English enthusiastically. However, we did not have regular English classes except for the first year of middle school, and most of our English lessons were idle due to the absence of teachers. I emerged victorious from the battlefield but lost at the table.

FAREWELL TO MY COUNTRY
Istanbul, Turkey, July 22, 2016

It was almost 10 in the morning when I arrived at our house in the Taurus Mountains. As soon as I entered the house, I hugged Hatice and the children tightly. The night before, during the entire trip, the idea of being unable to return ran through my mind, and I kept asking, "What would they do if something happened to me?"

Fatih was 18 years old and had had seizures since he was five due to his Lissencephaly disease. Hakan was 11 years old. He had spent most of his childhood separated from me for seven years because of my sea deployments. We were getting to know each other again, perhaps for the first time, in America. Nilgun was only eight months old.

After two sons, God gave us a daughter. Although the doctors often screened her as healthy, she was born with the same illness as her brother Fatih. We were getting over this trauma and had not shared this news with anyone. If asked about her progress, we would say, "She was born prematurely, and her development is slow." However, this was a bleeding wound for us and another heavy burden added to our shoulders. Hatice was a powerful woman. As a military spouse and a mother of a disabled child, she had made many sacrifices during our 19 years of marriage. This time, we were in the middle of a dead end, perhaps even worse, in Turkey.

Hatice had prepared something to eat for breakfast, but I had no appetite. "The news is bad," I said.

Almost all staff officers were arrested one by one, and images of torture were shared on various social media accounts right after. It looked like some undercover government agents were instigating violence among the crowds, and these " civilians" were treating their military members worse than enemy soldiers. I called the NATO HQ, where I was assigned, and informed them that the situation was complicated and that I could not return to duty because all flights were canceled. I had not gone down to the village square for two days. "Should I speak with people?" I thought to myself. Before, I used to go to the village and chat with the villagers in the coffee house. Meanwhile, my father-in-law, uncle, and aunt had arrived. They were all nervous. The images on television were heartbreaking. My uncle's son-in-law was a military judge, and they were anxious about his fate.

"What will happen after this?" They implored me.

"Hopefully, this doomsday will end soon, and those involved will be held accountable," I replied.

I didn't want to make things even more frightening. On the other hand, I repeated the same question in my head dozens of times. "What is going to happen after this?"

When the guests left, I decided to go down to the village square. As usual, I greeted a few people, went to the coffee shop, and sat down. I looked around, wondering if there would be a different reaction than expected. A few people at the following table asked questions about the attempted coup. I said that I did not fully understand the situation and followed the events on television just like them. "Commander! All leaves for military personnel have been revoked, and everyone had orders to return to their duties. Why are you still here?" One of them asked smugly.

Perhaps the second question that crossed his mind would be, "Or are you hiding here?"

I said I could not get on a flight ahead and would return to my unit as soon as I found a ticket. One of them asked this time, "You are a high-ranking captain. Shouldn't you at least be in Ankara?"

One by one, the doubts in their minds turned into questions, and they were questioning my presence with an increasingly real doubt.

In those days, the regime gave everyone unlimited free texting and calling rights on their phones to snitch on someone they suspected to be affiliated with the coup or even talk against the regime and its handling of the situation. With messages sent with the name of Erdogan, citizens were asked to "report anyone they deem suspicious." Until that moment, no one had come to our door. As can be understood from these questions, it was suspicious for a high-ranking officer to be in the village in such a confusing environment where all official leaves were revoked.

I returned home and told Hatice that, as a precaution, we had to pack our bags and get ready to leave. In the meantime, I called the airline several times, saying that military personnel had been ordered to return to their units immediately and that I had to fly to the USA as soon as possible. I tried to get a ticket as early as possible. The airline stated that the flights still needed to be opened, that they could not do anything under these conditions, and that they had to prioritize passengers whose flights had been delayed. As a military personnel and diplomat, I would typically be very persistent in such a situation. However, after July 15, the roles had changed completely, and being in the military and serving your country abroad began to be perceived as a potential crime. From the first day, a perception was created that the USA and NATO might be behind the coup attempt. Thus, I became one of the "usual" suspects. I thanked the attendant without being too persistent and hung up the phone.

During an uncertain wait, I watched the state of current events and the uncertainty of my fate, just as I watched my grandfather and mother leave from the window of my house when I was a child. This time it was my life that was falling into uncertainty.

The smell of Taurus pine did not smell like peace anymore, and time slowed down with each second that passed. Uncertainty and waiting desperately without doing anything were suffocating me. I couldn't watch the news anymore.

Years of hard work were brutally murdered, and for political gain and power, thousands of people in their own country were treated so that even an enemy should not be treated.

Although the uprising was over in a few hours, the regime's coup against civilians and the opposition continued growing at a terrifying pace with each passing day.

People gathered in the squares, heroic anthems were sung, and strange characters in the guise of religious clergymen issued fatwas (religious permissions) that the life, property, and chastity of the "traitors" were halal (permissible) for them. Some, out of fear, some in anticipation of power and property, ignored and applauded what was done to their soldiers, citizens, and dignity.

Dozens of military personnel, who were killed during the night of the coup, were buried in places called "Traitors Cemetery" without allowing a funeral to take place. This would later become the de-facto practice in Turkey for any deceased person affiliated with the coup.

We had witnessed the brutal executions posted by ISIS on social media and questioned how these people could become so monstrous. We started to see similar images of atrocities at the hands of people sprouting like mushrooms all over the country after July 15.

The level of brutality on the Bosphorus Bridge was mind-blowing. The crowd had beheaded a few soldiers and tried to throw Military Academy students from the bridge into the sea. These acts of brutality were portrayed as a heroic struggle. The hypnotized people on the so-called democracy watch did not even realize they were killing democracy. Watching these events was hard for humans, and I could no longer take it.

I called the airline again an hour or two after my previous call. It was the only option, and I had to find a way to get out of the country somehow.

The regime continued to implement what seemed to be pre-planned measures very quickly. It became obligatory for government workers to obtain written permission from the institution they worked for. Otherwise, they would not be allowed to leave the country. They had presented these permissions at the checkpoints established at the airports.

I began to think that getting permission from the Navy was impossible because I couldn't reach anyone at the headquarters. Even if I did, this would mean giving my location to the newly appointed "witch hunters" who had complete allegiance to the regime—in this uncertainty, six long days had passed.

On Thursday, July 21, the airline official said they could "book an earlier flight ticket for a convenience fee of approximately $2500". In this case, money didn't matter. I could book an earlier flight date by providing my credit card information.

What a priceless thing freedom was! In the movie Septembers of Shiraz, which tells the story of a businessman during the Iranian Revolution, the protagonist offers his entire fortune to a guard to get him out of prison and escape to Turkey. The movie ended with the liberation of his people in exchange for this great fortune.

In my case, my freedom was this $2500 plane ticket. At that point, $2500 or $25,000 did not matter.

That ticket was the only hope of escaping from my beloved country, which dragged me into an inextricable situation with each passing minute. We said goodbye to my father-in-law at around eleven at night and set off for Adana from the Taurus Mountains. We had taken one last look at our home and taken the first steps of a journey that may have no return. The road was a dirt road full of cliffs. It was unwise to take this road in the darkness of the night. We had to catch the flight in the morning. Missing our last chance would be the biggest mistake we could make.

I was worried about possible police and military police checkpoints at the entrances of Feke, Kozan, and Adana. However, we could only reach Adana with checkpoints in the night's pitch-black darkness.

It was seven in the morning when we arrived in Adana. Even though we didn't sleep through the night, I continued to the airport without wasting time since our flight was at 10:00 AM. When we reached the airport, we arrived at the ticket booth and asked for the printout of our new boarding passes. The attendant told us to wait and asked for our IDs and old tickets. Even though the minutes had passed, our transaction still needed to be completed. There were more police and security guards than ever before, and passengers' tickets and IDs were being reviewed at a second checkpoint. Even though I asked the officer several times, he repeatedly said, "The process is going on." I was trying to understand why the process that would typically take a few minutes could not be completed in an hour and a half. I told Hatice to continue with our children if they arrested me. "I'm not going anywhere without you," she replied. I did not want them to stay here when my fate was uncertain. She was resisting. "What would I do alone in a foreign country? How would we survive? How would we see you again?" We couldn't convince each other and were having the same conversation repeatedly.

With less than 10 minutes remaining for our check-in time, the female attendant, who had been taking care of our process from the beginning, came to us with our tickets and said, "Sorry, the system has slowed down due to new precautionary practices, but we were able to get the approval." The rush to catch the plane and the joy of getting our tickets ran through my head. We immediately handed over our suitcases and headed to the boarding gate. When the plane took off from Adana to Istanbul, my hopes of completing this journey were a little higher.

There was no negative result from the control procedures that lasted for hours. I was now thinking of the security checkpoint set up in Istanbul. I had no approval from the Navy, and our flight could have been canceled.

Dozens of questions were running through my mind, and I was busy trying to find answers. If they asked, "Why didn't you get permission" I would say, "I was already working abroad. The flight was within the scope of a pre-planned annual leave." With these thoughts in mind, I opened the newspaper I had bought at the airport and took a quick look. The pages were full of photographs of the Prime Minister, Heads of Military Services, and Chief of General Staff. They were portrayed as heroes of the night; ironically, some of these people were hiding somewhere safe, and others were taken captive by their men on the night of the coup. There were also reports about the ongoing "witch hunt," the arrests had reached thirty thousand suspects. Security checks at airports, ports, and border gates were maximized to prevent people from escaping abroad. One article had the headline "Traitors caught on their way abroad."

I closed the newspaper and tried to forget my situation, even if it were just for a moment. Nilgun was the cute baby she is, unaware of everything, while I was kissing and smelling her head with the fear of never being able to see her again. She had a tough life ahead of her, and I was worried about how she would survive without a father because we knew how difficult this road was in Fatih's life. Fatih and Hakan were again enjoying the joy of getting on a plane. Hatice, on the other hand, was holding my hand tightly as if she were saying, "I will continue to be by your side no matter what." The plane was on its way to the skies of Istanbul at full speed. We didn't say goodbye to anyone except one or two people when we left. We thought that if we could go abroad, we would call everyone and explain the situation. At this stage, no one should know that we were leaving.

Especially if the supporter of the regime officers realized that I was in Turkey, it would ruin my exit plans.

Due to my academic and professional achievements, I received early promotions and became a captain long before my classmates, and this had already made many people green with envy. The "Lists" who would end thousands of innocent people's careers, dreams, and lives were prepared by a group of resentful officers working in cooperation with the regime. All the prized accomplishments, successful military careers, studies, and duties at Western/ NATO institutions were held against these innocent people who had nothing to do with the coup or had any links to organizations other than their military chain of command. Soon thousands of officers and non-commissioned officers from all service branches who had successfully advanced in the professions were first purged from service and then arrested. They were the victims of vengeance from the past years and were stabbed in the back by their brothers in arms.

The new measure of merit in the government was not based on professional and academic success but on how many people someone had slandered and added to the Lists with false denunciations.

Many officers, who were subjected to similar treatment by Erdogan the regime during Ergenekon and Sledgehammer trials just a few years ago, were now siding with Erdogan (who openly declared that he was the prosecutor of these trials at that time) and leading this witch hunt were targeting innocent people. Many officers who were taken into custody were tortured for days by active and retired officers convicted in the Ergenekon and Sledgehammer trials. They were so reckless that retired Colonel Ali Turksen did not hesitate to talk about the tortures he committed with pride and joy on a television program he later joined.

While lost in my thoughts, I was startled by the flight attendant's announcement. "Can you fasten your seat belt? We have started to descend for landing in Istanbul."

I had come to the last stage of my forced departure from my country. Whatever path fate has laid for me would soon become apparent. Hatice and I looked each other in the eye once again. This time only our eyes spoke.

After landing at Istanbul Airport, we headed from the domestic to the international gates. An officer was directing transit passengers to another entrance. We came to a different checkpoint without going through security with other transit passengers. This also meant that we would not enter the government worker checkpoint. We were very excited. There was one last obstacle ahead of us. A young policeman stood at the transit checkpoint. We started to present our passports one by one. The children's and my wife's passports were stamped with an exit approval within minutes. When it was my passport's turn, the officer carefully looked at me. "Have you received permission to exit?" He asked. I handed over the permit I received in the USA and said I was returning to my unit. Even though I tried to suppress my anxiety as much as possible while waiting for the result, storms broke out inside me. He was not content with my answer because he started talking to someone on the phone. The process, which should generally take a few seconds, was not ending. He looked at me while examining my passport's entry and exit information. My wife and children were waiting at the checkpoint even though their passport control was over. "You guys should go on," I said to Hatice. Something was wrong. Almost 15 minutes had passed, and less than half an hour remained before departure. Hatice insisted on not leaving my side. Nilgun got tired of this long wait and started to cry. It felt good to stop thinking momentarily and hear nothing but Nilgun's crying. This feeling felt like I was out of breath underwater, and I lifted my head to the surface at the last moment to inhale all the air into my lungs.

Even momentarily, I felt relieved from my suffocating thoughts, and I was trying to calm Nilgun by hugging her tightly. The policeman raised his head once more and looked at us. Fatih was leaning on his mother, and Hakan was waiting by his hand luggage while I tried calming Nilgun. At that moment, he hung up the phone, stamped my passport, and said, "Have a nice trip." We had been waiting for these words for minutes, but I was unresponsive, probably because I was preparing for the worst-case scenario. The police officer held the passport again and said, "Your plane is about to take off. You'd better hurry." I tried to get back to reality, and we quickly headed to the exit point.

We were running, but it felt like this rush resulted from the desire to escape from the security point as soon as possible rather than hurrying to catch the plane.

At the end of a troublesome journey in the Taurus Mountains, we finally reached the plane's gate that would take us to America.

It was a sad run from my homeland to a foreign country, but it was a run toward freedom. It was a strange and intense feeling.

When we arrived at the boarding gate of the plane, we showed our passports and tickets to the attendant. Fatih was already heading towards the door of the aircraft. I was more comfortable there since this was only ticket control. After all, we had passed through all the checkpoints. I was shocked when the attendant said I needed to go through a second security checkpoint.

What was going on?

Why were they taking me for a new security check?

"You get on the plane," I said to Hatice. I had given her the car keys and the credit cards beforehand, but we didn't have a detailed plan B until now.

This check could have been a better sign.

"Raise our children freely, and never worry about me," I told her, heading to the security point.

This time I was alone. Hatice and the children were watching me. I later learned this was a check on randomly selected passengers, independent of my identity and profession. Indeed, after a glance at my backpack, passport, and tickets, they said, "Here you go. You may board the plane."

Excitedly, I threw myself at the plane door without thinking about what was happening. We took our seats on the plane as a family. We were living our joy internally to avoid attracting attention. I could put the evil thoughts aside. After we stowed our suitcases, we started to wait for the plane to take off. Hatice was busy on her phone to relax and distract her thoughts. At that time, we saw the Facebook post of our relative, who came to say goodbye to us in the morning. He took our photo while boarding the plane in Adana and wrote, "We will miss you very much. We hope you will complete your flight to America without any problems." We were left with a bitter smile, not knowing whether to laugh, get angry, or be happy. While we were cautious and did not call anyone, she announced our departure to thousands of people. Fortunately, we were sitting in our seats on the plane, and soon we would leave all this chaos behind us.

This relief was temporary. Although 45 minutes had passed since we boarded the plane, the plane had yet to take off. What a never-ending nightmare this had been. It was as if we were waking up from a suffocating nightmare and finding ourselves repeatedly in the darkest part of that nightmare. As a child, during every bad dream, I would somehow find a hill to jump over, where I would wake up leaving everything behind. It was a protection mechanism that I had subconsciously developed. If only everything were that easy now.

We were in a nightmare with my wife and three kids. Hatice asked the flight attendant passing by, "When will we depart?"

"We are waiting for the security units. They must take someone off the plane," the flight attendant replied.

Was that someone me?

Maybe someone had acted against us when they heard we were going abroad.

Time did not pass. I had no place to run to and nothing I could do to change my situation.

What a strange turn everything took.

How happy and hopeful we were when we boarded the US plane together last year. We planned to represent our country and return to Turkey two years later. With our diplomatic passports in our pockets, we were going abroad as one of the country's most trained and distinguished officers. We drew a painting where we had one last Turkish coffee before boarding the plane, bought some souvenirs, and dreamed about how we would shape our new life in America.

This painting was shattered in the darkness of July 15th. Now we were trying to leave the country as if we were fugitives.

I have completed many missions in NATO in the past year and have been rewarded with a certificate of appreciation for my duties. We have fulfilled our duty to represent Hatice and hosted dozens of foreign diplomats and officers in our house. In our friendly relations with distinguished friends from different countries, we emphasized that Turkey, a modern and democratic country, is one of the strongest allies of NATO. After this questionable coup attempt, our country was backsliding from a democracy into an autocracy at full speed. Erdogan established a new regime at the expanse of Turkey's longtime democratic gains and well-educated human resources.

This psychology had already exhausted me. We were sitting in the middle row. We were leaning our heads into the corridor and sometimes straightening up slightly, trying to look towards the front of the plane and understand what was happening.

I looked at the people around us for a while. Everyone had an expression of uneasiness and boredom on their faces. Some were spending time on their phones, and some were choosing a channel from the television. It had been almost an hour, and our plane had yet to take off. Three security guards with the words "Countering Terrorism" on their vests came onto the plane.

I held Hatice's hand tightly and said goodbye with one last glance. I was ready to throw myself into emptiness from that hill as I did as a child and end this nightmare. Suddenly, they stopped a few rows in front of us. They asked a passenger in his thirties for his passport. Next to him was a woman of the same age, who seemed to be his wife and a four or five-year-old girl. Before long, they handcuffed him and took him off the plane. I could see all the regime's cruelty in the last glance of his wife and the tears in his eyes. The plane door closed, and we were left to take off.

Neither Hatice nor I could get over what we had just seen. We were numb, frozen. I could no longer be happy in the face of the scene I witnessed. When the plane took off, I looked out the window for the last time at the beautiful seven-hilled Istanbul. We were flying to freedom, but tens of thousands of people were caught in this fire. A cruel regime that showed no sign of mercy was throwing each of them into the fire one by one; the crowds in the squares applauded this situation with joy, and they entered a race to carry wood to the fire. Along the way, only one thought crossed: I must find a way to extinguish this fire!

The List

PURGATORY

Norfolk, USA, August 2016

My first day back at NATO HQ in Norfolk, Virginia, was quite hectic. My colleagues were happy to see me return to my job safely. On the other hand, they were trying to understand what happened in the coup attempt.

All Turkish officers serving in the NATO were following the news coming from Turkey. With each passing hour, we were informed about new arrests and various unlawful practices of the regime. Meanwhile, a German officer, a close colleague, came to me. After a short conversation, he said, "Mehmet, this is your Reichstag fire. We experienced the same scenario in Germany in 1933."

Although I am interested in history, I needed to learn the details of this event. The first thing I did when I got home was look up the Reichstag fire. This was the name given to the possibility that Adolf Hitler used to gather all state powers into his own hands and destroy all the opposition.

In February 1933, just before the German elections, someone set the German parliament on fire. The prime minister of the time, Hitler, declared that "this was an act of the communists" and started the biggest witch hunt in German history. Hitler described this incident as "the gift of God," and had tens of thousands of dissidents arrested in Germany and became the only man to win the elections thanks to the chaotic environment. Afterward, massacres followed and went down as a black stain in the history of humanity, including the Holocaust and the killing of opposition politicians and journalists.

For Erdogan, the July 15 coup attempt was the Reichstag fire of Turkey. Erdogan, like Hitler, stated that July 15 was "a gift from God." While the information regarding the nature of this so-called coup attempt was behind a dense cloud of dust, Erdogan declared that what happened was "an attempt by the Gulen group." Tens of thousands of civil servants were discharged based on pre-prepared lists, their diplomas were canceled, thousands of institutions and workplaces were looted, and the biggest witch hunt in the history of the Republic of Turkey had started.

While Hitler murdered his opposition and Jewish people in concentration camps, Erdogan tortured thousands in closed gymnasiums and secret detention centers for days or months. The families of these people also faced discrimination and injustice from the government and society. They were excluded from the community; people refrained from communicating with them and were not given jobs, housing, and other basic human needs. Thousands of children were either put behind bars with their parents or left uncared for since relatives and neighbors refused to take care of them. This was technically a "social genocide" in the making.

The fact that the two events were so similar suggested that the Reichstag fire might have inspired the coup's plotters. With the death warrant issued by the regime under the name of Decree-Law, those who disobeyed the regime were condemned to social death.

Erdogan was at full speed to establish his new one-person regime in Turkey and saw the well-educated staff officers in the military, who were committed to democratic values, as a threat to his rule. These officers were purged from service in large groups through Decree-Laws issued briefly. There was no objection or resistance to this unlawful practice from any part of society, so this became the new apparatus for the state to purge anyone who would be perceived as a threat to the new regime from public service. The Turkish Military took the biggest hit, and even military academies and high schools, which have a deep-rooted history and tradition of more than 200 years, were shut down. The future hopes of all officers and military students studying in these institutions were shattered. The regime's hand did not only have access domestically. Admiral Zeki Ugurlu, a senior Turkish officer serving at NATO HQ in Norfolk, Virginia, was declared a coup plotter and dismissed. Admiral Zeki achieved numerous successes throughout his career, serving as a frigate commander, commodore, mine flotilla commander, the Head of Communications Electronic Information Systems, and Personnel Chief at the Naval Forces Headquarters. How could he plan or participate in a coup attempt thousands of miles from his homeland?

We entered Admiral Zeki's office together with Colonel Ozkan. He told us that "his conscience was evident, and he had no choice but to resign as honorable in the face of this decision." Even when all his hard work, which took more than 30 years, was suddenly usurped, he remained calm and ordered us to "continue to represent the Republic of Turkey in the best manner possible."

I will never forget when Colonel Ozkan, who would later be promoted to the rank of general by the regime, said, "We served under the command of a traitor for a whole year," as soon as he left Admiral Zeki's office.

He had suddenly abandoned all respect for a commander who was declared a traitor with a single statement and no investigation. His ambition was to take the office of Admiral Zeki, who was stripped of all his military and human dignity, as the most senior Turkish officer at NATO HQ. With each passing day, new people were being added to the decree-law lists, and orders for discharge followed one another.

Admiral Onder took the office of Admiral Zeki, who was also accused of treason by the same regime. He was imprisoned for four years during the Ergenekon trials, but the Ergenekon suspects had become the heroes of the new regime. However, he was too blind to see this contradiction. His first statement when he took office was, "So, it was in my destiny to sit on the seat of a traitor." What a contradiction, what a dark game this was. How could people serve such a filthy regime with enthusiasm to sit in a seat of authority?

The morning of August 8th was marked by an e-mail that Major Engin sent to all personnel at NATO. Major Engin received the news of his discharge and sent an e-mail to all personnel working in NATO describing the injustice he had been subject to. This e-mail helped the staff of other countries, shocked by what had happened, understand the gravity of the situation, and revealed the tragedy. Admiral Onder expressed anger at this situation and grumbled, "How could he send such an e-mail?"

Colonel Ozkan and Commander Aytac took the discomfort further, arguing that "this e-mail is great treachery." What a dark mindset that was! They couldn't even bear to see an e-mail sent by an officer who had been unlawfully stripped of everything he owned, explaining this to his friends and colleagues. They expected complete silence in the face of all the cruelty and injustice.

Commander Aytac was not a staff officer and was selected for a three-year assignment in a NATO post, which was a rare case. He was also sent to many courses and training in the USA and Germany. He usually kept quiet at meetings and treated the officers respectfully. Another trait he had was hosting newly appointed personnel at his home with his family and establishing close relations with them from the very first day.

We later discovered that Aytac was tasked with collecting information for the regime about the daily lives of the officers here, with whom they met, and what they did during their tenure. When the conjuncture changed after July 15, that quiet and polite officer turned into a self-confident and arrogant man. Aytac suddenly became the person who spoke the most in the meetings. He would not leave Admiral Onder's room, and the Turkish Navy officers would now report to Aytac instead of Colonel Huseyin, the Turkish Senior Officer. In return for his actions, his assignment was extended for one more year, and Commander Akın, who was supposed to replace him, had his orders canceled and was not allowed to leave Turkey.

What I experienced and witnessed that month was so painful that being on duty as a regime representative heavily burdened my conscience. Up to that point, nearly twenty officers had been discharged from the headquarters, and we were left with only a few people. I did not hesitate to keep in touch with my released friends and did not believe they were guilty. To remain silent in the face of this injustice would be the most dishonorable behavior. When we met with colleagues from other countries, I expressed that these practices were unlawful and baseless, and that NATO had to do something about these illegal practices. Speaking against the regime started to make my close friends uneasy.

A colonel from the Dutch Navy said, "Mehmet, I understand you, but if you keep talking like this, they will target you too."

How could I keep silent?

While I was still on duty and could reach people, I believed it was my responsibility to talk about these injustices while I still had the chance.

NATO should not have kept silent while these personnel, who had served alongside other NATO countries in Afghanistan, the Indian Ocean, Lebanon, and Iraq for years to serve world peace, were targeted one by one. The situation had gone so far that Erdogan claimed that NATO was behind the coup and even asked for the security camera records at NATO operational headquarters on the night of July 15 and the night before.

Any affiliation with NATO, having training in any NATO country or a Western school, or even being proficient in English could be used as proof of treason by the regime. This approach indicated the regime's desire to create a new self-defense army like Iran's "Islamic Revolutionary Guard Corps" by dismissing the trained personnel and closing the military schools.

A dark structure called SADAT, which was founded in 2012 under Erdogan's patronage, had the potential to fill this gap. The regime, with financial resources and government office positions, supported SADAT. It is publicly known that SADAT, a radicalized militia organization, had been giving armed training to thousands of people in camps in Turkey and abroad. SADAT was also an important player during the night of the July 15 Coup attempt. Despite all efforts to obscure the evidence, it was revealed that those who provoked the people on the night of July 15 and beheaded the soldiers on the Bosphorus Bridge were SADAT militants. Five years later, one of those militants could no longer live with his conscience and confessed everything they had committed that night.

Another danger for the Turkish Armed Forces was the promotion of officers supported by Dogu Perincek, the leader of the Vatan Party, which was now in full cooperation with the regime. Dogu Perincek had been a vocal critic of NATO for many years and supported rapprochement between Turkey, Russia, and Iran. He also had his share of being labeled a traitor by the Erdogan regime not too long ago, but now he was the closest ally to Erdogan. He was a mediator in resolving the crisis created by Turkish jets' downing of a Russian warplane in 2014. Although it is still unknown in which role and capacity he did all this. Still, he became a valuable guest on television channels and newspapers under the regime's control, appearing on a different screen every evening. He would praise the regime and the destroyed judicial system, stating that "everything is going as planned." He openly targeted the Turkish Armed Forces through the programs he participated in and through the media networks under his control. He accused thousands of people of being US spies. He stated that Turkey should leave NATO immediately, and a strategic partnership focused on Russia, Iran, and China had to be initiated. He was so intoxicated with a victory that he could openly speak on television that the arrests and dismissals were made according to the lists they prepared long before the coup attempt. With these statements, he admitted that they had orchestrated the coup. Newly appointed NATO personnel were selected from officers who supported pro-Russian policies, and Turkey was moving away from its

Western allies, democracy, human rights, and freedoms day by day.

As a patriotic officer, I was devastated to see this trend, and I tried to explain this danger to my colleagues at NATO as best as I could. In this context, one evening, we met with a few friends who were discharged. I said, "We need to write down the dangers posed by this situation in terms of the human rights violations and unlawfulness in Turkey and the risks and threats it poses for the European Union, the USA, and NATO."

I thought that if Turkey's rapprochement with Russia and Iran, the radicalization of the people under the leadership of SADAT, and Erdogan's secret connections with terrorist organizations could be revealed, international public opinion could be formed. For many years, Turkey had assumed the role of a bridge of civilizations connecting the East and the West. Erdogan targeted the people who were the guardians of this bridge. I hoped that if this danger were revealed, the international community would stop this unlawfulness. That night, we talked about these issues until late at night and reached common ground.

More and more Turkish officers were being discharged from service daily, and they had to adjust to their new lives. Many moved to smaller houses and sold some of their belongings as their salaries were cut, and their savings were confiscated.

My wife was a member of the Officer Spouse Association, and the association members gathered at our house to discuss how they could support these victims. What happened in Turkey was seen as an internal matter of the country in the official discourses of the member states. However, the military personnel serving here and their spouses were looking for ways to support their colleagues and families by showing a great example of loyalty and integrity. After the long meeting in our house, the spouses decided to organize a fundraising campaign and deliver the collected funds to the Turkish officers who were discharged from duty through my wife. The wife of a German colleague reached out to a journalist friend and requested to make a story of this tragedy to raise awareness among the international community. I told my wife we had to cut all our spending and put some household items up for sale. I knew the regime would soon realize I did not stand by this persecution and would add me to one of these lists.

Colonel Ozkan and Commander Aytac continued sending information about people discharged from their professions to Turkey. Strangely enough, these people were persistently called to Turkey, despite being discharged, their passports being revoked, and deprived of all their human rights and due process.

They were expected to trust the non-existing justice system. Rumors spread about people who did not return, stating that "if they were not guilty, they would have returned." Those who obeyed this call and returned to Turkey were arrested at the airport, in front of their families, and could not be heard from for days. The on-duty personnel were being called to the country on the pretext of a meeting that was going to be held in Turkey. They were being set up and arrested.

Commander Cafer, assigned to NATO HQ in Belgium, other strategic command, was called to Ankara for a meeting and was arrested on the day he set foot in the country. He was convicted for months. Returning to the country was even worse than surrendering to the enemy because the regime did not apply the most basic "laws of war" to these officers. The regime was subjecting people to the most severe types of torture without any discrimination between men, women, children, and older people. Human rights violations and torture were widespread, and the pressure on thousands of innocent people increased daily. Still, the expected reaction from Western countries and international institutions did not come.

Unfortunately, the Turkish state apparatus had committed similar atrocities against the Kurds for decades, and I could not stop thinking of the Kurds in this new light. Thousands of villages in Eastern and Southeastern Anatolia were evacuated, people were forced to migrate, their homes were destroyed, and most of their fundamental rights and freedoms, especially speaking their mother tongue, were taken from them. The state covered every crime it committed with the excuse of national security reasons, and most of the public felt that what was done by the state was justified. Mahsun Kırmızıgul, a prominent Kurdish celebrity in Turkey, explained these events well in his movie "I saw the sun".

The Anatolian people, accustomed to believing everything said on television and in newspapers, closed their eyes to all the persecutions. While studying at the Military Academy in 2014, a general who was the Head of the Anti-Terrorism Department of the General Staff came to our class as a speaker and gave information about the operations carried out. In those operations, cities were raided, and many civilians were the target of bullets and bombs. Erdogan shelved all his promises of a democratic initiative to Kurdish citizens, revealing how ruthless the regime could be, with such hatred that it dragged the bodies of people killed behind armored police vehicles in the streets. The general described these as a great success story, and I told him, "Instead of eliminating terror, these actions fueled the fire even more. The state cannot kill its civilian citizens or destroy their houses for whatever reason; a historical mistake is being made." A cold wind blew in the 76-person classroom, and the general dismissed my words without answering.

It can readily be accepted that Erdogan mastered using different segments of society against each other and succeeded in maintaining and even strengthening his power by turning the masses against each other. These had been the "shadow governments" methods of controlling and holding power for decades in Turkey. Even though the rulers changed, the ongoing persecution never did. In the last 100 years, the state has alienated certain groups within society and labeled them as terrorists or traitors. Many innocent lives were lost, and the prisons were filled with political prisoners based on political affiliation, ethnic background, or religious beliefs. Muslims, communists, socialists, minorities, revolutionists, Kurds, Alevis, and many others have faced similar fates. It seemed impossible for us to reach peace and tranquility without changing this order fed by the blood of the people of these lands.

It was time to rise against oppression, injustice, and treachery. We had to be Ahmet Kaya and fight until our pencil broke, and we were out of words.

DAYS OF EXILE
Virginia, USA, November 22, 2016

When I opened my eyes that morning, I felt lighter, as if a heavy burden had been lifted off my shoulders. It was a strange feeling. My lifetime work, achievements, naval career, dreams, and more had been usurped a few hours earlier.

Now I could be a more vocal critic of the unlawful practices of Erdogan's authoritarian regime without any concerns. I believed it was a choice between good and evil, and I was finally on the right side. I felt like one of the passengers who had boarded Noah's ark before the storm.

I would not have felt comfortable wearing my uniform during these times, as this could have been perceived as supporting this illegitimate regime. Even the idea of this perception was embarrassing for me.

I would rather be a soldier in the ranks of good than a commander in the army of evil. After that day, whenever I was told to lead at work, I would refuse it by saying, "I aspire to be a leader in the ranks of the soldiers."

It was not rank or title that brought the satisfaction of my discharge. The peace and pleasure of doing the right thing were far more critical than any rank or title. Before working for the last time, Hatice and I walked.

Our home was in one of Virginia Beach's most exclusive neighborhoods. With the mental awareness of representing our country as a diplomat, I purposefully rented a house in such a neighborhood by stretching our financial limits. It was a little bigger house than we needed. We only used a few rooms. It had a magnificent pool in its garden. We could reach the seaside by walking a few hundred yards. There was a lone tree on the beach and a bench under it.

Hatice and I would often come here at sunset or the first light of the morning, smell the scent of the sea and would dream. These would be very modest dreams, mainly focusing on the days we would spend in our house in the Taurus Mountains. In normal circumstances, I was likely to be promoted to Admiral after completing my assignment in NATO and returning to Turkey. But these were never part of the dreams we had for our future. When we had guests from Turkey, we would take them to that beach and share our dreams. We had so many memories in this neighborhood and enjoyed spending time together as a family for the first time. I bought bicycles for everyone in the family, and we had bicycle races with Hakan and explored the places around the neighborhood. We had so much more planned, but fate had other plans.

We would set sail for a new life and soon had to leave our dreams, memories, and hearts in this beautiful neighborhood. I came home and put on my favorite white uniform for the last time. I stood in front of the mirror and corrected my rank insignia. I double-checked my buttons.

It was time to say goodbye to my uniform, which I have been wearing with honor since I was 16 years old. It had been over 24 years, and it felt like the uniform had become a part of my body and was integrated with my heart. Military service was not simply a job but a way of life and a combination of dedication and sacrifice. In our culture, when a soldier was martyred, his uniform would be his burial robe on his last journey to eternity.

When I entered HQ in Norfolk, I wasted no time and went to my desk. I had colleagues from the United States, Canada, Greece, and Ukraine. I gathered them first. Our relationship had become a friendship rather than a chain of command in the past fifteen months. We would meet as a family. I still remember their joy and relief when they saw me back at work after the coup attempt.

I told them that it was now my turn as of this morning. Strangely enough, I didn't feel the need to give a single explanation other than telling them that I was on a list. Almost every week, similar events were seen in different departments. Their first reaction was to ask, "You will not return to Turkey, will you?"

This illegitimate regime was not satisfied by ruining our lives here in the U.S., thousands ofmiles away from the homeland; they demanded that we return to Turkey immediately to face criminal charges. In the past few months, the regime in Turkey has ruined the lives of thousands by fabricated accusations without any evidence and no criminal investigation. The worst part was that everyone accused had to prove their innocence in a flawed judicial system. The judicial system was under heavy political pressure, and almost every fundamental right for a free and fair trial was violated.

"No, I will not return. On the contrary, I will stay here and shine a light on the dark face of this illegitimate regime to the whole world." I hugged and said goodbye to all of them. Even though we were wearing the uniforms of different countries, these foreign officers under my command proved that our friendship was honest and sincere with the solidarity and sympathy they had shown me.

Their views and feelings about me did not change a bit after I was labeled as a traitor by my own country, and they shared the bitterness of that moment with me with all their sincerity. On the other hand, all my friends still in the Turkish Navy had turned their backs on me and sided with the illegitimate regime's rhetoric. I was removed from the WhatsApp groups I shared with friends in Turkey, I stopped receiving calls from them, and my name was deleted from the contacts of thousands of phones.

Those who pretended to be friends were now trying to erase the traces of our pasts, in a state of panic like a criminal who tries to erase his fingerprints. After the meeting with the officers in my branch, I went to the Italian Colonel Luca, the head of our department. Since I was the

Deputy Head of the Department and the Branch Manager, we worked on many projects and had a good relationship. Colonel Luca wasn't surprised when he heard the news. When I had previously told him about the regime's intentions and the crimes it was involved in, "Something might happen to you; you shouldn't talk like this," he warned me. He said that he believed this issue was Turkey's internal issue. I responded, "As long as you continue to ignore Erdogan's crimes, this terror will soon come to your doorsteps, and you will understand that this is an international threat."

For these reasons and other similar reasons, the countries in NATO preferred to ignore what was happening officially. They allowed democracy, human rights, and freedoms to be massacred in front of their eyes. However, democracy and commitment to human rights were among the fundamental principles of NATO's founding agreement, the Washington Agreement. What a contradiction this was. NATO was ignoring all the crimes of a regime directly opposed to its founding principles and values and sacrificing its personnel to the barbaric practices of this lawless regime.

I tried to raise awareness among my colleagues in NATO about the Erdogan regime's potential threat to international law and order. Erdogan had been using Syrian refugees as blackmail against the European Union. He attempted to intervene directly or indirectly in the German elections through the Turkish population in this country. He ordered many unlawful abductions of Turkish citizens residing in foreign countries, and he made deals with various terrorist organizations, including ISIS, to destabilize Syria and violate the territorial integrity of this country in every sense. As the Western countries kept silent, the Erdogan regime got more assertive and bolder. Erdogan called closer to Russia and Iran, with every Western-oriented officer purged from service in Turkey, and NATO turned its head the other way. Moreover, many of the new Turkish officers assigned to NATO posts by the Erdogan regime to replace people like us support Turkey's rapprochement with Russia. They could threaten NATO's integrity and solidarity.

The news that I was discharged spread quickly in the headquarters, and many people came to my desk and asked how they could help. In the face of evil, goodness did not disappear. It only changed dimensions and became more visible. Regardless of their political stances, representatives of nearly thirty countries united to show solidarity and support. On the spur of the moment, even Colonel Ozkan and Commander Aytac, who were incompletely allegiant to this illegitimate regime, felt like they had bid me farewell and expressed their regrets. Colonel Ozkan asked if I would report to the newly assigned Turkish Admiral. I told him I would not say to someone who voluntarily became a servant of the illegitimate regime and was put in office for his service. I was not going to allow them to exploit the situation I was in.

During my service at NATO HQ I gained the friendship and trust of dozens of my colleagues from different countries. After taking a few personal items from my desk, I bid farewell to my colleagues and my naval career in the Turkish Navy. Not too long ago, I walked in here as a well-decorated Navy Captain, and today I was walking out without my rank, a job, and no idea about what life has for my family and me. These lyrics of Ahmet Kaya's song once again helped me express my feelings and gave me some comfort in this turmoil:

I want to run barefoot in the long meadows,

My hair was in harmony with the wind, and my face towards the mountains,

Captivity that tests the wall of my chest with death,

And the courage that forces my heart

I want to fight hard,

I want to run, darling; forgive me if I can't return.

The List

REUNION WITH MY MOTHER
Kayseri, Turkey, 1980's

My desire to excel was shared during my middle and high school years. I wanted to excel, accelerate the flow of time, grow up as soon as possible, and leave the years of hardship behind me. I fulfilled my promise to my primary school teacher, Mr. Dervis. In the first report card period, I became one of only three students who received a certificate of appreciation. This success boosted my self-confidence. I soon realized that my friends cared more about who I was and my success in classes than my messy outfit or young age. With my improved self-confidence, I told my close friends that we could get together on weekends to study and that I could help them with subjects they did not understand. A small group of friends started gathering at someone's house every Saturday. We had breakfast together, revisited the week's topics, played soccer, joked about each other, and talked about the girls in our class. We had unwittingly established Yahyali's first children's club. This relationship expanded our friendship and success at school, and our teachers appreciated us. Our weekend meetings continued until the second year of high school, and our group, which started with six people, grew to ten.

Besides tutoring my friends on the weekends, I also helped the whole class to prepare for the exams. We also had to prepare for university admission tests, which demanded extra studying besides schoolwork. There were weekly supplemental booklets for this purpose, but unfortunately, too much work for those living in the suburbs to get them. A relative of mine had given me some previously published booklets a few years ago, and I started finishing these magazines in 7th grade.

Summer vacations continued to be a time to explore new business opportunities and earn my pocket money. I would collect mountain tea, work on the farms, sell bags at the market on Fridays, and go to help with apple picking during the apple season.

I had such a fast and hectic life that I did not even have time to think about the financial difficulties we were experiencing, the emptiness of my mother's absence, r my father's problems. Now, I realize that this short and hectic life has helped me from negative thinking and pessimism.

My mom and dad had each remarried and started new lives. Unfortunately, my brothers Ramazan, Emrah, and I had never become a part of either family. Emrah was staying in Kozan with my grandparents. Ramazan and I still lived in my grandmother's one-room house. Although my father got married, he could never fully recover psychologically. He would get sick occasionally, fight with his neighbors, sell everything we owned, and engage in absurd businesses.

He suddenly disappeared on a winter day in 1988, and 20 days later, he showed up with Emrah. "I cannot be separated from my son," he said. Three brothers, we were reunited once again. These were one of the best times, and our greatest pleasure was putting corn or potatoes into the brick oven during the winter evenings and listening to my grandmother's life story. Since there was no television in the house, we would watch movies at my uncle's or neighbor's house. I used to call my uncle's wife "Mother Nazmiye" and my other uncle's wife "Sister Dudu." They took care of us in our mother's absence, never made us feel different from their children, and allowed us to taste the warmth of being a family. Thus, as cousins, we became like siblings who grew up together.

In Yahyali, a new job opportunity arose for young people. A businessman founded a company called ARMAS and offered young people the chance to get a job in the factory he opened in Istanbul. Many families, including my cousin Huseyin, took their children out of school and sent them to Istanbul. During holidays, these young kids would return to Yahyali with their best jeans and fancy-looking shirts and talk about their adventures and fascinating life in Istanbul. In addition to earning money, they were proud to support their families. This situation made it difficult for me to continue school, and the pressures increased for me to start working at ARMAS. My father and uncles were critical of my stubbornness at every opportunity, regardless of my success at school.

I had to find a regular job and finally got a job as a dishwasher and waiter in a kebab restaurant. I worked at the restaurant during the summer holidays and on weekends. "I, too, have a stable source of income," I would argue. This was good for me. Since Ramazan and Emrah were now of school age, I started paying for their books, notebooks, and clothes. I encouraged them to go to school under any circumstance, and I would help them do their homework. As three brothers, we continued our persistence to go to school against all odds.

Ramazan and Emrah called my father's new wife "mom." I called her by name. She never treated us like stepchildren and showed all the care and compassion a mother would have.

With Hacer's presence, Emrah and Ramazan finally had an opportunity to grow up in a family environment. My father was also tired of life's struggles and began to settle down. I lost myself in the rhythm of life flowing rapidly, and I finished middle school as valedictorian. In our small town, everyone knew me, my neighbors, relatives, and teachers, and they would set my success as an example to their children. Many of our relatives were encouraged by my success and enrolled their children in middle school. At school, they called me by my last name, "Dagci," which means "mountain climber." I enjoyed this very much, and like a climber, I had a growing instinct and desire to climb new and higher peak points in life.

I worked in a kebab restaurant during the summer break of 8th grade, but different from the usual, this time, I quit my job before school started.

Like every year, I bought a used suit, packed a few items in a small backpack, and decided to go to Adana to visit my mother. My mother lived in Kozan then, and I had two brothers named İbrahim and Ali from her new marriage. After traveling all day, from Yahyali to Yesilhisar, from there to Adana, and finally to Kozan, after changing three buses, I could find my grandfather's old house where we stayed when I was in third grade. Adana had sweltering summers; even in September, it was like an oven outside. Especially for someone in a suit! I was still in a suit; I wanted to appear as a grown, strong, self-reliant young man before my mother. I do not know the reason for this desire at the time. Maybe I wanted to say, "Do not worry about us. We are doing fine," or maybe, it meant, "Look at me. Your little Mehmet is a big man now!" Who knows?

I had just turned 14, and it wasn't easy to comprehend how my emotions were shaped. When I arrived at my grandparents' house, I first saw Uncle Ishak, my Aunt Ayse's husband. He didn't recognize me. When I said, "I am Mehmet, the son of Durdu," he was surprised initially, but then he hugged me and invited me inside. When my Aunt Ayse saw me, she could not hold back her tears and embraced me with a mother's affection. We had a long conversation. "Your mother lives in her village. I'll take you in the morning," Uncle Ishak said. That night, I had difficulty sleeping because I was so excited. Uncle Ishak prepared his motorcycle in the morning, cheerfully saying, "Let's reunite the mother and son."

Candık Village was a cozy place built on a small hill rising among orange groves close to Kozan. As I rode on the back of the motorcycle, my excitement gradually turned into anxiety. I was going to a place where everything and everyone except my mother was foreign. I did not know how my mother's husband and other villagers would react to my unannounced visit. Then I remembered Uncle Ishak was with me and relaxed a little. Her new husband greeted us when we arrived at my mother's house. After Uncle Ishak introduced me, he told us to come inside and that my mother was making bread in the neighbor's house. I was sitting in a corner timidly, listening to the conversations of Uncle Ishak and my mother's husband, waiting for my mother to come as soon as possible.

My heartbeat quickened, and my emotions were like a rollercoaster. Finally, I saw my mother at the door of the room. "Welcome," she said to Uncle Ishak from the door, then turned to me coldly and said, "You are welcome too," then went directly to the kitchen. At that moment, the room froze. A dry "you are welcome too" without even looking at me after all the years and challenging roads.

Was this the only reaction she had?

I was stunned, unresponsive, and didn't know what to do. The people in the room were just as surprised as I was.

They couldn't understand why my mother was so cold and unresponsive to me. Uncle Ishak got up and left the room. At that moment, everything felt so foreign; the first thing that came to my mind was to get out of the room, run with all my strength and speed, and escape from the village.

When I was about to leave the room, I heard my mother's voice: "My Mehmet!"

It was a call that would melt all the ice and calm the fiercest storms.

She ran to me and hugged me.

I was stunned but had already fallen into her arms.

I missed her smell and presence, and I wanted to stop acting like a grown-up for a moment and be as much of a child as possible. I wanted to be my mother's little son. I tried to find my lost childhood in my mother's arms, absorbing every moment of the seconds I was presently in. We hugged each other for several minutes without speaking. It turns out they had only said to her, "Your guest has arrived," without mentioning that it was her son, Mehmet, who had come to visit. When she saw Uncle Ishak, she casually greeted us and went to pour tea without even looking at me. Maybe I was too grown up for my mother to recognize me. It didn't matter. We left all that behind and talked and talked for hours. I didn't get tired of talking, nor did she get bored of listening. From that day on, I started seeing my mother regularly every year.

Life has many different paths for everyone. No matter how close we are, everyone goes their way at the end of the day. So, it was not fair to put all the blame on my mother for the past or their breakup. Who has complete control over their destiny? After that day, I buried my anger and resentment toward my mother and opened the doors of my heart to her again.

After losing everything I have ever worked for, I now wonder if I will be strong enough to forgive the people who have caused this, or even my entire nation who silently sat on their hands and did not raise a single objection against the injustice and oppression.

Will I ever find the answer to this question, even many years later? Or will I suffer the same fate as Ahmet Kaya, Yılmaz Guney, Nazım Hikmet, and many others, who had great love and longing for their country but were forced to live in exile? Who knows?

GABBY'S MAT
Virginia, USA, November 2016

When I came home, Hatice and I started planning our new life's initial steps. We had to move to a smaller and more affordable house. Our monthly rent payment for the home in Church Point was $3,000, and when we included the utilities, this cost reached up to $4000.

We did not have any savings. Furthermore, we had taken cash advances from credit cards to complete our house in Turkey. We decided to sell some furniture and move into a new home with as little furniture as possible. This way, we could make money and reduce the table to roll. We also had to change the children's schools.

How would Nilgun and Fatih's therapies and medications work?

Now we did not have any health insurance and some of the medicines Fatih had to use daily cost around $1,800 per month. It was clear that our new life would not be accessible at all. We needed somewhere to go since our official documents and passports were canceled. Even if I wanted to work, I wouldn't be able to. I had to get a legal work permit first. Our legal status in the U.S. had also vanished overnight, but life continued quickly. I overcame many unbearable difficulties in my childhood but grew stronger. However, this was different now, and I was no longer alone. I didn't know where to move with my wife and three children. The weight on my shoulders had never been this much.

My chest was being crushed, and I felt suffocating. Fatih and Hakan had not returned from school, and Nilgun was playing in her room, unaware of everything. At that moment, Colonel Yuksel, also purged from service previously, called and said he wanted to visit us. With a habit from the old days, we forgot everything and started to clean the house to host guests. Hatice went to the kitchen and made tea. I took the broom and swept the entrance. For a moment, Hatice and I met eyes and started laughing. The situation made us forget our feelings. It was like medicine for us to forget everything and prepare for guests like a typical day.

Colonel Yuksel, Colonel Bugra, Colonel Huseyin, and a few friends visited our house to wish us good luck and support us. Friendship and true camaraderie bonded so strongly that anxiety, despair, fear, and sadness melted away next to the people with whom you shared this bond. On the first day of our new life, we could stand straight with the strength and support we received from our friends.

After dropping the kids off at the school bus and returning the following day, I witnessed an incredible scene of solidarity and hard work in our house.

A delegation from the NATO officer spouses group came to help. When I went to the kitchen door, Brigette, the wife of a French colonel, was looking for rental houses online, Gabby, the wife of a German colonel, was preparing a list of materials needed for the move, and the wife of another French colonel was taking pictures of the items to be sold and uploading them online. Our Norwegian family friend was arranging the kitchen supplies with Hatice, and a few other ladies I didn't know were helping them.

I greeted them and thanked them for their support. I was looking for a company to help move and clean the house and told them they didn't have to do this.

Gabby said, "Mehmet, all we ask of you is to take care of the kids. We are a family, and this is our house too. We will all move out together."

"You're going to need money, so don't waste money on moving and cleaning," she added. God, what a strange feeling this was!

A diplomat, an officer, and his family, condemned to social death by his state and pushed around by his citizens, received support from many "foreigners" that now felt like brothers and sisters. These people felt our pain, and they sincerely shared the anxiety we were suffering. While doing this, they did not care how sensitive the situation was, that it could cause a political and military crisis and even the possibility of any personal harm they may be subject to.

The scene I had just witnessed strengthened my belief that good will eventually prevail over evil, no matter how weak we may seem. With a historical example of women's solidarity and loyalty, we were able to rent a small and affordable house in Cove Point. The houses' rooms, toilets, and bathrooms at Church Point were cleaned by the spouses of officers who had reached the peak of their profession.

In addition to our Turkish friends, who were previously purged from service, my Greek, Norwegian, Italian, Canadian, French, German, Dutch, English and American colleagues helped us move with their vehicles. Sometimes they even brought their children for support. I didn't know how to feel when I saw Gabby grab the mop and start mopping the floor after the landlord pointed out a dirty spot in the dining room before returning our security deposit. Everyone had one goal: to stand by us, share the burden of difficult times, and show that we were not alone.

Our house turned into a festival place on the day of the move. I thanked my colleagues and their spouses, and their response will forever be etched in my memory, "We thank you. You gave us one of the most meaningful days of our lives." This was the purest, most sincere form of friendship based on virtue and without any self-interest. Their presence and support served as a life-raft for us in the vast ocean as our livelihood boat sank in this storm.

A new life full of hardships and unknowns awaited us. Despite all this, we still had our freedom and were united as a family; this gave us great comfort and consolation. Thousands of families in Turkey suffered the same fate, but most were traumatized by the incarceration of one or more family members.

We loved our home in Cove Point. It was a two-story townhouse. It was less spacious than our last house, but it had three rooms upstairs, with the bedroom and living room overlooking a magnificent river view. The living room had a balcony, with trees adorning the riverbank right in front of it. We were very worn out and tired, both emotionally and physically. In the tiredness of the first evening, we spent our first night just putting sheets on the beds without opening any boxes. The following day, Hatice started to arrange the house, and I was sitting on the table among the furniture and preparing a to-do list.

I needed to prepare the necessary documentation for the application that would provide the legal basis for our stay in America. In the document, which had to be filled out carefully, it was necessary to clearly state the conditions and reasons that required us to stay here and to support the file with documents. It was not our choice to stay here. Like my other colleagues, we were forced into this choice against our will unlawfully. We were fighting for our life and safety. As the application process was long and complex, we needed legal support. Even the most affordable lawyer charges around $3,000. We didn't have any income. Every dollar we spent was very precious. I decided to fill out the documents myself. Majors Engin and Goksel, who had been purged from the service previously, helped me and only left us with their support.

Since we had to submit documents about our past during the application process, my whole life flashed before my eyes like a movie.

One lifetime!

It was easy to say, but every moment was filled with struggle, hope, and sacrifice.

One of the questions in the document was, "Is there any possibility of torture if you return to Turkey?" I had a hard time answering this question.

Torture and human rights violations were widespread in Turkey, and the pictures and videos of tortured people were on TV and in newspapers. Some people who committed torture crimes and human violations were so bold that they avoided discussing what they did on TV shows. It was a like a nightmare, and everyone in Turkey had lost their sanity. I feared losing my sanity and seeking ways to suppress my anger.

General Akın Ozturk, former Chief of the Turkish Air Force and a Turkish National Security Council member were one of many torture victims in the wake of the coup attempt. He was a 64-year-old and had served his country with loyalty, honor, and integrity for 46 years. He was a personification of what a true leader should be and was very respected by his subordinates. General Akin Ozturk was in Izmir with his family on the night of the coup. When the events started unfolding, General Hulusi Akar, the Chief of the Turkish General Staff, and General Abidin Unal, the Chief of the Turkish Air Force, called Akin Ozturk and asked him personally to fly out to Akinci Air Base in Ankara. Akinci Air Base was claimed to be used as the Headquarters for the coup. Hulusi Akar and Abidin Unal knew General Akin Ozturk could use his influence and authority to convince the officers who were claimed to stage a coup. Later General Akin Ozturk would be charged for being the coup's leader. Unfortunately, he had to suffer one of the worst mischiefs a soldier could face in his lifetime, betrayal by his chain of command. Hulusi Akar and Abidin Unal drew General Akin Ozturk into a trap.

General Akin Ozturk was arrested on the night of the coup and was subject to all kinds of inhumane practices and torture along with several other high-ranking Turkish military officers. They were stripped naked, and their pictures later served to the newspapers had visible proof of torture. What kind of villainy and what sort of hatred motivated these actions?

Thousands of high-ranking officers had been handcuffed behind their backs for days. They were subjected to unheard-of humiliations and mistreatments that would even constitute a war crime during the war if they were done to captive enemy soldiers. They were not even allowed to meet their toilet needs and were subjected to various tortures by inhumane thugs who introduced themselves as plainclothes police officers.

Captain Huseyin Demirtas witnessed this torture. He was the Turkish Military Attaché in Romania then and followed his orders to return to Turkey after the coup attempt. Captain Huseyin fell ill after his return to the country and had to be operated on urgently. He was taken into custody by the police while he was about to be taken to the operating room. Although he was in agony for a week under custody, he was not allowed treatment or surgery. He had witnessed all kinds of torture during his detention period. After being released and leaving the country, he actively used his social media account to increase international awareness about the torture and human rights violations through his personal experience and what he had witnessed.

The regime had arrested tens of thousands of people in a couple of weeks, and due to the limitations of the detention facilities, nearly 40 people were put in rooms that were purposed for a couple of people. For this reason, about forty thousand convicts, including thieves, murderers, and rapists, were pardoned so that they could continue the arrests and the manhunts.

Amnesty International and many other human rights watch institutions recorded this situation in official reports.

If I ever returned to Turkey, being subject to torture was almost inevitable as this had become merely a standard procedure.

Since thousands of innocent people who had nothing to do with the uprising were declared terrorists, every treatment done to them was justified by society. Erdogan did not tolerate little sympathy or compassion, even towards women, children, or older people among the accused people. He would repeat his rhetoric "If you show mercy to them, you will soon be in their shoes begging for mercy."

There was such a dire situation that a provincial head of the ruling party could become unscrupulous enough to say, "Let them eat tree bark" for the families and children of thousands of citizens who were deprived of their jobs, were prevented from working in other jobs, and were condemned to starvation. Torture wasn't just in police stations and prisons. It spread everywhere through cursing, humiliation, threats, and social isolation.

After adding all these human rights violations and torture as evidence to my application document, I could not come to my senses for a few hours. "Let's take the kids and go out for a while," I told Hatice. Virginia Beach was 20 minutes from our house. I hoped that the sounds of the ocean and seagulls and the smell of iodine would suppress the heavy feelings surrounding my soul. The children were playing on the beach, and Hatice cared for them.

Staring at the vast waters of the Atlantic Ocean, I took a deep breath. I fully appreciated the liberty and freedom I had here in the U.S. Unfortunately, many take this for granted and do not realize what a blessing freedom is.

If we had not been able to leave Turkey, I would have suffered the same fate as these thousands of innocent people whose photos I had seen a few hours ago. Even though we were far from our homeland, we were free and safe. We could freely breathe the ocean breeze, free from the possibility of someone knocking on our door to arrest and torture us at any moment.

While so many innocent people were persecuted in Turkey, nothing we experienced brought us joy. Our friends and innocent people came to our minds, and the smiles on our faces became dull.

We were physically living a life here in the US, but it felt like our souls, hearts, and minds were still in Turkey, and our sadness exponentially increased with every bad news we received. Virginia Beach is one of the most popular tourist destinations on the East Coast. People would come here to relax, forget their difficulties, and have fun, even for a few days. For us, this place now felt like an island where we had to take refuge after our ship had sunk. We were waiting for any good news or new development to save us from this island. I was able to complete the application documents in a week. The house was starting to settle down. We hosted a few of our friends who supported us during the moving process for breakfast to thank them.

Only a few days were left until Christmas. The decorations of the houses in the vicinity were completed, and the street turned into a street fair. Fatih enjoyed this the most; his happiness was as if he saw it for the first time as he passed every house. Although he was 17 years old, his development was behind his peers due to his illness, and he could not comprehend what we went through. Whenever I looked at Fatih, I learned new life lessons from him. Despite heavy seizures, surgeries, and medications, he never lost his enthusiasm for life, and the pure child-like happiness on his face never faded. He was brave and resilient, focusing on what life gave him, not what it took from him. We did not restrict Fatih in any way. We would take him everywhere we went and make him participate in every activity we did. This interest and love gave him life; he could be happy with the little things around him if we supported him. I wanted to be in Fatih's place, to immerse myself in the decorations and lights of the houses we were passing by without being aware of the tragedy we were living in. That evening, Hatice was quieter than usual. She had not had time to think about the hectic environment that lasted for days, and the specters lurking in the corners of her mind had just found the necessary space to come out. There was a look of pessimism mixed with worry on her face.

"What will happen now? Will we ever return to Turkey again?" She asked worriedly.

I hugged her softly and said, "I don't know." I didn't want to give her false hope.

Despite six months, no international sanctions and significant reactions to the regime's horrific crimes against its people and humanity had come to the fore. This tragedy was ignored, and despite his crimes, Erdogan continued to be greeted with the same magnificence during his foreign visits. Under these conditions, the regime became more robust, and its radical supporters became irritable and militant.

I thought of the tens of thousands of people who had to leave their country after the 1978 Iranian revolution. Did they keep asking each other the same question: "Will we ever return to our country again?" Despite 38 long years, the regime in Iran managed to survive and silence all the opposition despite all the poverty and lawlessness.

The Erdogan regime also started to set up a system like the one in Iran, calculating that they could continue to hold power if they followed the same path.

More than a million people were armed with a structure similar to the militia forces in Iran, and a parallel armed system was established under the leadership of SADAT. By removing the people's trust in each other, a ground was created that allowed even the slightest oppositional movement to be declared an act of terrorism, and every dissident individual was arrested.

The Erdogan regime also laid the foundation of a structure similar to the Iranian Revolutionary Guards. Again, the shady organization SADAT played a leading role in this process: tens of thousands of police officers, special operations members, officers, non-commissioned officers, and specialist non-commissioned officers were recruited. The essential pre-requisite of this recruitment was loyalty to Erdogan. This code also led the state's law enforcement and armed forces unfortunately, the rule of law, the constitution, and many other guiding principles needed to be revised.

Just as the religious leader was sanctified in Iran, Erdogan was declared the leader and caliph of the Islamic world. SADAT's founder and Erdogan's adviser, retired general Adnan Tanrıverdi, admitted that the Turkish Armed Forces had been transformed within the scope of his projects, declaring that their duty was to "prepare the ground for the coming of the Mahdi" and presented to the world that everything was implemented with a perverted agenda.

A deputy of the regime went to the extent that he stated, "Erdogan has all the attributes of God."

The regime aimed to gain people's unquestioning obedience to Erdogan with a spiritual bond by exploiting religious feelings. In Iran, the religious leader was able to control entire political institutions. Erdogan also abolished the office of the prime minister with a constitutional amendment. As the president, he rose to a position to control the entire legislative, executive, and judiciary on his own. There was no separation of powers or checks and balances left.

Like the Iranian regime, the Erdogan regime was also supported by Russia. Under these circumstances, it would be too optimistic to expect the situation in Turkey to improve in the short term.

"I can't take you to Turkey, but if you want, we can go on a journey," I told Hatice. My cousin lived in Arkansas and had been inviting us to his house for a long time. They have constantly invited us to visit and stay there since I was purged from the military. We moved house and completed the application documents. We didn't have school priorities as the kids were on Christmas break. We both prepared our suitcases and believed this trip would benefit us. Arkansas was 14 hours from Virginia Beach. Hatice and I had planned to arrive in Arkansas without stopping at a hotel by taking turns driving.

Our route passed over the top of the Blue Ridge mountains. It had a magnificent view; one could stop and watch it for hours. The farmhouses lined up along the road, and the cows enjoying the vast greenery reflected the peaceful picture of a calm flow of life. While watching the scenery, we compared these to the Taurus Mountains and discussed our childhood memories. The trip was also perfect for Hakan. Our youngest son Hakan was 11 years old and caught in all the events. Since his siblings were disabled, he tried to support us as much as possible. He had a strong character and a developed sense of compassion. He was reacting to events with a maturity well above his age. However, he also needed clarification and to learn how to explain the situation to his friends at school. He did not know how to answer the question "Is your mother or father in the military?" On the form he filled out to determine his elective courses. He tried to collect the puzzle pieces in his mind and asked me, "Dad, are we kicked out of being a military family as well?"

"No, son, your father had served honorably in the military for 24 years. We were unjustly dismissed, but no one can erase those years," I replied.

Those who accused us of treason were those who did not even send their children to mandatory military service in Turkey. In short, these imposters who pretended to be patriots have plundered Turkey's resources for their interests and grew fatter, richer, and filthier as the people became poorer and weaker. Even if they unjustly usurped what we had, it was inevitable that they would not be able to erase our past and our memories.

As we talked about the past, Hakan continued asking questions and went on a journey roaming his parents' childhood and trying to discover them.

Strange sounds from Nilgun interrupted the ongoing pleasant conversation. She couldn't breathe. She was trembling noticeably. I pulled the car over. As soon as Hatice got into the back seat, she took Nilgun in her arms and started shouting. "Mehmet, Nilgun is dying! Nilgun is dying!" We were familiar with these kinds of emergencies with Fatih, but Fatih never had a seizure until he was five. Nilgun, on the other hand, was not even one year old. We couldn't do anything and witnessed Nilgun's struggle in our arms on a roadside amongst the mountains. The seizure lasted over a minute, and Nilgun's face turned red. Her body was burning in flames. She suddenly opened her eyes with a cough. It seemed that the seizure was over. She closed her eyes again without the slightest sign of life in her innocent gaze.

We immediately started to check her pulse and listen to her heartbeat. Thankfully her heart was beating. We couldn't hold back our tears. This was not a good sign; 80 percent of lissencephaly patients died before they were a few years old due to severe seizures. Since Nilgun was born prematurely, her condition was more sensitive. She stayed in the intensive care unit for 14 days after her birth, and her tiny body was tired on the first day of her life. The truths we tried to bury deep in our minds in the middle of the storms stood before us with all their weight and coldness.

The possibility of losing Nilgun was a very harsh feeling. Although she had just entered our lives, she became the joy of our house and illuminated our world with her smile, gaze, and pure and precise nature.

At that moment, "Oh God, isn't the situation we're suffering already harsh enough that you're putting us through this?" I thought to myself. My reproach was about to turn into a rebellion. I could not find the strength to restart the 17-year struggle with Fatih. As these thoughts captured my brain and soul, I became unresponsive and froze.

Hatice gave Nilgun a fever reducer, removed some of her clothes, and monitored her condition. The nearest hospital was almost an hour away, and we had to keep going. When Nilgun's fever dropped, she relaxed and opened her beautiful eyes again.

The rest of the road passed in silence. Nobody spoke, and we were trying to get over what we had just experienced. My eyes were stuck in the rearview mirror. I was relieved when I saw Nilgun's smile. We arrived at my cousin's house in the evening. He welcomed us with his wife and two daughters and prepared one room of the house for the children and another one for us. It was a relief to see the face of a friend and relative.

We chatted until late at night. How complicated everything was. Our emotions were changing dimensions with the pressure of the severe traumas we experienced. Sometimes we laughed, and sometimes couldn't help the tears that suddenly flowed from our eyes. As we talked, our troubles became tears and found their way out, flowing down our cheeks. I cannot recall what time we slept that night, but the friendship and closeness we experienced were perfect for us.

We were there for almost two weeks. They were both teachers and had bought their house and settled in.

The cost of living in Arkansas was cheaper than in Virginia, and it might be relatively easy to make a living here. We talked about job options with my cousin's wife, Goksel, and she told me about her experience in America. We discussed many options, such as driving an Uber, delivering pizza, selling supplies in the flea market, translating, preparing website presentations, and selling on Amazon.

Since I did not have a work permit, I could not search for a registered job.

I graduated from the Military Academy with a degree in electronics engineering. I fulfilled distinguished, prestigious duties that required talent and merit, including command at sea on board a warship and teaching at the Military Academies. I completed my MBA with honors from Purdue University, Krannert School of Management. With my military and academic experience and knowledge, I could have been a suitable candidate for many jobs. However, I could take a step after the official procedures were completed.

While I was still on active duty, we met with the owner of a Turkish restaurant. He had a brother with health problems, and when he saw Fatih, he chatted with us for a while, and we became very close. When leaving the restaurant, he gave us his card and said he wanted to stay in touch with us. We met several times afterward; they had visited us as a family at our home in Church Point while returning from vacation. When he learned about our situation, he called and told me I could work in one of his restaurants. He called again when we were in Arkansas and asked if I had considered his offer. It was a unique opportunity, given the circumstances I was in. I would have a job and gain experience in a new field.

Since Hatice loves to cook, we even thought we would open our restaurant. I wanted to know how right taking on such a responsibility without a work permit would be. How would we manage the legal process afterward if something happened to a customer or employee? It was inappropriate to endanger ourselves and someone else who had become our family friend. Therefore, I thanked him once again for his kind offer, saying that I would wait for the legal process to finalize and try to somehow manage everything until then. He understood the situation and told me that his doors were always open and that we should let him know if we needed anything.

Doing business online on Amazon stood out as the most viable option. I opened my first Amazon account in Arkansas and partially learned from Goksel how to package the products, ship them, and decide on what products to sell. Tears filled my eyes when my cousin said we could stay with them until we got our work permits and saved on rent and kitchen expenses.

We had grown close to my cousin while he was working at the Naval Forces Headquarters in Ankara, Turkey. He was studying at the university and would visit us almost every weekend. He would sleep over sometimes. After all those years, he opened his home and heart to us, showing a great example of friendship and loyalty when we needed him the most.

We knew this was a heartfelt offer but could not accept it. In Turkey, we have a proverb that states, "Two households cannot get on in one house," and we were already seeing the wisdom behind this saying. The children had already started to fight about which channel to watch etc. So, no matter how sincere and well-intentioned their offer was, we stated that it would be better for us to return. We did not want to be a burden. We thanked these beautiful people and returned to Virginia Beach.

We would try to sell the household items we could only sell and use our credit cards once we had an income again. Our return to Cove Point was good in many ways. We could continue gathering with our colleagues and maintain contact with our friends from NATO HQ.

Meanwhile, our American friends did not leave us alone. They organized social activities and language courses for our spouses and supported us in adapting to our new lives. Especially the couple Mary and Ken helped us with everything and supported my efforts to find a job as much as they could. Mary had arranged a phone call with a friend, previously an executive at Sears. She gave me a lot of advice when I told her I would go into sales at Amazon.

Meanwhile, Fatih and Hakan's school principals also closely monitored our situation. One day when I went to drop Hakan off at school, the assistant principal said that he was aware of our situation and that they had decided not to charge the lunch fee for Hakan and Fatih until I found a job. I couldn't control the tears that streamed from my eyes. It was a very complex feeling. I have not received any support from anyone for my children until now, and I have tried to offer them the best opportunities I can. I still needed foresight about what the days ahead would bring. I had to accept this support hand for my children. The school principal also had tears in his eyes and tried to calm me down by saying, "These days will pass. Now it's time to think about these children together."

That day, I once again thought, "I must earn an income as soon as possible." On the way back, I pulled the car in front of a Goodwill store. I had opened my Amazon account but had no idea what to sell. When I arrived at the book aisle at Goodwill, I saw that the books were only selling for $1 to $3. After examining hundreds of books, I bought nearly 20 books I thought I could sell on Amazon. According to my calculations, I could earn between 3 and 7 dollars per book, calculating the commission and shipping fees. In the evening, Hatice, Hakan, and I arranged the books on the table in the living room and added them to our Amazon sales list. We named our store "Books-and-More." We thought that if we could make money from selling books, we would also start selling other products. I couldn't sleep that night.

I would frequently check my Amazon account. "I wonder if we will be able to make a sale?" I was thinking anxiously. It had been more than two months since I left my profession, and we did not have a single penny of income. We could sell one of the sofas in the house and some of Hatice's handbags. That was all. The next day, after a long wait, we got the news of our first sale on Amazon with a notification on my phone in the afternoon.

What a joy this was! We repeatedly looked at the phone, rejoicing as if we had made the first online sale. Towards the evening, I packed the book, put a thank you card in the packaging, and shipped it out.

If all had gone well, we would have made around $5 from this sale. "If we can sell ten books daily, we can pay our rent!" I was explaining to Hatice. The following weekend, as a family, we wandered into every Goodwill store in Virginia Beach and found nearly sixty books.

Without wasting time, we put them into our inventory in the system. We sold nine books in the past week, prepared each package with great care, and sent it to the mail with thank you cards. Every morning after I dropped the kids off at school, I wandered around the stores and looked at the book sale aisles of the libraries.

In a short time, we had increased the number of books on our list to three hundred and started selling two or three books daily. I felt a familiar excitement awakening in me: the excitement of little Mehmet, nine years old, walking around with a crate of shoe paint on his back.

Even if it was only enough to cover our kitchen expenses, earning money through hard work was a good feeling. Within a few months, we had listed nearly 1000 products in our store on Amazon, including toys, bags, picture frames, books, and pens.

We sent seven or eight packages daily, visiting outlet stores or businesses with discounts to find new products. The rooms of our house were filled with products to be sold. Since no space was left, I took some large boxes up to the idle attic, accessed by a small ladder. As sales increased, our dreams got bigger. After a while, we opened an eBay account beside Amazon and started selling from there. Finally, in March, we could pay our rent not with a credit card but with the money we earned from Amazon sales. It was impossible to support a family of five by making $1400 a month. Every month, the credit limit of one of our existing credit cards reached the maximum limit, and our debts increased.

Whenever we spoke to our relatives in Turkey, they asked why we did not return. Some of them were beginning to believe the fallacy that we would have returned if we weren't guilty.

Our families sent us financial support by collecting money among themselves. This money, which they found and brought together by pushing their limits as much as possible, had very high moral value. But it only corresponded to $900 when it reached the US due to the exchange rate, and it could not even cover the rent of our house. I was very touched by the fact that they thought of us and wanted to support us in this challenging period, and I accepted the money with the thought that one day I would pay it back.

Selling on Amazon and eBay must have honed my business skills. We increased our earnings by putting new products on sale every day. Still, we needed to earn more to cover our expenses. We had reached the limits of each credit card, and the amount of interest we paid was increasing exponentially. Hatice also started to make decorative handcrafted items for additional income. Our friend, Sofia, the spouse of a colleague from NATO, was taking these products to activities attended by other military spouses and trying to sell them.

Together with Hakan, we set up kiosks at flea markets. I was trying to sell products outside of online platforms. These efforts yielded few results. Every night, after the children went to bed, I did research. I constantly searched for what else I could do for more income. It had already been six months, but I needed to get my work permit. Therefore, I could not apply for a regular job.

When May came, our situation got worse. I had nothing to sell but my watch, which was rewarded to me by then President Abdullah Gul for my achievements in the Turkish Military War College. I decided to put that up for sale. It was impossible to support a family of five by selling possessions. While removing my watch from my wrist and sending it to the customer by courier, I thought of a classic Turkish movie, Zugurt Aga (The Broken Landlord). It is a movie about the hardships and struggles a pure-hearted Agha (Landlord) from Eastern Turkey faced after he set out for Istanbul after a series of mishaps in his village. I was experiencing the same feeling he felt when he had to sell his leather boots, which he had identified himself with for many years, to the junk dealer. Despite everything, having my wife and children by my side was my most incredible wealth. I was determined to do everything I could with dignity to support them. As in my high school years, I would keep my head high, no matter how rough the conditions were.

MY FATHER'S TEARS
Kayseri, Turkey, 1990s

When I started high school, life seemed to accelerate, and years flowed like water. Three years later, I would be taking the college admission exam, which could have been the turning point of my life. In Turkey, the college admission exam was administered once a year, and millions of students would sweat bullets over this exam as their future depended on the outcome of this couple-hour-long test. My classes were going very well, but it was obvious that more than this would be needed to be successful in the college admission exam. I would compete against millions of people, and most had extra help, such as private tutors, private classrooms, and study centers to support them.

My hometown Yahyali had no extra support for students preparing for college admissions. Historically the college enrollment rates had been meager in my hometown, and there was not much demand to this end. Most of our teachers in high school had been working at the same school for many years, and they had internalized the convenience of holding students responsible for this failure. Two new younger teachers were assigned to our school as part of their mandatory military service, one was teaching physics, and the other was teaching a math class. They both used to give private lessons for university admissions exams and agreed to help us prepare. They would help us solve the questions from previous years' admissions exams in their free time from classes. I got along well with both of our teachers, and I followed their lectures with great pleasure and attention as they explained their solutions to questions.

"I wish the classes were longer and they could show more questions," I thought.

Since the high school years were when we stepped into adolescence, many of my friends spent their time and energy trying to impress the girls in the class and did not focus on their courses. They didn't believe they could be successful in college admissions. I thought I had to do something to change this mindset and make everyone believe that we could get admissions if we worked harder.

In our weekend study group, we continued to study on Saturdays, but the time allocated to games, conversation, entertainment, and talks about girls decreased considerably.

Students choose between science and literature curriculums at the beginning of the second year of high school. I chose the science curriculum along with 35 other students. The science curriculum was more challenging, and many friends preferred the literature curriculum. Most students with college enrolment aspirations were enrolled in the science curriculum, which gave me the opportunity I sought.

One day, at the end of the class, I returned to the classroom and started speaking out to my peers. "Would you listen to me for 15 minutes?" I told them that we would take the college admissions exam a year later and that if we did not study harder, we would be part of the unemployed high school students' tradition and be stranded here for the rest of our lives. I offered them my offer: study together for two hours every day after school and prepare for the admissions exam. They were convinced that if we did this, we would have a better shot at it. I would teach mathematics, physics, and chemistry; Sevgi would teach biology; and Murat would teach literature. We would study our subjects first and introduce them to the rest of the class when it was our turn. There was tremendous support from the course, and everyone said, "We can do it!" We were excited and wanted to bring this to life soon.

We had a problem; the school closed after classes. I told them to leave the matter to me and that I would ask Mr. Vahit for help. I knocked on Mr. Vahit's door the next day with a petition. Our acquaintance with Mr. Vahit had now turned into a friendship, and whenever he saw me, he would ask me how I was doing. When I handed the petition to him, instead of making me wait, he said, "Sit down." After reading the petition, he muttered with a humble but bewildered expression, "I have been teaching for all these years. This is the first time my students have received such a request."

"So, you mean that classes will end, but you will continue to teach among yourselves, right?" He felt the need to confirm what he had read.

"Mr. Vahit, we promise you. Our goal is to do our best and get into college. I assure you we will succeed," I said.

Mr. Vahit was convinced. He said that we could use the classroom for two hours after the classes ended and that he would hold me responsible if there were any problems. Despite the responsibility on my shoulder, I was thrilled I could get permission. Thus, we were starting Yahyali's first college preparatory program and would prepare for the exam together by continuing this program for six months.

Even the families who initially hesitated to let their daughters stay in the school after the classes started to support us. We were all determined to try our best and work harder.

Our friendship has also thrived during these classes; we had a bond of unity deriving from destiny. Our teachers supported us by bringing college preparatory books and practice exams they could find. The program had become popular, and some of our friends from the literature curriculum would soon join us. Taking this development as an opportunity, I assigned one of them the responsibility of philosophy and logic courses and expanded the program's scope. These efforts soon bore fruit. At the end of my second year of high school, I ranked third among five thousand students in the practice exam administered in Kayseri and the surrounding provinces. Four of our classmates managed to be ranked in the top five hundred. We were hopeful, and our self-confidence had increased.

I continued my summer job tradition during the summer vacation after my sophomore year in high school. I found a job at a rest area called PETNAK on the Adana-Kayseri highway and started to work the night shift to support the household.

There were few customers in the evenings. I was alone and had the responsibility of the night shift. I didn't struggle much since there were at most seven or eight customers simultaneously. I witnessed the sunrise every morning, looking at the passing buses and dreaming of my journey to college on one of these buses. The restaurant owner's two nephews, who were mining engineers, often visited the facility. With the excitement of seeing someone who had graduated from college, I asked them about college life, how they succeeded in the admissions exam, and how to prepare for it. I listened to what they said. They were like heroes to me. Until that day, I didn't talk to someone who grew up in my hometown, Yahyali and graduated from college to get a professional job.

The summer vacation was about to end, and a significant change was about to happen in my life. My success in the practice admission exam drew much attention and appreciation from teachers and faculty, who talked about how to support me to this end better. Attending a high school in Kayseri for my senior year was one of the options which would give me a better opportunity for success.

Mr. Vahit, our school principal, believed that even though I was first in Yahya Gazi High School, the bar for success and the competition was much higher in big cities and that I would be better off attending a high school in Kayseri. My achievement here in Yahyali was like being a champion in the third league. However, I was going to compete against teams playing in the premier league, and even the worst team in that league was better than the champions of the third league. As always, there were discouraging voices from some people who despised my achievements. They would try to belittle my achievements in high school and claim that getting college admission would be absolute proof of academic success. So, I made my decision; I was going to study my senior year in Kayseri at any cost.

Mr. Vahit said he knew the principal of Sumer High School, one of the leading Kayseri leading schools, and wrote a reference letter for me. I took the letter, kissed Mr. Vahit's hand, and left the school. My father was against the idea of going to Kayseri. Since I was used to ignoring his objections, I jumped on the bus and hit the road to Kayseri to enroll in Sumer High School.

When the school principal received Mr. Vahit's greeting and letter, he told me to come with my parents for enrollment. I told him I had no guardian, came alone, and wanted to enroll myself. Although the principal was surprised, he was impressed by my determination. "Ok, let's find a solution. Since I am the principal, I cannot be your guardian, but let's ask Mr. Rustem, who served as a janitor at the school. Maybe he will agree to be your guardian." He had found a solution for me.

He called Mr. Rustem to his office and "I want you to be the guardian of Yahyali's most successful student. Will you be his guardian?"

"Sir, of course! I couldn't reject your request," Mr. Rustem said and signed my enrollment documents. From that moment on, I became a student at Sumer High School.

The number of senior students at Yahya Gazi High School was, at most, 60. At my new school, I was one of five hundred students. Not only did I come to Kayseri, but I also enrolled in one of the best high schools in the city. My father had distant relatives in Kayseri. I somehow wanted to get support and make it through the year. It was tough to leave my high school and friends in Yahyali. "Who will lecture us now for the exam?" They asked me.

"Don't worry; it's only a two-hour drive. I can come back before the exam, and we can go over the topics together," I replied, promising not to break my ties with them.

"There are many private studies centers in Kayseri. I can send you their practice exams," I said as I tried to comfort them.

We had set big goals together, worked hard, and set out on this path.

Over the past year, this belief has grown, and the desire to get into a college has become a passion.

The fact that I was going to Kayseri, like always, caused many negative comments among our relatives and neighbors. Some thought I was embarking on a reckless adventure, and some argued that "the city life is not like it is here. How will you go there and survive on your own?"

They weren't wrong. The money I earned in the summer was not enough to stay in the dormitory. My father was not able to support me. No one from my relatives could support me. Sometimes I was angry, "What a thoughtless decision I made." As if all the difficulties weren't enough, I started to shoulder the weight of the big city.

While going back and forth between my decision, an acquaintance of ours who worked in finance said, "The governor's office gives scholarships to successful students whose financial situation is insufficient. Why don't you apply?"

I wrote a petition and went to the district governor's office promptly. I gave the petition to the clerk and told him I wanted to meet with the Governor. After looking at the petition and scrutinizing me, the clerk said, "Give me a moment. If the Governor is available and accepts to meet with you, I can get you 5 minutes."

A few minutes later, I found myself in the office. This room was more significant than our school principals, and when I was in front of the Governor, I got very excited. The Governor was a young man. He listened to me carefully as I briefly explained the situation and said he would approve the scholarship, but he wanted to confirm by calling the school. "Connect me with the principal of Yahya Gazi High School," he said to the clerk, and he gestured for me to sit down out with the corner of his eye. Before long, Mr. Vahit was on the line.

"I have a student of yours with me, and he applied for a scholarship from the governor's office to study in Kayseri. I am calling to get your confirmation," he said. I could hear the conversation from the speaker on the phone.

Mr. Vahit said, "Dear Governor, I have been monitoring Dagci closely for five years. He is enthusiastic, successful, and our school valedictorian. If you find it appropriate, this scholarship will be rightfully deserved," and he gave me his complete support. I was leaving the governor's office, which I entered with hope and excitement, having received an education scholarship. Life does not offer equal opportunities to everyone, but if you work hard for a goal, it will open new doors and opportunities. That day, Mr. Vahit and the Governor were my heroes who saved me.

My senior year of high school was one of the fastest years of my life. My first day at Sumer High School went better than I expected. I was sitting in the same row with two other students, Semih and Bulent. I had good feelings about both. Our class was 48 people, and I was a stranger to everyone. Almost everyone in the class has taken private courses since their first year. The emphasis was on college admission exam-related subjects rather than school lectures. In most of the classes, the teachers talked about the topics that could be on the admission exam. I had to work very hard from day one. Even though I understood the subjects, I had no private course practice. Other students were answering the questions before I was able to solve half of them.

Succeeding in the college admissions exam was my number one priority. Many would say, "We told you so," if I didn't. After school, I studied seven or eight hours a day with very short breaks. On the weekends, I took practice exams and tried to test my level. I scored between 400 and 420 out of 600 in the first practice exams. I was behind many of my friends with these scores. I had never experienced the feeling of being behind until that day.

My biggest passion in Kayseri was to buy pickles and pastries from the mobile kiosks waiting in front of the park. I had to use the money I earned from my summer job carefully. One day my father came to visit me unexpectedly, and we spent a whole day together.

This was towards the end of autumn, and Kayseri had dry frost. Despite this, for the first time, spending time as father and son warmed my heart, and we wandered all day long, regardless of the cold. While saying goodbye to him from the Kayseri bus terminal, he hugged me and said, "Son, study well and become a man. You see the situation we are in." My father's support, six years later and in a very unenthusiastic sentence, still meant a lot to me.

After that day, I would get more successful results in my classes and practice exams. I began to attract the attention of my teachers, and my friendships were improving daily. I enjoyed finding the spirit of the mountain climber in me again, and I continued to study after school without interruption.

One day, when we went outside for recess, I saw one of my close friends, Kemal, arguing with someone I did not know, and I couldn't help but get involved in the fight. The kid who punched Kemal was about my size, and I hit him back. Other students stepped in and separated us, but this kid threatened me and warned me that I should be prepared for what was coming after school. He said he would make me regret what I had done. When we went to the classroom, my close friends asked me how I dared to punch him.

The boy Kemal was arguing with was a bully involved in many incidents. Since I was new, I did not know him, and I now understood why Kemal did not return the punch. I would be in trouble if everything were sorted out. A few friends sitting in the back rows of the class, who were not very interested in the lessons, comforted me. "Don't worry. We'll be with you." The support of my friends gave me some relief, but the person I was against was a complete bully.

I considered reporting the situation to the principal, but this case would reach Mr. Vahit. He trusted me and referred me. I eliminated this option. I would accept my fate and wait for what would happen after school.

When the classes were over, four of my friends stayed with me. The infamous bully was waiting for us with seven or eight people. He was playing with a butterfly knife in his hand with rapid movements. The situation was more difficult. Getting into a fight with someone with a knife would be the dumbest thing I could do. The friends who said they would support me were also scared in the face of the scene, and I knew they were afraid even if they tried to hide it. It was utterly pointless to drag them into a fight. I told them to wait for me there, and I would go and face him one-on-one.

I started walking towards the group about a hundred meters away. When I got close enough to call them, "If you're brave enough, you can come by yourself, and we can figure this out one-on-one." He was shocked.

"You think I'm afraid of you?" He said, gesturing to his friends to stay and started walking, waving the butterfly knife in his hand. When he approached me, I said, "My name is Mehmet. My friends call me Dagci. It was not my intention to humiliate or challenge you. When I saw Kemal being punched, I responded without thinking. Wouldn't you do the same for your friend?" He was surprised. He stopped turning the butterfly knife in his hand.

"You didn't know who I was?" He asked.

Maybe he thought I was challenging him.

"I didn't, and I apologize for today's incident," I replied. "I don't want to fight with you. I want to be friends if you accept," I added.

This apology and my unexpected reaction softened the mood. He put the butterfly knife in his pocket, came to me, extended his hand, and shook hands. "Since you are new to this school, if you need anything, let me know," he said.

Both groups were watching the situation. They couldn't understand what was happening. After that day, I became friends with the school bully and learned one of my life lessons. It was foolish to jump into the center of an event without understanding and listening to the issue.

When winter break arrived, I received a certificate of appreciation. I became one of the most successful students in my new school, just like in Yahya Gazi High School. My success caught the attention of vice principal Mr. Mukerrem. He also chose me for the two-person team to represent the school in the knowledge contest held throughout Kayseri. Nearly 30 high schools would compete, and after the eliminations, a male and female student from each city would meet with the president in Ankara. The selection was a two-stage process. The first three schools would be determined through the elimination rounds, and an interview would select two students from these school teams. Mr. Mukerrem reminded us to wear our best clothes on the day of the competition and said that he trusted us and believed we would succeed.

The students came with their families. Mr. Mukerrem brought me. The results of the 100-question written exam were announced towards noon. At Sumer High School, we were in the top three, and if we passed the interview, we would represent Kayseri. Our teacher congratulated us and said, "Well done; you have made me proud."

In the interview, they asked where I lived, what my parents did, and if I had a relative with whom I could stay if I were selected for the group that would go to Ankara.

I needed clarification on what kind of interview this was.

Our financial situation was questioned rather than our success and ability to represent.

My answers did not satisfy the delegation, and I could not pass the interview. State institutions were supposed to offer equal opportunity to everyone, but that was different. Your effort, hard work, and success will get you to a certain point. You would need wealthy relatives or acquaintances with authority and power to move beyond this point.

Mr. Mukerrem was aware of everything.

"You're among the top three schools in the big city, and now it's time to celebrate." He took us to Zumrut Patisserie, the biggest patisserie in Kayseri, and we ordered dessert with ice cream. Even though I did not show it to my teacher, my anger did not subside. "Despite these injustices, I will be a great man in the future," I thought.

The days chased each other quickly, and the exam day was fast approaching. As promised, I visited my friends at Yahya Gazi High School, went to a class, and gave them the practice exams I had brought. I was pleased and delighted that their desire to succeed did not fade.

I did not neglect to go to Mr. Vahit's room, and I once again thanked him by showing him the certificate of appreciation I received. I also visited Ramazan and Emrah's schools and talked to their teachers. Even though going to Kayseri separated us, I always kept their well-being and academic success, and future in my mind. Not only mine, but all our destinies were dependent on the school.

In those years, the college admission examination had two stages: the Student Selection Examination (OSS) and the Student Placement Examination (OYS). To enter a four-year college, success in both was necessary. My dream was to become an officer, a doctor, or a teacher. There was a large military housing in the city center of Kayseri, as there were two large military units, a tank factory, and an airborne brigade. Every time I passed in front of this facility guarded by two soldiers, I would look through the bars and wonder about the life behind the wire mesh. On the other hand, I felt like I was born to be a teacher. I started teaching when I was in middle school.

Teaching, guiding, and motivating people was one of my favorite things to do. My dream of becoming a doctor was an attempt to challenge poverty. Since there was one hospital and a couple of doctors in my hometown Yahyali, patients were referred to Develi or Kayseri in important cases. My Uncle Mehmet, whom I was named after, had a cerebral hemorrhage that could not be treated in Yahyali. He was transferred to Kayseri, but unfortunately, he passed away while being moved. He could not be treated on the road, and it was already too late for him when he reached the Kayseri State Hospital.

My grandmother always supported me in going to school. Maybe that's why she wanted me to be a doctor. I had to decide. After a year in Kayseri, I realized how difficult it was to study without financial support. If I were to get into college, money would be required for housing, food, books, clothing, tuition, and more.

I was beginning to think that attending a military school would be the best option. I had written Gulhane Military Medical Academy as my first choice and Bogazici University as my second choice as a mathematics teacher. I also applied to the Naval Academy since the Military Academy had an additional exam at that time. The exam results were a victory for me. I ranked 2011th out of over one million participants.

While waiting for my university placement, I got on the Istanbul bus to take the Naval Academy exam on a hot July evening. The Naval Academy was in the Tuzla district on the Anatolian side of Istanbul. I planned to arrive in Istanbul early and return to Kayseri on the first bus after taking the exams. After a fourteen-hour journey, I arrived in Istanbul, which I had only seen on television. At around seven in the morning, I got off the bus at the Tuzla entrance on the highway and reached the Naval Academy with two transfers on the public bus.

A second lieutenant stood guard at the school entrance. I said I came to take the exam and handed over my documents. After looking at the papers, he shook his head and said, "Young man, you hit the goal post but missed the shot!" I didn't understand what he meant, except something had gone wrong. I was about to have a rude awakening. "Your exam group is over. Your exam date was yesterday," said the second lieutenant with an indifferent look. The test takers were divided into five groups, and a group was taken every day. I could enter with any group during the week. Did I come all this way for nothing?

For a moment, I was angry with myself for wasting money for nothing. Just as I thanked the second lieutenant on duty and was leaving, he said, "Don't worry, you will get into a college," and asked, "How did you score in the exam anyways?" When I told him my score, he couldn't believe it. He repeated his question: "Did you get this score?"

I took out the result document I was carrying in my bag and handed it to the second lieutenant. "Come and sit here," he said and took me inside. He was on the phone with someone: "Commander! He got a very high score on the exam; what is your order? Should he take the exam with another group?"

After hanging up the phone, he smiled and said, "So, your shot did hit the goalpost, but I was able to score the goal for you."

Once again, I tried to understand his meaning until he explained: "Come on, you're in luck. You're going to take the test with tomorrow's group."

"Remember, you must be here at exactly eight o'clock tomorrow morning," he reminded me.

Although I was thrilled with this news, I was once again stuck in my pessimistic thoughts when I thought about where to stay until tomorrow. I didn't know anywhere or anyone in Istanbul. I needed a place to stay or eat. I turned back to the highway and took a minibus to Topkapı, which I was familiar with from the movies. I crossed the Bosphorus Bridge from Pendik, Maltepe, and Kartal routes and reached Topkapı in an hour and a half. I saw the sea for the first time and admired the deep blue waters as I passed the Bosphorus Bridge.

Istanbul was much more beautiful than it appeared in the movies.

"I wonder if I'll see someone famous," I thought.

For a moment, I forgot that I did not have a place to stay for the evening and that I would take the exam in the early morning hours. I walked excitedly from Topkapı to Eminonu, saw hundreds of tourists in Beyazıt, and ate fish and bread on the seashore. It felt like a dream.

The crowded streets were filled with people worldwide; some dashed, and some tried to catch the ferry or bus. The Golden Horn Bridge was full of people trying to put aside the stress of the daily rush and go fishing.

I was trying to explore my surroundings with a childlike curiosity, my steps taking me from one street to another. After getting very tired, I started looking for a hotel to stay in. I found a suitable hotel in Topkapı and instructed the receptionist to wake me with the morning prayer. "Don't worry, I'll wake you up in the morning," the man replied reassuringly. It had been almost 30 hours since I left Kayseri. I fell asleep as soon as I laid my head on the pillow.

The first thing I did when I opened my eyes was to look at the clock. I was shocked! No one woke me up, and it was almost seven o'clock. The exam started at eight, and I was in a hotel room in Topkapı. I threw myself on the bus. I don't remember running like that ever again in my life. It was eight forty-five when I finally reached the Naval Academy. The second lieutenant, whom I met the day before, was preparing for the change of guard. When he saw me, "Well, brother, it seems you are determined to bounce off the goalpost again; where have you been?" He asked reproachfully.

I told him that the hotel attendant didn't wake me up. After staring down at me from head to toe and shaking his head, the second lieutenant on duty took me to the building where the exam was administered. When I entered the room, there were only 40 minutes left to complete the exam. I was used to answering questions quickly from the college exam. I had done one of the fastest runs of my life that morning, and apparently, I had to finish this marathon like a hundred-meter sprint. When the exam period was over, I had completed almost all the questions and missed only a few. The exam was the first step in a three-stage process. An hour later, the results were announced, and I was qualified to take the second stage, the physical aptitude test.

The physical aptitude test consisted of running, push-ups, and sit-ups. It was almost 11 o'clock, and I hadn't had a bite to eat that day. I gathered my strength and passed all the tests. I came to the last stage of the day, the interview part.

It was almost evening, and I was interviewed last because I was included in the exam of another group. The gym cafeteria opened, and while I was waiting, I ate a croissant and drank a Coke. It felt like a full-course meal. The delegation in the interview consisted of four people. They asked why I wanted to be a naval officer, how I scored in the college admissions exam, and some of Ataturk's founding principles and reforms. They must have liked my answers because I was called for the knowledge exam, which was the final stage of the selection process to be held two weeks later.

I caught the Kayseri bus and returned to Yahyali after a two-day adventure in Istanbul. I was excitedly waiting for the process to conclude and dreaming about this new chapter in my life. Two weeks later, I went to Istanbul again for the science exam, and I passed this stage successfully and earned the right to enter the Naval Academy.

The university placement results were announced, and I learned I had been placed in GATA (Gulhane Military Medical Academy) as a first placeholder. I had a tough choice before me. Both options were military schools. I would graduate from one as a naval officer and the other as an army doctor. GATA was in Ankara, and the Naval Academy was in Istanbul. I had to study for six years to become a doctor and four years to become a naval officer. I wanted to finish school immediately, have a job, and make money. Six years seemed like a lot, and I fell in love with Istanbul. I decided to go to the Naval Academy.

In August 1992, I said goodbye to my father, aunt, grandmother, and siblings and got on the bus to take me to Istanbul. When I looked out the bus window, I saw my father wiping his tears with his hand. When the bus came out of Yahyali, I couldn't help myself and sob. There were dozens of emotions from every age that filled my eyes with tears that flowed from my eyes—joy, hope, pride, fatigue, longing, and separation.

The List

I CAN NOT STAY SILENT
Virginia, USA, 2017

The constant stream of bad news continued from Turkey, and it was nearly impossible to turn on the TV, open a website, or scroll through Twitter without seeing a scene of torture or a human rights violation. The injustice inflicted on victims was spreading every day. Almost all opposition journalists were arrested, and newspapers and televisions were shut down. The regime managed to silence all opposition, even objective perspectives, and social media was the only venue where we could follow the suppressed people's views and news. The regime had turned into the worst crime mafia. It targeted government officials and individuals from all segments of society who were not totally obedient to them.

This continual exposure to bad news devastated my mental health. A businessman who owned a driving school in Diyarbakır was detained for weeks after the coup and was later arrested for 28 months based on accusations of being a member of a terrorist organization. While he was in custody, not yet found guilty of any crime, the regime confiscated his businesses, seized all its vehicles, and transferred them to regime supporters at no cost.

His long-time "friends" and relatives cut their ties with him since he was charged with being a member of a terrorist organization. Some people bought the regime's promoted lies, and others were scared for their well-being. He was a successful businessman with a good reputation, and overnight he was broken, and when he was finally released from prison, he could not even pay the rent of his house in one of the suburbs of Diyarbakır. His wife and children were exposed to humiliation and insults, which caused severe psychological problems among them.

After spending 28 months in prison, this businessman was acquitted of all charges as there was no evidence to support the case. However, he never got his illegally seized assets nor was compensated for his losses. As if this was not enough, his teacher's wife had her college degree revoked, and she was not allowed to practice her profession. The family was sentenced to social death.

This and similar devastating events had become normal in every city, town, and street of the country, and people were left with no choice but to seek refuge outside their country. Turkey, home to millions of refugees from Syria, Iraq, and many other states, had become a country whose citizens had to flee.

The Erdogan regime had also either confiscated or revoked these innocent people's passports thousands of people were trying to leave their homeland by secretly crossing to Greece through the Maritsa River and the Aegean Sea. They had to leave their friends, families, homes, cars, and everything and risk their lives to pursue liberty and freedom.

People, who until that day had not even been at the door of a courthouse or the police station and who had no criminal records, were trying to escape their homeland like illegal immigrants. They had to surrender their fate and their families to the hands of human smugglers.

During these dangerous journeys, dozens of innocent people drowned in the Maritsa River's dark waters, including children and women. The bodies of some of them could not be found. Despite this, tens of thousands of people left the country, risking death to live freely and with dignity. Those who made it to Greece were held in refugee camps for weeks or even months, and many continued their journeys to European countries, the USA, and Canada.

Despite all the Erdogan regime's efforts, intimidations, and slanders, neither Greece nor the other countries were convinced that these people were terrorists or criminals. On the contrary, these countries provided safe havens for these oppressed masses where they found the opportunity to make a fresh start.

Unfortunately, world history has many mass atrocities committed by despotic regimes who sought to solidify their power. However, there have always been benevolent administrations that would side with innocent, oppressed people.

In 1593, the Ottoman Empire welcomed Sephardic Jews fleeing the persecution of the Spanish King. Millions of Jewish people who fled Hitler's genocide spread worldwide to places that would become their homelands. People fleeing Erdogan's persecution were also trying to establish a new life in countries where democracy, human rights, and the rule of law prevailed. These unfortunate events have also triggered Turkey's most significant brain drain. Almost all of these people who sought refuge in other countries were well-educated, experienced, and well-trained professionals in their fields of expertise.

According to official figures, more than 6,000 academics and scientists moved to European countries in this process. Although their religions, languages, and cultures differed, these countries' peoples embraced and supported them.

There were also many touching stories of human kindness that we heard about in our conversations with our friends. These random acts of kindness have restored our hopes and faith in humanity, and we found strength in ourselves in the face of the depressing news from Turkey.

The landlord of our friend, who was dismissed while serving at NATO, had cut his monthly rent in half for a year. Another landlord of another friend of ours only requested rent from him once he found a job and could make a living. Our American friends and neighbors in Virginia Beach competed in loyalty and charity.

In the spiral of all these feelings, we moved Hakan and Fatih's beds to our room many nights and slept together. As I inhaled the smell of my children with a bitter peace, I thought of the thousands of innocently imprisoned people in Turkey in solitary cells or cramped wards, separated from their children. Who knows what feelings they had every morning? They spent the best years of their lives in cold and dark dungeons without hugging their children or spouses. Not only that, their families, whom they left behind, were struggling to survive.

What about the women in prison? Thousands of women were separated from their children, some thrown behind bars with a few days-old newborn babies in their arms. The number of babies who opened their eyes to their first days in this world behind bars, without seeing the sun, adds up to thousands.

The images of the police waiting to handcuff a mother who just gave birth at the door of the maternity services and hospital rooms haunted my mind. Could justice be expected from this regime, which has lost its humanity and showed no mercy, even to a postpartum woman and a baby that hasn't yet opened its eyes to the world?

It was upon us, who enjoyed the liberty and freedom of speech, to be the voices of these oppressed people and to tell the world about these persecutions. One of my wife's friends said she knew a local journalist and could arrange an interview for us so we could explain what happened in Turkey. We were very excited about the possibility of making our voices heard, even if it was on a local scale. We made an appointment with the journalist without delay, and we had the opportunity with a few of my colleagues and their families to talk about what happened in Turkey, why we had to stay here, and how we felt.

We were all happy to have taken steps to do something and not remain silent against the prevailing oppression. After the interview was published in the newspaper, The Virginia Pilot, people we met at school, in the hospital, and in various places we went openly expressed their support. On the one hand, we were trying to build a new life; on the other hand, we were struggling to be the voice for those oppressed in Turkey. We contacted NPR radio, also known as the Voice of America, and had the opportunity to talk about what was happening in Turkey to the entire US public.

During the interview at Colonel Yuksel's house, the journalist asked, "Do you have any concerns about the US expelling you from the country for political reasons?" I responded, "We are officers who have come to serve at NATO headquarters to contribute to world peace and security. We are soldiers who have fought against terrorism, smuggling, and piracy worldwide and put our lives on the line. We are staying here because we were dismissed from our profession, not voluntarily, but illegally. US officials and the public have the common sense to see this. If the authoritarian regime in Turkey collapses one day, and we are called back to duty again, we will take our luggage and go back without thinking for a second."

Colonel Yuksel and his wife Nergis showed their usual hospitality that day, and we continued talking about the country's issues after the interview. The journalist kept his promise and promptly delivered the interview to America on NPR radio.

While trying to make our voices heard, the United Nations Rapporteur and Amnesty International also published reports on human rights violations in Turkey. With these documents, which were recorded in history, the tortures carried out during detention and arrest were revealed to the eyes of the world's public opinion.

Despite the news reports and documentation, there was no sign of an international sanction or a significant reaction against the Erdogan regime. On the other hand, the government was carrying out police raids on the families of those living abroad in Turkey. The aim was to intimidate families with repression, intimidate society, and reinforce the perception of terror and security they were trying to create.

I was a teenager when I pledged my alliance to my country and swore to sacrifice my life for the sake of my country. No despotic regime or its perpetrations of various atrocities would be able to wither my love and loyalty for my country. Even if the Erdogan regime does eclipse the sun, the truth will shine through one day.

The List

LIFELONG PROMISE
Istanbul, Turkey, 1992

I was 16 when I stepped through the door of the Naval Academy. The school was built on a peninsula in Tuzla, Istanbul. The Naval Academy was like a small city, with an indoor swimming pool, a boathouse, two football fields, a vast dining hall, a library, and many dormitories and academic buildings.

The midshipman was trained here for four years to graduate as a naval officer in the Turkish Navy. The Naval High School, which provided four years of education, was the leading human resource for the Turkish Naval Academy, and 90% of the student body were graduates of the Naval High School.

Like me, the remaining 10% were graduates of regular high schools and had to go through a rigorous admissions process. Our class had 276 midshipmen, and female students were admitted to the Naval Academy for the first time.

Every incoming class had to finish a challenging forty-day summer camp called induction training to be sworn in as a midshipman. Those who wanted to quit before the end of the training were allowed to leave. Still, after completing the induction training and taking the oath of duty, it was harder to leave the Naval Academy, and penalties were involved.

In forty days, I had to make a decision that would affect my entire life. Induction training was intense from day one. We received our uniforms and military equipment.

We all got military haircuts. It was a very fast buzzcut by an emotionless barber, which took less than 5 minutes. I was never interested in long hair, but one other candidate tried to hide the tears streaming from his eyes while his long blonde hair was cut. Military service meant sacrifice, and we started it by sacrificing our hair.

The hardest part of the induction training was not the intensive and busy physical training but the attitudes of the Naval High School graduates toward us, the students who came from the regular high schools. These attitudes amounted to humiliation, questioning, and even bullying.

They came here after four years of military training and were subjected to many hazing by their superiors in the Naval High School. They had to mature at very early stages of their adolescent years in a very formal and disciplined environment, which resembled a semi-closed prison in Princes Island Istanbul, where the Naval High School was located.

It was hard for them to accept those of us as equals since we had not been through these hardships. While we had only sacrificed our hair until then, they had reached this point by offering four years of their youth.

As we got closer to them, I listened to hundreds of stories that confirmed what significant trauma they had been through. They were expected to become adults without ever being a teenager, and their adolescent years were cut out of their lives. A few students were trying to inflict the same trauma they had experienced in the Naval High School onto the other students. Most of the class started to accept us as equals as we continued the induction training, and we laid the foundation for many friendships that would last a lifetime.

During this period, I met Murat. His father was a policeman, and he was from Yahyali. Although we had lived in very close neighborhoods, we had not met until that day. Due to his father's profession, he had been far from his hometown, and after middle school, he decided to enter the Naval High School and become an officer. He had a calm and humble disposition. He introduced me to his group of friends and provided shelter for me against the hazing that most regular high school graduates had to endure. I don't know if the pressures were part of the induction training, but two weeks later, two friends had already decided to leave, and the number of those considering quitting was starting to increase daily.

While this process pressured the regular high school graduates, it also created a sense of solidarity among us. I met Murat and Hakan on the first days of the induction training. When friendship takes shelter in a lifetime, the first moments bore that company is emotional to think about. Both had attended high school in Istanbul. Hakan had a maturity well above his age, and Murat had a swagger reflecting the storms that broke inside him. At meals, Hakan, Murat, and I always sat at the same table, finding strength in each other. As days passed, I adjusted well to the military environment. A week before the swearing-in ceremony, I was about to embark on a road of no return. On Monday morning, the unit commander called me to his room. I entered his room with a strange rush and hesitation inside me.

"Mehmet, your financial obligation document is missing. You need to complete it before the swearing-in ceremony," he said. This was a deed and a bill of obligation regarding the compensation I had to pay if I decided to quit the Naval Academy after I took the oath of duty.

The financial obligation indicated on the document was worth a fortune. I called my father and told him he had to fill out the paper, get it notarized, and find a guarantor. Although three days had passed, I did not hear back from my father. It was now Thursday, and it was only possible for me to attend the swearing-in ceremony if I turned in this document.

When I reached out to my father, I deeply felt his deep sadness and desperation: "My son! I asked all of our friends and relatives. No one wants to be a guarantor for such a high amount," he said embarrassedly.

I was angry.

I did not have time to think about this.

"Get on the first bus, come to Istanbul, and let me think about it tonight," I told him as I hung up.

My brain began to think of all sorts of possibilities and possible solutions at an almost reflexive speed.

Meanwhile, I had missed a point that I find selfish even today. My father didn't have a regular job for years, and I told him to be here in the morning without thinking about whether he had the money for the bus or if he could find a bus from Yahyali to Kayseri at that time of the evening.

Since there was no cell phone then, I could not get any news from him during the night.

Tired of the thoughts and anxieties swirling in my mind, I fell asleep. I opened my eyes with a wake-up call in the morning. When I went to the breakfast formation, I thought this could be my last day here.

I didn't tell anyone about my situation. "What could they even do if I shared it with them?" I thought. Training would begin after breakfast, but I was expecting to be called by my company commander about the financial obligation document.

It was already 10 AM, and I still had not heard from my father. "I guess he couldn't come," I thought. With the thought that I had to complete my last day here in the best possible way, I was running with all my strength in training. I was staggering through the obstacle course, which I had been struggling with until that day. I was going through this challenging course as if I had been familiar with it for many years.

It was almost lunchtime, and I heard the announcement. "You have a visitor." My heart was about to burst out of my chest. I couldn't hold back my tears when I saw my father in the gangway.

I had never hugged him so tightly before. Despite all the impossibilities and desperation, what he had done and sacrificed. He had traveled over 700 miles just because I asked him to on the phone, and here he was, in front of me.

We asked for permission from the company commander and went

to a notary public in Pendik. I was going to try and persuade the notary to ratify the document with a single signature. When I explained the situation, he said, "You already have two signatures, you and your father."

At that moment, I again saw that everything happens for a reason in our lives, and sometimes it takes years to see the wonders of destiny.

My father made a mistake when he was registering my birth certificate. As we did not have an integrated system in Turkey at the time, the parents' declaration was used to register the birth date of a newborn. Some parents would wait years before they registered their children's birth certificates. Although I was born in 1976, my birth year was registered as 1974. So legally, I was 18 years old and could sign the official document. This had not occurred to me until the notary told me. We completed our job quickly and returned to the Naval Academy before the end of the shift.

I was with my father all day, but we could not find time to chat as father and son for even five minutes. On the Pendik-Tuzla bus, when I was going to ask my father how he had gotten here, he had already fallen asleep, perhaps from exhaustion or perhaps with the feeling of relief from having completed a difficult task. I kissed his hands at the door and hugged him tightly once more. He couldn't hide the tears dripping from his eyes when he said, "I trust you, son. You will be a great man."

I handed over the document to my company commander, took an oath of duty on August 30, 1992, and set sail for a long and arduous journey. I was only partly aware of the storms, challenges, and trials I would encounter on my route. Not knowing that the end of the course would end with a treacherous ambush, I had dropped an anchor at the edge of my life.

If I were to describe my entire four-year Naval Academy life, it would be a series of books. My first year was a period of exploration: discovery of Istanbul, one of the most beautiful cities in the world, the discovery of myself and discovery of a new world that I was a stranger to. I was learning new things every day, getting more robust, and improving my character.

English classes were the most difficult for me. The English program in the Naval High School was intensive; the students had one year of English preparatory courses and took all other major classes in English. So, they had a great advantage over those of us who came from a regular high school. What I had to do was to close this gap as soon as possible. While looking for a solution, I discovered many used bookstores in Beyazıt, an old Istanbul district known as a "used-book bazaar" among college students. Beyazit became my favorite weekend destination; I would spend the whole day looking at books and return to school with two grammar books and two beginner-level English novels. When I was in middle school, I wouldn't sleep until I finished the book that I started to read. I remember staying up many nights.

I returned to those days when I started reading my first English book. With great enthusiasm, I opened the first page of the book. In each sentence, I only knew a few words. I found the meaning of each word in the dictionary and took notes in the corner of the book. Even though it was midnight, I had only progressed three or four pages. I was straining my mind, trying hard until my head exploded, but I was struggling more and more with each page. Before I could finish the book, I fell asleep and lost a big field battle. When I woke up in the morning, I had a terrible headache. Since it was Sunday morning, my friends were on leave, and I was alone in the four-person dormitory. The sound of seagulls rising from the seaside broke the morning's silence. The English book and dictionary at my bedside caught my eye. They seemed as if they were some victorious commanders.

They seemed to be saying, "It's too late. You can't learn English."

I dressed quickly and rushed out of the dormitory. I started running like crazy, each step faster than the one before. If I remember correctly, the area around the peninsula was around three miles. I was running and crying at the same time.

I had dared to stand firm all alone in the vastness of Istanbul.

The burdens I was shouldering were starting to feel too heavy to carry. I don't know how many minutes I ran on that road, but my life flashed before my eyes while I was running. I was only 16 years old and had been through many hardships. At the end of the run, I stopped by the cafeteria and bought ayran, a traditional Turkish yogurt drink, and simit, a Turkish bagel, and made my way to the dormitory. I started writing down the words I did not know the meanings of in an empty notebook. I had made up my mind. I would study for another class when I got my English courses in order. I secretly pulled out the grammar book and learned English in my other courses.

In the meantime, I joined the judo team, pushing my limits with two or three hours of training. I would be better off mentally if I had better physical shape. Having my age registered as two years older worked at the notary public but not on the judo mat. When the people before me were a few years older, I often found myself stuck on the mat. I was so tired that I would eat dinner, attend the night formation, and soon pass out in bed with an English book; when the training was evaluation started to worry my dorm friends. I was not studying, and my life consisted of judo and English. One of my dorm friends, Erkan, who failed his classes the year before, said, "Don't worry, you'll fail for this year, and you'll get it back together. I failed last year's semester, but now my grades are above 3.40."

His words of consolation made me even more stressed. Losing a semester was not an option. I entered the exam week without studying and completed the midterm exams with mediocre grades. I got an "F" in English despite studying very hard. It was the first time I failed a course. Everything was going wrong. I had always been an exemplary student with the best grades and achievements, but not this time; I was flunking English and barely meeting standards in other classes.

"I wonder if I made a mistake," I thought. While struggling with various thoughts, I remembered when my father came to Istanbul one night and undertook a financial obligation greater than ourselves and said, "I trust you," with tears in his eyes.

I had no choice but to succeed. I would stand up again. I decided to change my perspective. I would admit defeat in the first round against English but would spread the learning over time by not giving up.

On the other hand, I would focus on my other courses, regain my previous academic success and renew my self-confidence.

When I look, I regret that I decided to quit judo. I had to study more, so I needed to end the tiring training tempo. One of the advantages of struggling to survive on your own is making many decisions without needing advice from others. I was a much different student in the second term of the first year; I was more like the Mehmet I used to be. I got good grades in all math, physics, chemistry, biology, and military courses. However, I continued to fall below a passing grade in English. I wasn't going to let this bring me down. I would continue to study English constantly and confidently. My degrees in my other classes had attracted everyone's attention, and I found myself tutoring my friends before the exams. Despite my lack of a good English score, I achieved a credit average of around 3.30 due to my success in other classes. The most challenging part of military schools was that we only had one month of summer break, while other college students enjoyed a three-month break. During the rest of the summer, we had to do military training camps and graduation ceremony practices, which was a big event since all top officials and ministers, including the president, used to participate.

While everyone else went on summer break, I had to spend two more weeks at school because I had failed in English and needed to retake English.

There were only about a hundred students left in the vast school. I was preparing for the English exam and tutoring those who had failed the other classes. This failure I experienced for the first time in my life was an opportunity for my friends and even for me. I had finished English books a few times and simultaneously learned how to use a sailboat, which I had longed for sometime. I was rediscovering myself in the Naval Academy and getting stronger daily. It had been a whole year, and I hadn't been to my hometown. During the two-week summer vacation, I went to Yahyali to see my brothers, father, and relatives and chatted with my childhood friends. I also visited my old high school and met with my teachers. I went to Adana to see my mother for the remaining few days.

When I started my second year at Naval Academy, I was much more confident, knew what I wanted, and was respected and well-esteemed among my classmates.

I chose electronics engineering as a major in my second year. I was getting good grades in all classes. Even though my grades in English class improved, I continued to study the English grammar book at every opportunity. On weekends, we met with my cousin, Huseyin, and wandered around Istanbul.

At the end of the second year of the Naval Academy, there was a two-week sea training onboard training ships in the Mediterranean. This training was a critical turning point for me that would shape my life in the future. Our cruise route included port visits to Canakkale, İzmir, Marmaris, and Mersin. We would stay in Mersin for three days, and I had planned to take a leave and go to Adana to visit my mother. The distance between Adana and Mersin was only 45 minutes, and since my mother was in Kozan, I had to take another bus for another hour. This distance was typically off-limits during a port visit, but my company commander allowed me to visit my mom. I didn't know if my good grades had something to do with this, but this grant had one requisite; I had to wear my uniform the whole trip. I put on my short-sleeved summer white uniform and set off. I had decided to briefly visit my relatives in Adana before going to my mother's.

This was when I met my future wife, Hatice, for the first time. She had a quivering, inquisitive gaze. She talked about what she did at school and said she had difficulties in her math classes.

The following day, I was on my way again to visit Kozan to see my mom. I was full of joy and a complex feeling I had never felt before. It was as if I was bounded with Hatice by an incomprehensible solid force. In the subsequent years, I would stop by Hatice's house before visiting my mother's house. I found some excuse to stay in Adana rather than stay with my mom in Kozan, and my mom would tease me about this. "Are you coming to visit me or someone else more significant?" Should say.

The time passed quickly. We were now juniors at the Naval Academy. Our friendships were getting stronger here at the Naval Academy and turning into companies of destiny. Since everyone had to stay at school, we would chat until midnight after the night formation. Some of us would talk about a book we were reading, some would talk about a girl we met, and others would speak about the movie we watched. Now we were all mature, adapted to the military way of life and service, and, more importantly, well-equipped with the training we received.

Two of my cousins settled in Istanbul in my third year at the Naval Academy. I started visiting them frequently on the weekends.

Istanbul no longer felt like a stranger. It made me fall in love with it every day. I continued my habit and spent most of my weekends in the used bookstores in Beyazit and Kadikoy. Every week I bought a book in English, and at the same time, I read books on political topics with interest and curiosity. Books on the politics of Turkey were right by my bedside, and as I read through them, the lyrics of my favorite singer, Ahmet Kaya, made more sense and gained more meaning.

When I read opposing ideas, I liked to interpret them. As the child inside me grew, my world of emotions also changed. I was trying to understand why Anatolia was so helpless and underdeveloped. The injustice and discrimination I witnessed firsthand was the reason behind this underdevelopment.

There were about twenty midshipmen in school who had military families. Every Friday, a special shuttle bus was scheduled for them to visit their families in Golcuk, a small city homeport to the Turkish Fleet. These midshipmen and some others with solid connections were all part of a small exclusive club and would always enjoy special privileges and favors. They were entitled to more liberties; the company commanders would always prefer to give them high-visibility tasks, and any problems they ran into would be solved with a simple phone call from their parents. Other students, like me, were usually looked down upon. No matter how hard or successfully we worked, we never got any of these privileges or were never given responsibilities or tasks that would bring us to the fore.

This discrimination would continue for most of my naval career. These exclusive few would always get the best assignments and high-visibility billets so they could shine at work. However, I was never disheartened by this discrimination and continued to work hard. I knew this would not continue forever. Time proved me right, and the Turkish Navy adopted more meritocracy-based and transparent promotion and assignment practices. This allowed many well-qualified officers like me to get better assignments and promotions.

Unfortunately, this meritocracy-based practice would also be targeted after the July 15th coup attempt. While thousands of well-qualified officers were being purged from the Navy, those underqualified but privileged officers were promoted to these positions and ranks.

I reflected on the memory of Lieutenant Akif, our company commander. A student military delegation was to be sent to the NATO headquarters in Belgium during the midterm of my second year at the Naval Academy. I had one of the highest grades but was not selected for this delegation. When I asked why this selection was, he tried to escape the situation by saying, "We looked at your grade point average from a year ago."

The rules, guidelines, and everything else would be adapted or changed if necessary to favor or choose these privileged few, and the ground was always soft and slippery for the rest of us.

I did not lose hope and was determined to show that there are Anatolian children, like me, who are not greedy and want nothing other than what they deserve. We were taught from day one that there was no place for politics in the Armed Forces. However, during the Military Academy years, we encountered privileged classes, nepotism, and political games.

As part of the junior year summer training program, midshipmen at the Naval Academy go on a cruise onboard training ship, and as part of the training, they also make foreign port visits. In our junior year summer cruise, we visited Italy, France, and Spain onboard the training ship TCG Cezayirli Hasan Pasha. Every port visit felt like a different world. We traveled all over Naples with my friends Hakan, Yusuf, and Murat.

Italians were friendly people. The traffic of the city and the swindlers at the port entrance were the only bad memories I could recall. One of my friends bought a stereo with all his savings, and when he got on the ship, he found out that two big bags of salt were in the box. The swindler had changed the package with a sleight of hand right before his eyes.

We made a port visit to Villa France, near Nice. This was a tiny little port on the shore of the Mediterranean Sea. During the port visit, we went to Monte Carlo and decided to hitchhike for adventure. Luckily, a Frenchman who had worked in Turkey for a few years took us to his car, and we chatted along the way.

The best part of the trip was the port of Barcelona, Spain. Of course, we visited the Nou Camp Stadium where is home-field of famous soccer club Barcelona. The summer cruise onboard a naval training ship and the port visits gave us a sense of real sailor life and allowed us to explore different cultures. I knew that the Navy had always had innovations and reforms in Turkish History; now, I better understood why this was the case. The foreign port visits and interaction with different nations were the gifts of a sailor's life, and they would gain a broad vision and grow as an intellectual.

Now I am a senior at the Naval Academy. I would graduate a year later and start my career as a naval officer. Senior year was when midshipmen honed their leadership skills and were given more authority and responsibility to lead the student body, the Regiment. Midshipmen who excelled in academics, military conduct, and sports and had leadership skills were assigned leadership billets in the Regiment. The most successful in these areas would be selected as the regimental commander, and he led the entire Regiment command organization. A friend of mine, Levent, was chosen as the regimental commander. Levent also came from a regular high school like me, was consistently successful in all his classes, was excellent in military conduct, and was one of the best players on the soccer team. This selection bothered some classmates with a Naval High School background, but soon Levent managed to win the hearts and minds of almost everyone in our class and the Regiment through his success in this role.

It was a source of pride for one of us to come from a regular high school and be chosen as the regimental commander. I was selected as the Commander in Education. My responsibilities included the educational planning of all four classes and acting as the academic board's midshipmen representative. This task increased my dialogue with the faculty members and enabled me to gain significant leadership and headquarters work experience before starting my career.

The most important academic subjects in my senior year at the Naval Academy were thesis work and service selection, which meant choosing to be a surface warfare officer, submarine, supply officer, etc. I received my thesis from a professor at Yıldız Technical University. My thesis topic was positional satellite communications applications. We were going to do the thesis with my classmate, Cumali, and after our topic was assigned, we immediately started researching. Although we scoured the university libraries and even visited and consulted the

TUBITAK (Scientific and Technological Research Council of Turkey) campus, we could not find any Turkish source on this subject. Looking back at those days, I realize how much the internet has made life easier. The strange thing was that in 1996, even in Istanbul, where Turkey's best universities are, we could not find a Turkish source on satellite communications. We came across foreign resources in the libraries. This situation was a snapshot of where we were as a country regarding science, technology, and academic infrastructure.

Another thing I realized during the literature review phase of the thesis was that I still needed to feel more comfortable using English sources even though I had improved my English quite a bit. After this awareness, I focused on studying English in my spare time. I bought a more comprehensive dictionary and started following the weekly Times magazine. I often had to consult a dictionary to understand what I was reading, but I realized that it was not possible to fully master the English subject without pushing my limits.

I was a great example of Turkey's dysfunctional foreign language education system. On paper, we took many hours of foreign language. Still, due to a lack of qualified teachers and impassive administrations, millions of talented and intelligent students missed the opportunity to learn foreign languages in elementary, middle, and high school. Even some officials in authority and responsible for fixing this shortcoming would make negative, empty, and ignorant comments such as "Let the foreigners learn our language." The state did not seem to let its citizens learn or master a foreign language.

Turkey is a country at the crossroads of civilizations; many civilizations with different languages and cultures lived in these lands for thousands of years. Unfortunately, our society has lost its connections with these cultures over the years, one by one. The Turkish community first cut off its ties with the two ancient languages of our civilization basin: Arabic and Persian. Later, the state tried to make some local languages extinct, such as Zazaki, Kurdish, and Laz, that had existed in Anatolia for hundreds of years.

With a functional language education program and a systematic approach, most societies could grow up by learning a few languages. A community that grew up at peace with other cultures, languages , and civilizations could establish its foundation on tolerance and brotherhood instead of radical and ultra-nationalist feelings. But this was not what the deep government wanted in Turkey.

I was more than ever convinced of this idea when I heard about some of the dismissal criteria used by the Erdogan regime in the wake of the 15 July coup attempt. Speaking a foreign language education in a foreign country was among the essential criteria for dismissal from the Armed Forces after July 15. Erdogan knew he could easily control society. People in such a society would be content with what the regime provided and afraid to seek more rights, freedom, equality, or welfare.

My senior year in the Naval Academy was precious for me. I developed morally, mentally, and physically, and I felt ready to assume the highest responsibilities of a naval career. In the same year, fate also had a sad plan for me. At the beginning of June, I visited my cousin and his family on my weekend leave and learned that my grandmother had passed away. My grandmother raised me, and she was both mother and father to me. She supported me in my pursuit of education when everyone was against it. She sent me to school every morning with the warm flatbread she made with trembling hands. Her biggest dream was to see me graduate from the Naval Academy and become an officer. Three months before my graduation, she passed away to the other world. I was very upset because my family did not inform me about her passing. I could not even say goodbye to my biggest supporter and the strongest, most self-sacrificing woman in my life.

I cried for hours.

My childhood flashed before my eyes, and my grandmother's life story, whose book I wish to write one-day, one-day ears. This was my delayed farewell to my grandmother on an evening in June in Istanbul.

I was in such a strange, indescribable wave of emotions.

I had lost my biggest support in life. I felt lonely.

"Get up, you will graduate, and you will keep your promise to your grandmother and hold on to life," I said to myself.

I received an "A" in all my classes and succeeded in graduating in eighth place from the school we started with 276 students. Those who finished school with honors were given the option to choose their first service assignment.

The main combat power of the Turkish Navy consisted of frigates, destroyers, submarines, and gunboats. Most high-ranking admirals were surface warfare officers and had served on large combat ships like frigates for most of their professional careers. I was aiming high; I knew this would be a long and challenging journey, but starting on the right foot would help. So, I decided to choose an assignment onboard a frigate, where I could learn more about the Navy and would be working closer to future senior leaders of the Navy.

The German-made Yavuz-class frigates were the Navy's newest and most equipped ships. There were roles on these ships as assistant communications officers and operation center assistant officers. We had several training and induction visits to different types of Navy ships at Golcuk Naval Base. I decided on the combat operations center assistant officer billet onboard TCG Yildirim Frigate, a Yavuz-class frigate.

However, fate had other plans for many classmates who graduated at the top of our class and me. We were only a few days away from service selection. Our company commander informed us that all available billets onboard the Yavuz class frigate would only be open to female officers. Our plans, future dreams, feelings, and trust in the system were once again shattered. The rules and practices were changed overnight, and our well-earned right to choose our first assignment was taken away from us. Four years of hard work meant nothing; I was outraged. How could someone make career plans in a system where arbitrary rules and regulations were so con, and there was no mechanism to question these changes or hold someone accountable?

I decided to choose the logistics pattern instead of the frigates to express the irrepressible reaction I had inside. There were only two available supply officer billets for our class. My classmate, Naim, who ranked with me, had decided in advance and said he would choose to be a supply officer. If I decided on another supply officer position, there would be no more available billets for the rest of my classmates. I knew many other classmates were aspiring to become supply officers, and they were trying to change my mind.

Being a supply officer in the Navy was a relatively straightforward path. The supply officers had only two years of sea duty onboard ships. This pattern offered all the possibilities for a naval officer who wanted a comfortable life. However, this was not me. I was not acting rationally. I had bigger dreams and goals. I could not just give up on them as a reaction to another unjust practice. I had to move on.

I chose the communications officer role onboard TCG Ege, Knox class frigates. This was the final step before graduation, and soon, I would be commissioned as an ensign in the Turkish Navy.

That night I reflected on my past four years. I came to Istanbul on a bus with nothing but some pocket money, made many friendships that lasted a lifetime, visited many foreign countries, matured mentally and morally, and was about to finish a challenging marathon. I knew every ending was also a new beginning, but now it was time to enjoy the prize of four years of hard work.

My cousins Huseyin, Uncle Mehmet, Aunt Refiye, and their children, my father and brother Ramazan, attended my graduation ceremony. My father could not bring my brother Emrah, Murat, or Sefa because he could not arrange money to buy them tickets. My mother and other siblings could not attend the ceremony either. After graduation, we visited Istanbul with my family and had dinner in Kadikoy. It was one of the best days in my life, but like every good thing, it did not long.

I sent them off to my hometown on a bus. I was also going home after running some errands, like taking my belongings to my cousin's and finishing some paperwork at the Naval Academy.

TCG Ege was on rotation duty at Aksaz Naval Base in Marmaris then. I had two weeks off before I was expected to report to my new job. I was going to spend this time in Yahyali. Before I got on the bus, I went shopping and bought school supplies for Ramazan, Emrah, and Murat and some gifts for my father, aunt, and my other siblings.

I always dreamed of buying them new clothes before they started school. It was a great feeling to realize this dream for my brothers. "Don't worry. I will always be your supporter," I always told them.

I visited my school in Yahyali and talked to my teachers when I returned home. I felt great joy in buying a cup of tea and paying for all the students in line at the cafeteria, which I couldn't afford to buy a cup of tea when I was a child. About twenty of my classmates had gone to college. Some attend medical school, law school, education faculties, and the police academy. This was a first in Yahyali, and the number of graduates who got into a college was more than those who did not.

I was on my way home with these joyous feelings. I was only 20 years old; I had completed my education and stepped into my professional career. My success story gave hope to many relatives and friends, and those who wanted to send their children for education increased considerably.

Who would have guessed the Erdogan regime would steal this hard-fought and well-earned success with a single line in a list, which also shattered the lives and dreams of thousands? This regime was stealing decades of effort, hope, hard work, and dreams of Turkish youth who went to cities where they were strangers with nothing but pocket money.

I still have a hard time understanding why the people continued to be loyal to a regime that would hunt their children and take away their professions, dreams, and lives.

We are living in a twisted Era. Corrupt and inadequate officials stole public property and used the system for nothing but their self-interest. They are praised as patriots, and those who put their lives on the line for the country's best interests are declared traitors.

The List

MY NAVY YEARS
Golcuk, Turkey, 1996

The first months of my career as a young ensign were very difficult. My first duty was as a communications officer on the TCG Ege frigate. According to the ship's commander and executive officer, sailors usually categorized the ships they served onboard as good or bad. Our ship's commander, Captain Ferda Narinc, was a tough-tempered officer. The Executive Officer was Sinan Ertugrul, who would later be promoted to rear admiral. They both initially tested me, possibly testing my ability to work under pressure.

I oversaw the communication branch, and my branch was responsible for all incoming and outgoing messages and paperwork. At the same time, I had to know every detail about these messages and explain them briefly to the commander and executive officer, regardless of subject and section.

Sometimes I had to present dozens of messages that filled four or five dossiers and study the details of each message. My shift started before everyone else, and I was reading the incoming messages, taking notes, and meeting with the relevant department heads. Working 16-17 hours a day under intense stress intimidated me. In addition, I managed tactical communications during exercises and deployments. Since the continuity of combat liaison was vital, I spent most of the day standing at the bridge or the combat center supervising communications.

I had times when I used to lament why I didn't choose the supply branch when I had the opportunity. On the other hand, these difficulties matured me and enabled me to gain much more knowledge and experience than my classmates. I proved myself to my commander and executive officer a few months later. Every minute I spent with them, I turned into a learning opportunity.

Life on a frigate was harsh compared to other warships. Even in the officer's hall, designed as a resting place, dress code and discipline were sought, and the 120-meter ship would sometimes feel like it was closing in on me with all its weight and metallic coldness like a giant cage.

Even though we didn't stay in the port for long, I decided to rent a house.

Hakan and Cemal, my close friends, were also appointed to Golcuk. As three friends, we rented a house in Degirmendere, a lovely coastal town only ten minutes from the Naval Base. When we were at the port, we used to come home after work, even if it was late, and order dinner from Saray Restaurant, one of the best in the town. Since the frigates were on deployment for most of the time, we were rarely at home at the same time. We would have long chats on such days and relieve the day's stress with a cup of tea.

TCG Ege was scheduled for maintenance at the shipyard, so I was assigned various temporary assignments on other ships in the Turkish Fleet. These exposed different types of leaders, working environments, and much training. The Eastern Mediterranean exercise I participated in, in the TCG Karadeniz, would be unique in this respect. It would be the first NATO exercise I participated in, and the communications would be conducted entirely in English. This was a great opportunity and a challenge for me in the first years of my professional life.

To prepare for this exercise, I studied the relevant documents thoroughly and examined the communication logs of the previous exercises. The fourteen days of underway during exercise turned into excellent training for me. Besides practicing my English during tactical communications, I also had the opportunity to interact with foreign ships as a liaison officer during port visits. After three days of guiding

30 officers and non-commissioned officers from the Italian ship ITS Minerva in Antalya, I established long-lasting friendships with many of them. This was one of the best parts of the Navy life.

We saw many parts of the world doing joint training with the personnel of different countries and developing close friendships fostered by maritime and military culture. After each cruise, our perspective widened, and we learned new things.

TCG Karadeniz sent a detailed letter of appreciation for my outstanding performance during the exercise, and the commander shared this message with everyone in the officer's mess. My experience during this exercise in the early stages of my career further increased my self-confidence. I took advantage of the fact that my ship was in the shipyard and joined the training with many different ships, and in a short time, I became one of the well-known officers in the Fleet. After our ship left the shipyard, our first training would be the Seawolf Exercise, the largest and most sophisticated national exercise of the Turkish Navy.

After this national exercise, we would be joining in some multinational exercises. We also had scheduled Malta and Italy port visits. During our Malta port visit, we would participate in the Channel-98 exercise with the Maltese and Italian Navies. In this context, we would make a port visit to Valletta, Malta. A few hours after we entered the port, the ITS Minerva, whom I acted as liaison with during the Eastern Mediterranean exercise a year ago, docked next to our ship.

I soon found myself on the Italian ship, entwined with a group of about ten, celebrating this pleasant surprise. When I returned to our ship, the staff were surprised by the sight they had just seen. They were asking how I knew so many Italian sailors.

Jokingly, "I was running from task to task while you were shooting the breeze in the shipyard. This is its reward," I replied. On this occasion, I understood that although it was difficult, every task I did open different doors for me, gave me opportunities to learn, and made new friendships. At that moment, I decided not to shy away from any task, no matter how difficult, and I would always try to stay true to this decision.

As a result, in my 20 years of professional life, I would be a sought-after man for demanding tasks. Of course, while it was easy for a single naval officer to bear the challenges of this situation, things would start to change after marriage.

Since the story of my childhood is based on the separation of my parents, my biggest dream was to establish a peaceful family and experience the love that I have been deprived of for years. After I started my career, whenever I visited my hometown or my mother, I frequently came across questions such as, "Are you getting married anytime soon?" Or "Is there someone special in your life?" Even though I felt warm to the idea of marriage, I wanted to make this critical decision that would ultimately shape the next period of my life, with the right person, at the right time. Both my friends and relatives were trying to match me with someone they knew.

Finding the right person would take place after an event I never expected. In my second year as an ensign, I received a call from Kayseri when we were doing a one-week Marmaris exercise. My father was injured in an accident and was taken to intensive care.

His blood pressure had dropped very low several times, and the doctors had told us to be ready for the worst. All my memories with my father flashed when I put the phone down.

Tears began to flow down my cheeks once again. Although I blamed him from time to time for the difficult years of my life, the prospect of losing him hurt me terribly. I took the first bus and made it to Erciyes University Hospital in Kayseri.

When I saw my father, I understood how serious the situation was. Although the doctors managed to control his blood pressure, his psychological problem had resurfaced, and the doctors feared that he would hurt himself.

A doctor explained that his psychological state was a priority at this stage and that if he did not realize his situation and did something wrong, nearly forty stitches could burst. He added that the right decision would be to refer him to the Psychiatric Hospital. I strongly objected, stating that "to refer my father to another hospital in this state would be to sign his death warrant."

Ultimately, the doctors decided to refer my father to Adana Psychiatric Hospital.

I spent almost a 200-miles road between Kayseri and Adana thinking about how my father would survive under these conditions. Although the name of the hospital he was sent to was Mental and Nervous Diseases, I knew that heavy treatment methods, including electroshock therapy, were tried on patients.

I couldn't get the question out of my mind. How could they send someone with 40 stitches on his body and who had just escaped death to this hospital? It was one of the most challenging moments of my life.

I was trying to stay strong as I said goodbye to my father by recovering my strength for the last time. When I left the hospital, I considered buying a ticket to Marmaris to return to my ship with the first available bus. But some force stopped me at the last moment, and I decided to visit my mother while I was in Adana.

I had been on the road for three days, writhing with a terrible headache due to the thoughts and concerns occupying my mind for days. I thought it would be better to spend the evening in Adana, unaware of fate's best gift, so I got on a minibus that took me to Hatice's house. When I got home, Hatice opened the door. We had met several times before, and every time I saw her, I found peace and serenity in her face, and when I was with her, I felt my troubles and anxieties would fade away. It happened again.

The smile in her eyes made me forget the three tiring days I had just been through, and I let myself free in her usual magical atmosphere. I was trying to describe this feeling, which had been recurring for a long time, and to make sense of my emotions.

When I first saw her, I felt very different emotions that I was unfamiliar with, and I tried to ignore the fact that love was blooming inside me.

I would learn later that Hatice had also fallen in love with me at first sight and often talked about me in conversations with her friends.

We met once again, covered in the emotions of a fledgling and shy excitement.

I was trying to avert my eyes so those around me wouldn't understand. When Hatice's mother asked, "Are you on leave?" I had no power to explain what had happened, and I dismissed her question by saying, "Yes." That night, we talked with Hatice until the morning. Although we did dare to up to each other, our souls were already entwined. I was sure that the person I was looking to spend the rest of my life with was standing before me, and I felt the excitement of the possibility of spending the rest of my life with her in my heart.

Life was full of uncertainties and too short to waste. In the morning of that night, I told Hatice I was in love with her and wanted to be with her for the rest of my life. She couldn't hide the sparkle and smile in her eyes when she heard this. Thus, in February 1998, we decided to walk together and take a step toward life's journey.

It was a big surprise for everyone when we opened our decision to our families. After the traditional family meeting, we were engaged. How strange life is. I hit the road with the possibility of losing my father, and I was now returning engaged with the woman who lit up my world and gave me life. Throughout the journey, I looked at the photo she gave me at the beginning of every mile, praying that this magical feeling would last forever.

Navy was not only a job but also a way of life. I needed more than an education and a diploma to perform well in the Navy. You had to be much more: a great follower, a leader, a hard worker, a learner, etc.

A ship was a couple of hundred-foot long. However, two hundred and fifty sailors lived in it, and the ship's commander was responsible for the life of each of them and what they did and did not do.

For this reason, navigating the stormy seas required someone to establish and maintain military discipline, avoiding many personal conflicts during the months-long deployments.

It takes years to acquire these abilities. To be a frigate commander, one must prepare at least twenty years, including school, and be trained in this profession. Looking back, I need to address and interpret what I have experienced and observed throughout my professional life after July 15. Each officer dismissed from the Navy, or free government in general, by the architects of the July 15 conspiracy represented the hope and future of the Turkish Nation.

Those who set this treacherous trap never once pitied all these years of hard work and had dismissed tens of thousands of trained soldiers with this relentless treachery. At this point, the following question came to mind: If these people were such well-trained officers, why couldn't they notice this trap set for them, or why didn't they show resistance when they could? The simple answer to this question is that they were lured into this trap by some of their leaders, and everything seemed normal due to the country's state at the time.

Before July 15, due to the bloody terror attacks in Ankara and Istanbul, it was a common practice for all military units to conduct counter-terror drills at unexpected times. This was the case for most soldiers and cadets who took to the streets that night, and their statements could be understood. Many were called back to duty due to a terror threat and were directed to the previously planned positions. In the meantime, Erdogan announced this was a military coup and called on the people to take to the streets and resist these "traitors."

Oddly, the civilians were more prepared, organized, and better guided than the military for that night. It looked like Erdogan and his party knew exactly what to do on the night of July 15. The municipal vehicles were closing every critical road that military assets could use, and the public announcements on the local mosques were used to call and direct people to the streets; there were even heavily armed civilians who were leading the crowds on the streets. This all looked too odd to be a coincidence or just a simple reaction by the public.

The soldiers understood this was a trap once faced with their nation on the street. Then they did everything to prevent bloodshed and did not harm innocent people at the risk of their liberty and lives. Those who set up this treachery were in safe and sheltered places, hoping to watch bloodshed that night. Their hopes did not come true, and these self-as the country's self-sacrificing and prudent sons get their troops in this treacherous plan, ignoring the harm that would come to them.

Of course, Erdogan controlled media that did not cover details about that night and broadcasted the made-up stories of the regime. The nation's heroes have declared traitors and were subject to torture and imprisonment.

The truth will shine one day, and these innocent people will be cleared of these charges and remembered as heroes. In those dark days, the regime was in a hurry to fill the pages of history with its lies. Truth has a habit of coming to the surface sooner or later. When the light of the truth illuminated all sides, the fake history written by the traitors would be erased first, and then the real history would be rewritten in a way that would give credit to these heroes.

After two years of naval service as an ensign, I was assigned as Communications and Electronics Warfare Officer to Naval Surface Strike Group HQ. There were 18 frigates in the fleet, and I was responsible for the combat planning, training, and encrypted security of all these ships. Our fleet commander, Admiral Metin Atac, would take me to every training and exercise he participated in. It was the first months of my marriage, and every deployment meant being away from home, away from my wife. Every time I went away, I would send Hatice to Adana so she would not be alone.

Admiral Metin took only some of his staff to this tactical training, and the burden of the whole headquarters would be on my shoulders.

This was quite a difficult task for a young officer. On the other hand, as the only staff officer next to a two-star admiral, I was learning something new, gaining more experience, and honing my management and communication skills. I spent most of my time interacting as a liaison between the admiral and the commanders and executive officers of the ships, which significantly boosted my self-confidence.

Since the Admiral was trained as a communications officer, he often talked about communications in English through NATO publications. He exchanged ideas with me on increasing the tactical communications skills of other combat officers. It was a unique opportunity to work closely and exchange ideas with two stars Admiral. This situation made me more experienced in the profession than my peers and prepared me for the task that I would unwittingly undertake.

Meanwhile, time passed quickly, and it had been six months since our marriage. We started the day of August 17, 1999, with good news, unaware of what would happen later that night. Hatice learned that she was pregnant with our first child, Fatih. Our whole day was filled with the joy of this sweet surprise, and we dreamed of our future. The night of the hot summer day, which started brightly, we ended with a terrible earthquake in Golcuk.

We were awakened suddenly by a violent jolt accompanied by an infernal roar. The ground was shaking, and the building we lived in was shaking like a cradle. While I was trying to protect Hatice, she screamed, her hand on her stomach. "My baby!"

We quickly managed to find a way out of the building. The area was covered with a cloud of white dust. It was around four in the morning. It was like an apocalypse. People gathered in the parks in front of the lodgings in astonishment and fear. Everyone's hair and face were covered with a layer of white dust.

We became the first witnesses of a heartbreaking and terrible scene with the breaking of dawn. All the eight to ten-story buildings just across the lodgings were flattened. There were screams, and the smell of death was in the air. The epicenter of this catastrophic 7.6 magnitude earthquake was Golcuk, and more than twenty thousand lives were lost that night. Even though we survived this apocalypse, we could not get over the shock we had just experienced. We didn't have a home to go to. Hatice was devastated by the anxiety and fear of losing our baby and the impact of the disaster she had witnessed.

After getting over the initial shock, we took refuge on my old ship TCG Ege, thinking that nothing would happen to the ship even if there were a severe aftershock. While trying to understand the earthquake's destruction, we thought about what to do. No matter how great the tragedy was, I was a soldier, even if our own families were affected. We needed to coordinate what must be done after the earthquake, including search and rescue activities, as soon as possible.

First, I had to send Hatice away from Golcuk to ensure she and our baby were safe. She didn't want to leave me. Although it was difficult, I convinced her to go to Adana.

The balance sheet got heavier as the days progressed, and Golcuk became a ghost town. We coordinated search and rescue activities and organized food and clothing distribution to the survivors. Every day, we got news of more losses and reached the dead bodies of one of our friends or relatives under the rubble.

It was a severe trauma. We were trying to protect our mental health while working with all our efforts. We were like bodies running from place to place with their emotions taken away. Perhaps it was one of the most basic requirements of being a soldier. To live but not to feel. I was ignoring the pain, worry, and anxiety and focusing on the task I needed to do. I would talk with Hatice from time to time, and I was relieved by thinking that she and our baby were safe. I had no sleep schedule. I couldn't sleep without seeing the sunrise.

Meanwhile, the Navy moved the Strike Group HQ from the earthquake zone and transferred it to Marmaris. I was assigned to coordinate this move. I set out with a truckload of materials and documents. When we arrived at Aksaz Naval Base, we converted an old barge ship into a headquarters since there was no building dedicated to the strike group. Our enlisted staff members, NCOs Nusret and Ali were helping me with this task. Both were in the last stages of their careers, and I learned a lot from them.

As a young officer, having petty officers with professional backgrounds and long service experience was a great chance. I knew many officers who disregarded this experience and were deprived of the knowledge of their subordinates just because they misunderstood the power and authority of being an officer.

I was not looking at professional activities from a purely hierarchical framework. Getting the opinions of the team I worked with and showing them the value and respect they deserve made me stronger and contributed to my leadership development and the foundation of my military personality.

Together and with teamwork, we overcame many challenging tasks. I would continue to work the same way throughout all my years in the Navy. When the relocation was completed, Hatice also came to Aksaz Naval Base in Marmaris. We were together again after a long time.

It was time to start a new life in Aksaz. My workday started at six in the morning and continued until midnight. After the earthquake, the busy working tempo was normal. However, the Chief of Staff was ambitious enough to become an admiral, and the Chief of Operations Division wanted to become the commander of a Gabya-class frigate. He created work and jobs out of nothing because he was blinded by status and promotion. They often made the headquarters staff wait many hours for a simple document or message. Military service was a grueling and self-sacrificing profession. However, these greedy and over-ambitious people turned this profession away from logic and order and into a chaotic state of work.

These people should have evaluated professional success by efficiency or how much can be done during regular working hours, but by extended overtime and after hours someone would work. This counter-productive and outdated management and leadership held the Turkish Navy back if they took it forward.

However, this toxic leadership style was widespread in the Turkish Navy, and I was always worried about how to be both successful and keep my clear conscience at the same time. This was something beyond being a workaholic; these people were blinded by their career advancements and ambitions. During one religious holiday, my wife and I visited the Chief of Staff's house to celebrate Eid al-Fitr, the festival after the month-long Ramadan. It is a custom that younger couples visit their relatives and friends, and they have something to eat or drink together. I was shocked when the Chief of Staff met us at the door with a cold welcome and said, "We'll celebrate at work anyway," and did not invite us inside.

The simplest human values were trampled underfoot, and people's lives were under the personal calculations of a few intrepid individuals. This had not changed even after a terrible earthquake, the pain of which was still very fresh.

Many months passed this way, and I had no time to spare for my wife. One day, Hatice asked, "Can we have dinner together for one evening?" She was right, and I couldn't stand it anymore; I decided to raise my voice. "Why do we have to wait for hours after hours?" I asked the Chief of Staff. Of course, there was no logical answer to this, and I got the answer, "We are the backbone of the fleet. We have to work harder than anyone else," and I had to leave his room.

These people played a crucial role in setting people up on the night of the July 15th coup attempt, and in return, they were appointed to important posts regardless of their merits or achievements.

A person can realize many things, even if he is not involved in the events, and the missing pieces fall into place after a while. Between 1998 and 2000, frigates known as the Gabya-class were procured from the USA. The selection of personnel to work on these ships was of great importance. Working on new and improved ships was considered a valuable experience. This would constitute an essential reference in the career advancement of the personnel. Interestingly, almost all personnel selected to receive the ships from the USA consisted of officers who would later be investigated in the Sledgehammer and Ergenekon cases. Many officers were far more successful than them academically, professionally, and in terms of English proficiency. The officers who selected as crew of new ship would stay abroad for six or seven months, and including the courses they had taken before and the ship boarding processes, would gain significant advantages over their peers, both financially and professionally.

Oddly enough, some of these people were assigned to other relatively easier posts a few weeks after the ships arrived in Turkey. This time, that compassionate hand that protected them made sure they were exempt from the preparation of the ships for training and inclusion in the inventory, which is one of the most challenging and undesirable tasks.

The star of most of these personnel had shined once again after July 15, and they were appointed as military attachés, which is part of the staff officer cadre. These greedy and underqualified people set up a treacherous trap against their friends, whom they saw as successful, and plundered the positions and ranks vacated by them. The damage these unqualified people did to the Naval Forces would surely come to light one day.

After two years of service in the HQ, I was appointed the combat operations center officer on the TCG Kocatepe frigate. As the second senior officer of the operations division, my duties and responsibilities on the ship were quite demanding. TCG Kocatepe was one of the Knox-class frigates procured as a grant from the USA in the early 1990s. For the reasons I mentioned, although I was at the top of the list, I was not selected to be among the crew who went to the US to transfer the Perry-class ships.

Many of the younger officers, who came from small towns in Anatolia and were successful in this system, were a source of discomfort for this group of privileged officers. This privileged, exclusive group was used to an order in which positions and ranks were passed down from father to son and shared among "their children," so these successful and well-qualified "outsiders" threatened them and the old system.

My job onboard the frigate became even more critical after unusual case between the commander and the operations officer. The ship's commander, Colonel Sadi, brought the Operations Officer Lieutenant Suat to court and accused him of not coming on time for work and not fulfilling his duty. The Operations Officer had not been doing any work for a while, and all the work was left to me as the second senior officer in the department. So, I was technically serving as the operation officer, a billet that requires at least five-six years more experience and rank than I had.

Of course, this came with a price. It has been a year since Fatih was born. Due to long shifts and deployments, I could see Hatice and Fatih very little for a minimal time. It was a problematic sacrifice that I could not explain with the standard requirements and sacrifices of the military profession.

Although Fatih was one year old, he was not crawling or walking. While this situation made us very sad, I was trying to do my job under challenging conditions while worrying about what I could do for Fatih.

In April 2001, we hit the road to GATA Military Hospital in Ankara to find answers about my son. He had to undergo 40 days of examination and diagnosis until the doctors discovered the problem. We were staying in Gazi Officers Club and jumping from bus to bus to get to appointments so that the doctors could conduct the dozens of tests required.

It was a very rough period for us, and it was tough to remember or write about those days.

After completing the tests, we went to the health board to get the

146

results. Four or five doctors briefly explained that there was a structural defect in Fatih's brain called white matter. They stated that the risk of losing Fatih in a few years was very high and that, as parents, we should stand as strong as possible and be prepared for the worst. We could not control our tears.

We came to the hospital hoping everything would go well and encountered a result that turned our lives upside down. The doctors prepared a report stating that it was vital for me to be with my family, and therefore it would be more appropriate for me to be assigned to shore duty rather than on the ships. I had no idea how our life, suddenly turned upside down, would take shape in the coming days. For years, I tried to succeed in the Navy, fulfilling only the most demanding duties, and I became a prominent officer among my peers.

This sacrifice was nothing compared to the sacrifices of my son, who, unaware of everything, entered the first year of his life in the corridors of a hospital—the sacrifices of my wife, who believed in me and shared this destiny with me.

I had made my decision. I would follow the doctors' advice, request to be assigned ashore, and be excused from my duty in the Fleet Command. The next morning, I left Hatice and Fatih in the Gazi Officers Club and went to the Turkish Naval Forces Command to meet with the Head of the Personnel with the health board report in my hand.

Commander Tunc, the branch manager in charge of service assignments, would later be dismissed due to his poor conduct. When I explained the situation to him and presented the doctor's report, he said that the operations officer role at Mediterranean Regional Command was available in Mersin. We could also get family support as it would be close to Adana. He added that he would make sure to include my orders in the general appointment list, which was scheduled to be issued in two weeks.

I was surprised he showed so much interest in my situation and would do his part to get my orders on time for shore duty. I thought that it would be difficult to be assigned to shore duty and that I would encounter some obstacles. However, Commander Tunc sent me off from the headquarters, saying, "The most important thing is your son's health, don't worry about the rest."

When I shared the news with Hatice, the possibility of being with her in the complex process ahead and being close to her family in Adana calmed her. On the other hand, a burning flame had already fallen inside us and begun to burn our hearts.

Before leaving for my new assignment, my last task onboard TCG Kocatepe was participating in the "Top-on 10" exercise hosted by Spain. The operations officer had managed to find an excuse not to join this exercise. Captain Sadi's English was not good, so I would be the one who would coordinate and execute everything related to this operation.

Within the scope of the exercise, a visit to the port in Rota, Spain, was planned for the first time in my professional life. I would sail out of Gibraltar's Strait and into the Atlantic Ocean. Each sea has a different meaning for a sailor, but navigating the ocean and being responsible for this entire operation meant much more to me. The Atlantic Ocean was turbulent for almost the full deployment, and we were caught in the most severe storms I have ever seen. We had very heavy seas, and the Spanish authorities advised all participating ships to take shelter in the nearest port. We had to get approval from the Turkish Naval Headquarters to return to the port. We had to wait in the storm for two days for an unknown reason, even though all the ships had returned to the port.

I couldn't forget when we entered the port of Rota after the approval finally came. There is a saying, "Sailors always forget the pain of storms, and mothers always forget the pains of childbirth." This was very true. While wandering around the port of Cadiz, a small port city on the opposite side of the Bay of Cadiz, I had long forgotten about the storms. Moreover, I could talk with Hatice and Fatih on the phone.

When the exercise was completed, on our route to Aksaz Naval

Base, Captain Ali Sadi summoned me to his cabin and handed me my certificate of appreciation. He said he was proud of me for successfully conducting such an essential operation at this junior rank. Accomplishing this demanding task gave me a great sense of pride. When we returned to port, the crew hosted a farewell dinner in my honor, and we said goodbye to TCG Kocatepe and the crew. Despite the fire inside us, we had overcome this heavy duty, but more difficult days were ahead of us.

We started our life in Mersin on a scorching July day. Since we could not get lodging, we stayed in the officers' club in Mersin. It was impossible to go outside because of the humidity and heat. Yet we were excited. I hadn't been able to spend much time with Hatice since we got married because of the earthquake, Fatih's health problem, and extended deployments. We were happy that we would be together at least in the evenings and on the weekends, and most importantly, I could be with Fatih during his many hospital visits.

From the first day I took office, things would get more complicated again. The Commander of the Mediterranean Region was Admiral Hasan Hosgit. He was known in the Navy for his toughness and disregard for those under his command. When we first met, he asked me, "Why did you choose to come to this billet from the Fleet Command ?" My appointment was rather strange and unconventional for those unfamiliar with the internal issues I was having. Mersin was an undesirable region, often called a place of exile. "I asked for shore duty due to my son's health problems," I said. He looked me up and down. I could see the distrust in his eyes, in all his simplicity. It was tough for me to be met with distrust from the first day. Up to that day, I had received perfect performance evaluation scores from my superiors and had been awarded many verbal and written appreciations. "Well, I'll put up with anything for my wife and child," I said, and I tried to ignore this situation and started learning my duty.

On the other hand, our first job in Mersin was to have Fatih get physical therapy and occupational therapy. Hatice devoted all her time and energy to Fatih. We thought that he could crawl or walk if we kept the faith.

Each day, I was learning and adapting to my new task. In the meantime, Fatih got sick frequently, and we had to get a referral from the naval base's dispensary to take Fatih to the university hospital or the public hospital in Mersin, as there was no military hospital.

Admiral Hasan had made arrangements for a small dispensary in the Mersin Naval Base and appointed a civilian doctor through his connections. Under normal circumstances, he could not make such an official assignment. As the Mersin garrison commander, he declared his kingdom here and made his own rules.

His twin brother Admiral Huseyin Hosgit was serving as the chief of staff of the Southern Sea Area Command. Again, I came across an example of a scene I have witnessed many times throughout my professional life. These twin brothers, who did not value their subordinates and were devoid of merit and competence, were not only protected by a mighty hand for years but were promoted to admiral ranks.

With the courage they got from the power behind them, they crushed those under their command as they oppressed them, and they did not encounter any objections. Our first conflict with Admiral Hasan was when the doctor he assigned to the sick bay made my wife wait hours for a referral to the hospital, which usually takes a few minutes. Hatice was not only kept waiting with Fatih in her arms but was also threatened with being kicked out of the sick bay when she asked why the wait was so long. When she could not stand her treatment, she informed me about the situation, and I immediately went to the dispensary. I wrote a complaint petition by recording the statements of those who witnessed the incident. Admiral Hasan called me to his office the next day and ordered me to withdraw my complaint. "I will not take back my complaint about this doctor who neglected his duty and insulted the wife of an officer trying to get a referral for her sick child," I said.

As a young lieutenant, my failure to comply with the command of the unit commander in the rank of rear admiral meant signing my death warrant. However, I felt I would be a disgrace as an officer if I succumbed to injustice and lawlessness.

I was facing an admiral protected by the system. I knew it was illegal for him to appoint that doctor in the sick bay. Finally, he asked me to leave his office and "be prepared to pay for my actions!"

In the next few weeks, he would target me at every opportunity. He did not hold back from attacking me; in our weekly meetings with the unit commanders, he said, "There are those among you who are ruining the military to protect their spouses."

Despite everything, I continued to do my job in the best way without changing my attitude, and I managed to come out of the inspection by the Naval Forces Inspection Department with great success and dignity. The supervisor was surprised by what he witnessed and congratulated me, saying, "How can a branch subject to much criticism during the last inspection now perform at this level?"

In the face of this success, Admiral Hasan stopped targeting me and had to close the dispanser due to my complaint. While these events were taking place, I hadn't told Hatice about them. While Fatih's situation upset her enough, I did not want her also to be affected by the unfair treatment I was being subjected to. Even though the situation we were going through was challenging, I had no idea what surprises fate had planned for us.

It had only been a couple of months since I was appointed ashore. Still, I received new orders as the Navigation and Operations Officer onboard TCG Iskenderun, which would be commissioned into the Turkish Naval Forces. When I first saw the message, I read it repeatedly, thinking it had to be a joke. Moreover, the ship was in Istanbul, and the transfer process would take at least six months, which meant I would be away from home again for a long time.

I immediately called the Naval Forces service assignment branch manager, Commander Tunc and requested them to correct this mistake.

They were committing injustice in plain sight and throwing an officer assigned to shore duty back on a ship due to a family health issue. When I got home, I didn't know what to say to Hatice. I left my duty in the Fleet Command to be with and support them. I was now assigned onboard a logistics ship. I still couldn't believe it.

Despite all the phone calls, objections, and applications I made, I could not change the situation and came to Istanbul on a snowy January morning and joined the ship.

It was a painful feeling to leave Hatice and Fatih alone. We had been supporting each other for a few months despite everything. However, they didn't think I deserved this and punished me ruthlessly. It was as if they were saying, "How dare you go against an admiral?"

Life had become so hard in the span of a moment. A hand was finely planning and laying out all the conditions for me to give up.

What should I do?

Should I give up on the Navy?

Should I run away?

In our phone conversations with Hatice, the words of love were replaced by arguments. We couldn't find any other means to relieve our pain.

Fatih's condition worsened during the winter, and he had to deal with asthma. Hatice, all alone, had to spend more time at the hospital with Fatih.

Despite everything, my new ship had a friendly atmosphere of friendship. We became a family with crew who shared similar fates. We were trying with all our might to make TCG Iskenderun, the largest ship in the Turkish Navy, comply with naval standards. We had to make the entire organization of this ship, which sailed as a ferry within the Maritime Enterprises, from scratch. This task rescued all the experience I gained in the Fleet Command. I prepared the entire mission organization, training orders, and department organization from scratch without support.

Our Ship Commander was Commander Ali Karadal, who was respected by all the officers more than I'd ever seen. Commander Ali had an extremely calm disposition and a leadership style that united the people he worked with. He assumed a hefty responsibility and took command of such a large ship after only a few days of trial underway periods. Commander Ali and I oversaw almost every task onboard since the other person had previously served on small boats. This situation helped me hone my seamanship skills, and I could drive this large ship in and out of many ports, such as Istanbul, Golcuk, Pendik, Famagusta, and Mersin.

In my spare time from deployments and work, I started to prepare for the Naval Staff College exams. To advance and be promoted to the rank of an admiral, I had to get the Naval Staff College education and become a staff officer. No matter how hard life was upon me, I was determined to complete what I had started.

Hatice visited Istanbul with Fatih, and we had the opportunity to be together for a few days. It was April, one of the best times in Istanbul. I took Hatice to the Naval Academy in Tuzla. I could show her these places where I spent four years of my youth. In the meantime, all our efforts and prayers paid off, and Fatih started to crawl. He could even stand for a few seconds. This development felt like a kiss of life to us. Two hearts madly in love with each other, we started to enjoy our conversations again.

My hopes for the future sprouted once again. Day and night, I focused on the staff college exam preparations. I was reading the documents over and over again, taking notes, and underlining the important points. Other officers teased me occasionally, saying, "How do you find this energy between all your work?" They could not hide their curiosity. This energy came from someone who had to hold on to life from childhood and fight like a warrior. For as long as I can remember, I never thought I had an alternative but to be successful. Even though life presented me with difficulties, I continued to play the Glad Game, look for the positive aspects of my situation, and hold on to them. But June of 2001 would be the day when my Pollyanna spirit died.

While we hoped to return to Mersin Naval Base after the shipyard period in Istanbul and stay in port for extended periods, we were bombarded with deployments and tasks that the Mersin port had almost turned into a foreign port for us. We carried logistics supplies to Cyprus Island and military equipment to Albania and Croatia. Just as we thought that the cruises were over, this time, we were assigned with the sailing of the officers of the Naval Staff College.

Usually, this was a unique opportunity for me. We would host the faculty members and students of the Staff College that I had dreamed entering. I could have learned a lot from them. However, the ship had just docked in Izmir port when I received Hatice's phone call with tears. Fatih was in the hospital for several days. The news got to me late because I had been at sea.

Hatice was rightfully reproaching me and accusing me without hiding her anger. I had never felt so helpless and stuck. I had to do something. I had to take a step to stop this trend.

When I hung up, I was going to make one of the most radical decisions of my life. Almost all my friends who graduated from the Turkish Naval Academy with a good ranking chose to go to graduate school and gave up on their dreams of being staff officers. Going to graduate school meant studying at a reputable university in the USA for two years, getting a master's degree, and living a comfortable life in the land of dreams, albeit temporarily. This opportunity was beautiful to many successful officers but came with a catch. Those who had a master's degree were transferred to the restricted line and would not be able to become staff officers or be promoted to the rank of admiral.

I had always aimed to be a staff officer from day one, and I did not want to go to graduate school in the US and give up on my dreams. I would always tell myself, "I did not enter the Naval Academy to be an engineer, and I will learn this profession in the best way possible and become a frigate commander; I will be a good officer, staff member, and a good sailor." My friends' letters, postcards, encouragement, and persuasion efforts from abroad had not deterred me from my goal until now.

The last straw was Hatice's voice on the phone, full of anger, reproach, and despair. As soon as I hung up the phone, I returned to the ship. I asked my personnel to immediately send the paper shredding machine to my cabin. Almost all the walls of my cabin were filled with my study notes. As if spewing out the anger that had accumulated in me for years, I began tearing each one apart until no page was left on the walls. I had gone crazy.

My personnel froze in the rush of seeing me like this for the first time. Within a few hours, I had destroyed all my lecture notes, documents, and worksheets. It was like cutting a flower I had grown with care for a long time with my own hands.

On the other hand, I knew it was impossible to make a fresh start without extinguishing this fire in me. I threw myself off the ship before it got dark. I had to get high grades in TOEFL and GMAT exams to get admission to graduate school in USA. Both were challenging exams that required months of preparation. Whatever I did, I had to succeed in these exams and go to the US with my family. This seemed like the only option to bring me to Hatice and Fatih. Otherwise, I could only guess how long I would stay on TCG Iskenderun. I completed the necessary exam applications before the ship left Izmir.

I told Commander Ali what I had been through and informed him that as soon as I returned to Mersin Port, I would take a day off and go to Ankara. Although Commander Ali did not want to lose me, he understood my family situation. For this reason, he did not try to change my mind. When I went to Ankara, I immediately went to the office of the service assignment branch manager.

When he said, "I have a meeting right now; I can't meet with you," I opened the door, stood before him, and said, "You will have a meeting with me first."

Commander Tunc had lowered his tone in surprise. He probably didn't expect such an attitude from me. After offering me a chair to sit on and closing the door, he said, "Mehmet! Every time I think of you, I lose my sleep. I tried to prevent your assignment to sea duty, but a large ship like TCG Iskenderun needed a successful officer who had served on a frigate before. We had to recommend you," he said.

He was confessing his sins in his way, and when I heard these words, I got even more upset. "Look, Commander Tunc!" I replied, "I am the one who has been losing sleep for months, who is worried whether his son will be able to get out of the hospital, and who has not even been able to see his house and family. If you don't fix this mistake right now, you will start to lose sleep!" I said, and I slammed the door and left the room.

Before leaving the Naval Forces Headquarters, I also went to the office of Admiral Metin Atac, the Chief of Staff of the Naval Forces at that time and presented the situation to him. I informed him that I had been away from home for months, even though we had health reports for the treatment of Fatih. I have always believed that not seeking justice is just as bad as forcing injustice. I had been separated from my sick child for months for unknown reasons. I was ready to sue the service assignment branch manager if necessary. Fortunately, I was appointed Social Services Officer to the Naval Headquarters Personnel Directorate, and I would get my orders in August.

This ended our one-year-long Mersin adventure. We had suffered so much in such a short time. However, I had fought in a way worthy of a naval officer, completed my duties successfully, and above all, I had been victorious in the struggle for justice I had embarked on. Although I thought we would be happy when we left Mersin, leaving my colleagues onboard TCG Iskenderun and my colleagues in the Navigation and Operations Department was difficult—difficult times brought people closer together. The one-year mission in Mersin brought us great friendships that would continue for many years.

As with many other things, July 15 had put a black veil over most of these friendships. If we met one day again, the seeds of hatred and grudges they tried to sow among us would rot in the shadow of trustworthy companies that grew by sharing difficulties.

Who knows, fate will allow me to test this one day.

My new job in Ankara was the shirt of Nessus. The Service Assignment Branch Manager took revenge on me and appointed me to a difficult task that had plagued several officers before me. As the Social Services Officer, I was responsible for allocating summer and winter camps. These camps were military social facilities and hotels where military personnel and their families could stay during their vacations. They were popular travel destinations and were affordable compared to other alternatives. I had never been to a camp before, but I knew these military camps were very popular, and it was always the talk of the day when the allocations were announced. Almost everyone talked about who got a camp and where, during which period, and at which camp and room. The week I took office, I understood why the issue was so open to gossip.

In theory, a system oversaw the allocation of the camps. Still, in practice, nearly forty percent of the camp periods allocated to the Navy were distributed to specific individuals with the directives of the higher authorities without being subject to the principles outlined in the system. Since the system needed to be more transparent, it was unknown who would go to which camp with how many points. Only the beneficiaries were informed due to the application in closed envelopes. My room was filled with about twenty folders of camp complaints pending action.

Before I was appointed, Petty Officer Ali handled the camp applications and allocations, and two civil servants handled the paperwork. The week I started my duty, Petty Officer Ali said, "It would be good for you to learn the job as soon as possible because I am retiring in a few months." He said that he was tired of hearing insults from dozens of phone calls every day, and he was talking about how impossible it was to please people. There was very little professional satisfaction in the job in the current conditions.

This system had no justice or transparency, and people assigned to this branch had to deal with each case individually. It was impossible to make people happy or even get the system working. Even worse, I felt that fulfilling unfair and favored camp allocations would negatively affect my moral values. I could never stand injustice, let alone be the one participating in injustice.

To maintain this system based on injustice, camp allocations were only kept in dozens of folders that only branch personnel could see. One day, after discovering the root of the problems, I asked Petty Officer Ali, "Would you support me if I wanted to change this system?" Despite his timidity, he got excited and said, "I have already made up my mind to retire. I have nothing to lose. After this time, I will not be afraid of anything. I am with you," and he gave me his open support. When Commander Tunc appointed me to this position, he knew that one of a hundred complaints would jeopardize my professional future because these complaints and petitions were full of concrete cases of injustices and irregularities.

Not taking action against them meant admitting all these wrong doings. Immediately, we reached a civil official working in software development in the Department of Communications and Information Systems. We told him we wanted to make the camp allocation system transparent, and we needed software that minimized human intervention and was based on objective criteria. He said he would gladly support it without hesitation.

We pulled out all the camp allocations made in the last five years from the archive and started working on them. We planned to share this work with everyone when it reached a certain level of completion. Camp allocations were a tool of power for many people in the headquarters, and it was possible that people would want to mess with our project to keep this power.

As we examined the files, we realized that certain privileged people were allocated camps every year thanks to some interventions and favors from senior ranking officials in the Headquarters. The allocation system was based on each individual's camp points. Every year personnel would get specific points, and once an individual was allocated a camp, particular issues were deducted from their cumulative points. So it was almost impossible for anyone to get camp allocation every year. However, the system was open to human intervention and only served some privileged groups.

We decided to build the system on the pension fund registration number and entered all the camp records of the last five years into the system. When the actual records were entered, the camp scores of many people, especially those serving at the Naval Headquarters, suddenly dropped to negative numbers. Considering the new situation, it was easy to predict that a camp distribution would create an earthquake in the headquarters and that we would face and answer many influential names.

I was in a complete dilemma. We would either ignore all injustices and complaints like the previous ones, or open the new system for use transparently and explain who entered which camp, with how many points, and in what order. In this case, we needed the approval and support of our department head and the Chief of Staff.

Our branch manager Commander Musa gave us his support. With the strength I got from this, I prepared a presentation about the problems in the system, the petitions, and the allocation method we designed and presented it to the Chief of Staff. "Honestly, I'm tired of quitting all that important work and trying to respond to the camp requests. Let's make it transparent. " Everyone can follow it from there," he said, supporting our plan. It was an extraordinary achievement for us, and without wasting time, we finalized our computer-based camp allocation system.

While our daily work was busy with this feverish work, each night when I got home, I spent as much time with Hatice and Fatih as I could.

After they fell asleep, I was preparing for the TOEFL and GMAT exams, which US universities require to apply to graduate education programs, until three in the morning.

For the first time, the Navy decided to send personnel to graduate programs in social science programs as well. Previously only engineering degree programs were accepted, and all the officers who received their degrees were switched to the restricted line as engineering officers. However, if I could get a degree in social sciences, I would still have the opportunity to take the Naval Staff College and become a staff officer. It was as if fate had begun to smile upon us after years.

My goal was to get high grades in both exams. I bought a few workbooks for these exams from the used bookstores in Ankara. I was taking a practice exam every week and studying regularly as if I was preparing for the university exam. The day came, and I took both exams a few days apart. Hatice was also very excited. Like the parent of a child excited about their child's exam results, she came with me and waited outside until the end of the exam. We almost cried joyfully when the results were announced a few weeks later. Both my TOEFL and GMAT grades were well above the threshold score. I had been rewarded for working until three in the morning for months. Of course, this was only the first step in a long process. Next, I had to apply to one of the reputable universities in the US and get accepted.

The Naval Forces announced the list of universities that can offer a master's degree in social sciences. They put universities in the top 50 in the list of related programs. The list included world-renowned universities such as Harvard and Stanford. Although getting accepted for graduate education from these institutions was difficult, I had some advantages that made me an ambitious candidate. I had an excellent GPA of 3.81 out of 4. These were plus points for my applications. After I prepared a letter of intent that included these, highlighting my strengths and motivations, and completing the necessary documents, I sent the application package to four universities on the list.

The more universities I applied to, the more I could increase my chances of being accepted. On the other hand, submission and application fees were required for each application, and it took work to afford the hundreds of dollars of application fees with an officer's salary.

We were already experiencing financial difficulties with the payments I made for the TOEFL and GMAT exams, moving Fatih's hospital, rent, and kitchen expenses. There were times when we couldn't afford gas, and we moved the sofa bed and Fatih's bed to the kitchen and spent a few weeks there. Despite the financial difficulties, we hosted guests at our house almost every week. We used the limit of our credit cards to avoid reflecting on the economic challenges we were experiencing.

My brothers Ramazan and Emrah had also started college, and we were trying to support their education expenses as much as possible. As an officer with the rank of lieutenant junior grade, I lived in a modest neighborhood in Ankara. Some days we could only buy bread and olives from the grocery store. I often asked myself where the state's resources were used and why I had trouble living despite all these years of education and experience.

If we were in this situation, even though our household had a fixed income of an officer, what was the case of those who tried to make a living on minimum wage or were unemployed?

As a soldier, staying away from politics was one of my most important principles, but it was not possible to ignore the grave situation the country was in.

Suppose the resources of the state were distributed fairly. In that case, if the plundering of politicians and a narrow circle of people around them and corruption could be prevented, people could live in better conditions. During Erdogan's ruling party AKP regime, which came to power with the promise of ending these corruptions, things got ultimately out of control; Erdogan thoroughly siphoned off the resources of the state and his supporters, nepotism and bid rigging were evident, and naturally, the economic conditions became worse every year than the previous one.

Investigations, known as the 17-25 December corruption operations in the Turkish Media, would create an opportunity to eliminate this dirty order; however, Erdogan crashed this investigation, and the regime was able to close the file despite all the clear evidence. While hundreds of police officers, prosecutors, and judges who wanted to stop the looting of public resources were sentenced to years of unlawful captivity, corrupt business people, ministers, and children of ministers would succeed in maintaining this dirty order.

This was the reason why the unfortunate fate of the country had never changed; the endless theft and corruption of the powerful had always prevailed. The corrupt government official would get away with their crimes, and the masses would continue to applaud them. Millions still continued to support this corrupt regime despite all these disclosures and exposed lies and plunder.

The peace and conversation in our tiny home, where we hugged each other tightly, kept us alive during our Ankara days spent in the shadow of financial difficulties. Difficult days in life sometimes lead to promising developments.

While we were in the grip of financial difficulties, a message came to my e-mail box that I was accepted into the business administration graduate program of Purdue University, one of the most respected universities in the US. After reading the acceptance letter over and over to be sure, I shared the good news with Hatice. Hard work bore fruit once again. This was a dream. Purdue was ranked 17th in the list published by the Navy, and I was accepted by one of the best universities in the US. It was time to submit the acceptance letter to the Personnel Department and enter the quota of six people. The best part was that I only had to study in the morning, at least for a while. While waiting for the decision of the Navy for the next few months, I would spend as much time with my family as possible.

The camp allocation period had come, and it was time to implement the new system we had been preparing for months. As usual, privileged allocation requests continued to pour in. Camp times were reduced from fifteen to ten days, and as a result, the number of personnel benefiting from this service increased by 30%. Thanks to the termination of the old system, the chances for those who did not benefit from this service also increased. That day, I worked overtime with Petty Officer Ali and programmer who prepared the software for the camp allocations. By running the application, we completed the assignments on the computer.

After comparing the hand-delivered privileged list of camp requests and the allocation results determined by the software with objective criteria, Petty Officer Ali said, "Sir, no one on the list sent to us received a camp allocation."

Explaining these results would mean messing with the established system that had been ongoing for many years. In some of the hand-delivered requests, there was unlawful guidance to mention the hotel door number, let alone which camp was preferred during which period. Taking strength from the support given by the Chief of Staff, I said, "Regardless, we will publish it like this." We would publish the results on the military internet system for the first time.

These privileged small groups had always felt they had the right to go to the camps they wanted, whenever they wanted. They were sure their demands would be fulfilled without hesitation, thanks to the power they received from their office, rank, and sometimes from acquaintances in high positions.

Petty Officer Ali was both anxious and excited. After taking a deep breath and opening access to the system, we left work around 10 PM. We all needed to rest before the storm that would break the next day.

As we expected, the phone calls were nonstop the following day.

Trying to keep my calm, I listed the camp periods that the person in the system in front of me had benefited from previously, and as a result, I explained that their current camp scores were in the negatives.

When the objections reached the level of threats, I said that they could write their complaints through official channels and correct them if there was an error in the records, and I hung up.

There would be no official objection petition from any of these people who hurled many threats, insults, and curses at us. In the following hours, calls started to come from the crew of my previous ship, TCG Iskenderun.

The staff we worked with, who were allocated a camp for the first time, thanked me individually and said in a surprised but happy tone, "I can't believe it. It's my first time gaining the right to a camp in years. Thank you very much for what you've done."

Even though I told them that I had no personal involvement in the allocation process and that the allocations were made according to the points they deserved and accumulated, they said, "Of course, sir, we understand what you mean." They could not believe that I did not interfere personally in their favor.

I felt like the main character in famous Turkish actor Sener Sen's film, The Honored, Dishonest. People who did not go camping for years attributed this allocation to the fact that I knew them personally. Well, that's how the system worked for many years. But we had the opportunity to stop a bleeding wound in the personnel system, which damaged the sense of justice among the Navy personnel, and we implemented a transparent camp allocation system.

Petty Officer Ali, who said he was planning to retire after a few months when I took office, would stay in the same post for seven more years after this development. In the following years, in each of our meetings, he would remember the old days and tell how relieved he felt thanks to the system we established, that everyone could access information from their page and that instead of the incessant phone calls full of reproaches and swearing, only one or two technical questions were received a day.

Integrity and courage were a talisman that could beautify anything they touched. Many other institutions and organizations in the Turkish government still needed honest and courageous leaders to stop corruption and bribery. However, the Erdogan regime did the opposite; they purged honest, selfless, and qualified officials from the government and brought in cowardly, greedy, and unqualified people to replace them. This way, the regime was able to continue its existence and power.

It was a pity that the public did not realize this. Just as the injustices in the allocation of camps in the Navy were internalized, irregularities and favoritism were normalized in many areas, from personnel recruitment to tenders, from credit utilization to appointments and promotions in other state institutions.

It became almost impossible for anyone without a political acquaintance to find a job or maintain a commercial standing. The regime abolished institutional transparency with its power and silenced all independent audit and surveillance institutions. The official statistical institution of the state had changed the fundamental macroeconomic indicators, data, and formulas such as inflation, unemployment, and growth rate. It published them in line with the regime's guidance.

The press, controlled by the regime, broadcasted fake news to support and promote the Erdogan regime's agenda instead of writing the truth. But as the realities came to light, the regime's lies began to attract the attention of even ordinary people. The people could not cope with their financial difficulties, so they questioned the regime's lies.

Many citizens who expressed their opinions on social media declared that the data announced by the regime was not accurate. As the system of lies and plunder impoverished itself noticeably, the faith and trust of most people in the government began to decline.

These people who started questioning the Erdogan regime's lies and deceits in areas related to their interests still did not see or dare to ask about the events of the December 17-25 Corruption scandal or the July 15 coup attempt.

How could a regime deceiving the nation in every field and at every opportunity be able to tell the truth about the country's darkest night in recent history, July 15?

How could the inconsistencies, contradictions, and dark spots regarding the official July 15 narrative, which darkened the lives of hundreds of thousands of people while the lies of Erdogan and his close circle were exposed, be ignored?

While independent sources have verified the evidence in the December 17-25 corruption investigations, why has no one questioned that the police and prosecutors who conducted the investigation are still held in prisons?

This insensitivity in society deepened the swamp the country was stuck in, and the whole country sank deeper a little more with every passing day.

Watching my country's and nation's current state pained my heart. What could I do to change this order? I wish I had the opportunity to change this system governed by corruption and lawlessness just like I changed the camp allocation system.

In this spiral of despair that tortured my soul, I felt that my emotions were beginning to atrophy, exhausted from wandering between the past, the future, and the present.

Despair was one of the most profound emotional pits one could fall into. To stay strong, I continued to shout using the strength of my word, write the truth using my pen's dexterity, and expose the regime's crimes as best I could without losing hope.

THE ANGELS AMONG US
Indiana, USA, 2003

It was June 2003 when the Turkish Navy finally announced the decision about officer selection for graduate school education in the United States. Two of the 6-person quota remained vacant, and four officers were selected to receive a two-year graduate education in the US. I was one of the four officers. From the moment the message was published, congratulatory calls began pouring in.

Without wasting time, I told the news to Hatice. She had dreamed of this with me, worked at least as much as I did on this path, and supported me to the end. It was our dream. Many of my colleagues, superiors, and commanders in the Personnel Department congratulated me and shared my joy with great sincerity.

It was Petty Officer Ali who shared this joy the most. During the period we worked together, we developed a sincere friendship. We met as a family, and he closely followed Fatih's situation.

The best part of going to study in the US was that we could find better medical treatment and education opportunities for Fatih.

For me, the educational adventure that started in the Yahyali district of Kayseri extended to America. Nothing was impossible. The order in my hand proved this once again.

That evening, I shared the news with my mother, father, and siblings. Of course, we did not neglect my father-in-law, mother-in-law, and Hatice's siblings. Our relatives who heard the news were as happy as we were. This was a first for the extended family and would set a precedent for many following us.

We were experiencing developments that we only saw in movies or heard in the success stories of lives that seemed distant to us. Going to America for higher education had been such a source of joy that we saw it as a reward from God in the face of the difficulties we had experienced until that day.

As soon as the celebration phase was over, we immediately started preparations. Purdue University held a one-month preparatory training before the graduate program. This training was going to begin in July 2003. We had four weeks to prepare our passports and visas and move house. After four weeks, I would go to the other end of the world with my family and be the first and only Turkish military officer here. Almost all Turkish naval officers who had previously pursued graduate degrees in the US went to the Naval Postgraduate School in Monterey, California. There was a large community, including families in California. In addition, graduates there were able to benefit from many opportunities in the US Navy, including housing and health care. At Purdue, the situation would be different.

The school was in West Lafayette, a small city in Indiana. It was about 2-3 hours from Chicago. Since I was the first military personnel to go to this university from Turkey, there was no one we could call and consult to get support. Lieutenant junior grade Levent also got admission from the same university and was one of the officers on the list of the Naval Forces. We talked about how we were partners in destiny and that it would be good for us to support each other.

I completed the passport and visa procedures. We packed our luggage and put them in a shipping company's warehouse. I sold our 1993 Renault Broadway car, less than its market value. We gathered Fatih's medical reports and all his medical files in a suitcase. Hatice started to make a second suitcase for things she thought she could not find in America. We had learned that the Navy would only pay for my airfare and health insurance. The state covered no expenses related to spouses and children. My salary there would be $2100. The first three salaries were paid in advance. We spent our debts with some of the money we received. After buying the plane tickets for Hatice and Fatih, I had about $4000 left. Looking back at it now, I wonder how I got the courage to support a family of three for three months with $4000.

Before I left Turkey, I had booked a two-night hotel room in Lafayette. I was planning to find a house to rent after I got there. We bid our farewells to our families in the last week of June, and we longed for the last time before our journey to a foreign country that would last two years.

It was time to travel. With three suitcases, Hatice, Fatih, and I boarded the plane that would carry us to our new life in America. Everything felt strange. We felt as if something negative would happen and everything would turn around. When the plane took off, all the feelings gave way to a sweet excitement. During the 12-hour flight, we discussed the new world we would set foot on. I remember looking down with childlike curiosity as the plane landed in Chicago. Seen from above, the houses were neat and alike, as if an artist had carefully crafted them. The streets were straight as if drawn with a ruler.

We arrived in Chicago on the first Sunday morning of July. Levent was single and had arranged a place to stay in the Valparaiso University dormitory, where we would study. At the airport exit, a vehicle sent by the university was waiting to pick him up. We had to go to the hotel in Lafayette. The first thing we learned about Chicago was that the public transportation system was less widespread than in Turkey.

We had to take a taxi or rent a car. When I asked a few taxi drivers at the terminal exit how much they would charge to go to our hotel's address, they looked at me strangely.

The hotel was 3 hours from the airport. This would cost at least $500-$600. We decided that the most logical option was to rent a car. A middle-aged man was sitting at the reception. I extended my driver's license and passport and told him I wanted to rent a car for a week. After slowly examining my documents, he said the total fee was $980, including tax and insurance.

I was shocked; I had no idea how we would spend the next three months if I had given a quarter of my pocket money to rent a car. I asked the officer to give me a minute to use the internet, saying that the prices we looked at online were more affordable. In response, he said I could only find a car at this price at the airport without making a reservation. I told Hatice to wait and returned to the terminal building. Using the paid internet service of a hotel there, I could rent a car for 40 dollars a day. After about 45 minutes, I told the same officer I wanted to rent the car with my online reservation.

It was his turn to be surprised; I had made the reservation for almost a third of the price he offered me. He said that the keys of the vehicles waiting in the parking lot were in the cars and that I could choose any vehicle I wanted. All the vehicles were automatic transmissions. Until that day, I had never driven a car other than a manual transmission. When I asked the officer, "Can you show me how to change the car's gear," he was shocked for the second time.

"What a strange man!" he was probably thinking. Luckily, he explained how to drive the car without any problems. Minutes later, Hatice guided me with a map, and we went to our hotel in Lafayette.

It was challenging to find your way in a country where you set foot for the first time when you didn't have smartphones and navigation devices. As we got to the highway, huge trucks and unfamiliar large and bulky vehicles quickly passed us from our left and right.

I was very nervous driving in a foreign country, on unfamiliar roads, and in this strange traffic pattern.

We decided to leave the highway and take local roads where the traffic flowed more calmly. Although our decision made the road about 3 hours longer, we reached the hotel in Lafayette at around 10 am.

This was our first test with Hatice in America. After sweet tiredness, a slight uneasiness, and a bit of delay, we completed this test without an incident.

Although the course at Valparaiso University lasted only one month, we made great friendships and memories that would last over the years. Initially, I thought we would spend this month in a hotel, but hotel fees were $80 per night on average, which was way above what I could afford. We were rediscovering life in an unknown world.

As the days passed, it became clear that starting a new life in foreign geography with limited opportunities was difficult. We started looking for a house to rent without wasting any more time. Nobody wanted to rent out their home for a month. And even if they did, we didn't have a piece of furniture to put in place. It was a few days before the rental contract for the car expired. Hatice and I were exhausted from looking for a house all day, and we were in despair. It was about to be evening. Before I found a hotel to spend the night in, a funny idea occurred to me. "Come, let's look at the city's most beautiful neighborhood. Even if we can't find a suitable house, it will be a different experience. We will see how the rich people live," I said.

After a ten-minute drive, we came to a neighborhood with very orderly streets, well-kept gardens, and beautiful houses. Although we had little hope, we entered a real estate agency, thinking we would see the inside of a few places.

A polite middle-aged woman named Angel greeted us. After introducing ourselves, I said we were looking for a house. She said they had an apartment that might be expensive because it was furnished, but I said we wanted to see it. When Angel showed us the apartment, Hatice sighed with admiration, accompanied by despair.

The three-room house had all the items a family could need, down to kitchen supplies. It was like a luxury hotel suite. When we returned to the office, I said we liked the house very much and wanted to learn more about the conditions for rental. The first question was, "How many years do you want to rent it for?"

With a daunted despair, I explained that we had come for a one-month training course and needed a place to stay. After Angel explained to us that it would not be possible to rent a house for only a month and that they had to lease it for at least a year, we thanked her and headed for the door.

As we were about to leave, Angel called after us and asked with sincere curiosity, "What are you going to do now? You will be at school all day. What about your spouse and child? What do they do in their hotel rooms?" And she finished without giving us a chance to reply, "Okay, I'll rent you this place for a month."

We couldn't believe what we heard.

"And, how much is the rent?" I asked excitedly.

She said that since the house is furnished, the rent is $1800 and that we would have to give a deposit in addition to the rent. This was equivalent to all the money we had.

While I was happy to be able to stay in such a beautiful and comfortable house at a cheaper cost than a hotel, it would only be wise to give some of our money.

Pushing my luck, "Frankly, we just got here, and we weren't expecting such high numbers." I told Angel.

When I looked at the university's student residences while I was in Turkey, I saw that the monthly rents were in the range of $500-600. We encountered a figure three to four times this amount.

"What will happen now," Angel said empathetically as if she were going to rent the house for herself. Her sadness could be read in her eyes.

"How much can you give?" She asked.

"900 dollars?" Without waiting for Angel's reply, I said, "By the way, can we waive the deposit?" I added.

I asked these questions without any expectations, thinking she would respond negatively anyway.

Angel, true to her name, was our angel that day. "My boss will probably fire me, but it's okay," she said.

Angel came to our rescue in our first week in America at our most desperate time.

"Don't pay for the hotel tonight. " You can start staying here tonight," she said, handing over the keys.

We couldn't believe what we had just witnessed.

Our happiness was over the roof.

We filled out the forms required for the contract and started staying at our first house in America that night.

Our experiences showed once again that although we divide people according to their country, language, and religion, good people are the same everywhere. There are good and evil, merciful and cruel, tolerant and disrespectful everywhere in the world.

We met one of the most compassionate people in the world, even if she was different in language, religion, and race. She empathized with us, even at the expense of her job.

The following day, I told Levent that we had rented a house and were expecting him for dinner as soon as we did our shopping. We also had Japanese friends in training. Each of them had worked in essential companies in Japan, and they had come for their MBA. I also invited them to dinner. Wherever we were in the world, we tried to preserve and show the hospitality we learned from our elders.

During the two years, we stayed in America; we hosted close to a hundred friends from dozens of countries, most with their families. We learned new things from everyone we opened our house and table to, reinforcing our friendships. Such strong foundations were laid that our company and communication with most of them continued even after many years. Kindness, friendship, and humanity always win in the long run. Enmity, grudge, and hatred were doomed to drown and lose in their darkness.

The second week, I rented a bike instead of a car to cut costs. Commuting the 8-mile road with a bike took much work. On the first evening I returned from school, I was about to faint from exhaustion, thinking about how I would go to school the following day. Hatice couldn't hold herself back any longer and laughed at me hysterically. We had a ridiculously tragic life journey. We were making fun of difficulties and finding a way to overcome them by gaining strength from each other, no matter how difficult the conditions were.

I often attributed this to the presence of Fatih. God entrusted us with His precious and unique creation. When He entrusted us with Him, he also commissioned us to Himself. He lightened the weight on our shoulders, gave peace to our hearts, showed us a way out when we felt overwhelmed by difficulties, and sent us relief.

The following day he had one of those relieving mornings. While taking the bike out of the garage, I saw a friend who was going to the same training. He lived in the same neighborhood, and his father brought him to school daily. When he saw that I was commuting by bike, he said, "We are going there anyway; why don't you commute with us?"

I accepted this tempting offer without hesitation. I put the bike in the car's trunk and returned it to my rented place when I got to school. Looking back at our current situation compared to our last week, full of despair and difficulties, it was like a miracle. I lived in a beautifully furnished house in the best neighborhood in Valparaiso, and a private vehicle took me to and from school every morning.

These unbelievable blessings indicate how unique and beautiful our days in America would be.

Hatice had completed our kitchen shopping. We had already hosted our Japanese friends from school, Angel and her husband, and the Iranian family who lived downstairs for dinner.

After returning the bike I rented, our first task was to buy a bike for Fatih. We wanted to teach him all the talents we could afford. After a month, my training in Valparaiso ended, and we moved into our second rented home in Lafayette. This house was a small 60-square-meter apartment. Its monthly rent was $700, including electricity, water, and internet. While trying to furnish a home with a limited budget, we also learned about the "garage sale tradition in the USA, and thus we completed our house furniture from these places at a very affordable price. Hatice bought a sewing machine, renewed the sofas' covers, and once again turned our house into a cozy home for us.

Finally, I managed to buy a 1992 model car for $1500. The Indian seller from whom I purchased the vehicle agreed to collect the payment in two installments. We decided to pay $800 upfront and $700 when I received my salary.

We could meet our basic needs with the money we brought, and we survived three months with very tight budget management.

After settling in, we enrolled Fatih in the university's kindergarten and Hatice in a full-time English course. In the morning, the three of us would leave the house together. Hatice would drop me off first, then Fatih to his school, and then go to her course. We often met for lunch and enjoyed our Panera Bread or Potbelly sandwiches.

Life was getting better, but the classes were challenging. The academic year consisted of four quarters. I took four courses in the first quarter: accounting, marketing, human resource management, and statistics. It was my first time taking classes in these subjects, except statistics.

I was intimidated by reading case studies which amounted to forty-fifty pages a day, participating in group work, and trying to complete homework.

One day, when Levent and I came out of accounting class, we looked at each other and said, "How are we going to pass this class?" We were worried. When we met with Hatice at noon, she immediately understood the anxiety on my face, "it's the first time I see you so worried," she said.

After many tough exams, I was chosen to come here. Until that day, whenever I faced similar difficulties, I told myself, "Work harder, sleep less, and you can handle just as others do." Now, I was in an environment where we competed with students selected from many countries of the world in courses that I had no foundational knowledge of.

Krannert School of Management was one of the few business schools in America. For this reason, they considered all grades below A and B unsuccessful and dismissed any student from the school with two courses below passing grade.

I had overcome many challenging processes academically, but succeeding in a foreign language was nearly impossible without a background in these master's degree-level courses.

With the permission of Hatice, I spent a few weeks studying and finished the textbooks from beginning to end. I was making lists of words I didn't know, reading case studies repeatedly, and creating separate notes for each course.

This hard work paid off, and I completed the first quarter with an A in two courses and a B in two classes, with an average of 3.5. I regained my self-confidence and spent more time with Hatice and Fatih.

Hatice had improved her English at an incredible speed. The guests who came to our house were amazed at the improvement she had made quickly. Two decisions we made had a significant impact on this improvement. First, we have yet to watch Turkish television channels at home. Secondly, we only spent time with friends from Turkey, except for special occasions.

We knew we were here for only two years and had to make the most out of it by improving ourselves and focusing on Fatih's education. Hatice enrolled in the kindergarten teacher program and assumed the role of social affairs coordinator at Fatih's kindergarten.

I also got high grades in the courses and managed to attract the teacher's attention in a group of about 250 people. After this success, the head of the admission committee began to take my opinions frequently, and he took evaluations as a basis, especially for applications from Turkey.

I worked day and night to get admitted to this university a year ago. Now, I have the opportunity to support many officers from the Navy in getting accepted. Krannert continued to broaden our horizons with an excellent educational program.

We analyzed dozens of companies in each lesson and made case studies based on actual events. Every week, senior company executives of large companies gave conferences and shared their experiences with us. I combined my knowledge and experience in finance, marketing, leadership, informatics, and law with my knowledge and experience in engineering and the military. I had the opportunity to expand my perspective and horizon.

The saying "Good days pass quickly" is true.

We had completed our first year without realizing how it had gone by. Hatice started complaining of severe headaches, and attacks became more frequent and incessant. When we went to the hospital, we were told that an MRI was required and that we would have to cover the $4000 because our insurance did not hide it. This was equivalent to our two-month salary; additional examinations could be required after the MRI.

We got together with Hatice and decided that the most logical way was to go to Turkey for a week and have the necessary examinations done there. The plane ticket and other expenses would cost much less than the hospital expenses here, and she would have the opportunity to see her family. I would stay with Fatih and wait for her return.

"Men plan. Fate laughs." Three days after Hatice went to Turkey, the US Consulate General in Istanbul decided to stop all visa procedures. Thus, our one-week separation plan turned into a long-lasting forty days.

During the forty days the US Embassy approved Hatice's visa, I spent most of my summer vacation with Fatih, far from Hatice. Although it was a hard forty days, it was very instructive in that it helped me realize something significant. Taking care of children was the most demanding job in the world, and it required much responsibility.

It was a full-time job to prepare breakfast for Fatih every morning, send him to kindergarten, take him to the park and swim class, and prepare dinner.

As a naval officer, I would go on long deployments and leave the entire burden of the children on my wife. I realized with all my heart what a great sacrifice it took to be both a mother and a father.

Military service requires a lifetime of sacrifice not only for us but also for our spouses and children. That's why it was challenging for us to be separated from our duties one morning. This was not just a profession but the central axis of our life. The result of so much self-sacrifice for the country and humanity should not be such great betrayal and disloyalty.

When Hatice returned to America, we went to Virginia and New York for two weeks. We especially enjoyed Virginia Beach. Extending our one-day visit, we stayed there for four days. It must have been a quirk of fate. We would come back to this state, from which we left with good memories, after being assigned to NATO headquarters.

While scrolling through the pages of the past and writing my memories in detail, I saw that the critical turning points of our lives were mysteriously connected, and yes, life was full of surprises.

I understand that a planner who is much more powerful and greater than us has brought together all the details and created a lifeline for us. We sometimes miss the big picture and fail to notice the connection that is mysteriously woven between what happens in the future and what has happened in the past. However, life always prepares a person for what's coming next. As we struggled to comprehend what had happened to us and pondered over the reasons, it was inevitable that we would find ourselves with mixed feelings.

Leaving myself in the hands of the Almighty God and surrendering to Him helped calm my feelings. This surrender wasn't just for protection from the crisis of emotions. Every innocent person persecuted and smashed by injustice and lawlessness has placed their hopes on the manifestation of divine justice. Although the persecution of the regime continued to increase, believing and trusting that divine justice would work when the day came was a relief.

This regime, which deprived hundreds of thousands of educated people of their duties, freedoms, families, and homelands with the fabrication of a coup, was getting dirtier day by day, and the country was being dragged into a thick and pitch-black state of darkness.

While conducting this massacre, they said the country got rid of its burdens and cleaned its intestines. They claimed that from now on, a much more qualified staff, defined as "domestic and national," would fulfill the government duties and that the country would advance at an unprecedented pace in all areas.

After all these years, it was the opposite of what they said. At the end of the relentless slaughter, the state and the nation had been dragged into a swamp where public debt had multiplied by six or seven, unemployment had risen from eight percent to twenty percent, inflation had skyrocketed from seven percent to fifty percent, the progress of joining the European Union had come to a standstill, and the Turkish lira had lost five to six times its value against foreign currencies.

As a result of the climate of oppression and fear, it became the second-last country in the world in terms of freedom of the press; bribery, lawlessness, and corruption were exposed.

To delay the economic collapse and create new resources for its supporters, the regime sold public assets one by one, confiscated the help of tens of thousands of people, and went arm-in-arm with the mafia, conducting the greatest wealth transfer in the history of the Turkish Republic.

More than half of the population, crushed under the incessant price hikes, were left to live below the poverty line. Even though the press, rosy paintings, and all kinds of lies, almost all of which fell into the hands of the Erdogan family and their trustees, tried to cover up this situation, the public, who started to realize the condition they were in, gradually expressed that they could not find anything to eat to their table.

Despite this dark and terrifying picture, the rate of those who said they would vote for the regime in the polls could reach 40 percent.

Was the whole nation really in Stockholm syndrome, and were they attached to the head of the regime like prisoners who fell in love with their captors?

Or was their ability to think and question lost due to the intense propaganda they had been exposed to all these years?

Perhaps because of their indifference to the persecution of innocent people, their eyes and hearts were sealed.

The history of humanity is full of stories of nations, tribes, and people who shared the sins of their oppressors in the past and ended up paying a heavy price for this.

In an environment where all kinds of torture are practiced in prisons, women are subject to naked searches, babies, the sick, and the elderly are kept behind bars, the tears of the innocent are ignored, and their laments are not heard, when divine justice is fully manifested, this could have devastating consequences.

For this reason, I always prayed: "O God, allow them to see the truth as soon as possible."

Our second year in the United States was passing quickly yet rewarding. I got an "A" in all my courses in all four quarters and was eligible to be included in the Dean's List three times with a 4.0 average.

Hatice had completed her kindergarten teacher training and started her internship at Fatih's school. Fatih understood everything spoken, walked, and talked, and the gap between him and normal children was closing daily.

While we were in our second year, four more officers from the Navy were accepted to the same university, and our numbers had increased to six with their arrival. We supported the newcomers as much as possible, so they did not suffer the same difficulties we experienced in our first year and welcomed them to our home. We were trying to help them adapt to this new life based on our experiences in housing, buying a car, and education.

After July 15, having a master's degree from a US university was seen as evidence of a crime by the regime. The most successful officers among their peers were targeted and dismissed based on this criterion. However, ten years before the July 15 plot, there had been a silent revolution in the Turkish Armed Forces.

Military service, once the profession preferred by the elites due to its benefits and privileges within society, started to lose popularity due to increased terrorist incidents in the 90s. Because it required grueling and actual sacrifice, the rate of intelligent, vigorous, and patriotic children coming from low-income families in Anatolia entering military schools increased, and the military profession spread to the grassroots.

During the coalition years, when no political view could be organized within the state, especially within the Turkish Armed Forces, a window of opportunity was opened for the country. A new generation of officers and non-commissioned officers started filling the ranks, forming the backbone of the Turkish military. They were well-educated, bilingual, open-minded, and had many years of experience working in NATO and foreign countries. They believed that Turkey and Turkish Military should walk together with the developed democracies of the world based on the interests of the country and the common interests of humanity.

Although a narrow, elitist clique tries to protect its power from the past and favors its cadres, many of the staff cadres found their actual owners due to the exams and successes achieved by poor Anatolian children, especially in the last ten years.

Although the July 15 coup setup might seem like a trap to liquidate these Anatolian children I mentioned above, it was a trap set for the nation itself. Instead of a merit-based promotion system that promotes being successful, knowing a foreign language, and studying and working abroad, total obedience to the regime was the only criteria for success, and these masses were brought to the state level with a predatory mentality and became the architects of today's dark period.

Hakan's birth was our second year's most beautiful surprise and gift. During Hatice's pregnancy, we always worried that our new baby would have the same disease as Fatih. The good news and positive signs we received during our visits to the doctor during pregnancy gave us great hope.

Hakan was born at the beginning of March 2005. From the first day, he illuminated our world with his long hair and curious eyes trying to explore his surroundings.

This may be how God rewarded us for our patience and love in Fatih. Moreover, he had blessed us with a second son who would support his brother for a lifetime.

Even though we were thousands of miles away from our homeland, our friends here did not leave us alone. The memory book we opened for those visiting Hakan had turned into an international gateway.

The notebook contained congratulatory messages in nearly ten languages, from English to Japanese, Arabic to Turkish, and Spanish to Korean. Humanity and friendship were beautiful, and many events we experienced once again confirmed this. After Hakan was born, as Hatice had a cesarean, most of the housework and looking after the children were left to me. While I was worrying about how to cope with everything alongside school, our friends had already prepared a menu and shared the responsibility amongst themselves without our knowledge.

Every day, our friend brought food and asked how we were. Celeste, the American wife of a Turkish professor at Purdue University, visited us daily with her daughters Deniz and Derya. When Celeste came, I had the opportunity to get some sleep. On the other hand, the time to return to Turkey was approaching, and I was also preparing for the Naval Staff College exams.

These two years in America allowed Hatice and me to rest or at least be together.

We re-energized and decided to continue our goals from where we left off. I was keeping up with my graduate courses with great determination and preparing for the staff college exams when Hatice and the children were asleep. Interestingly, a person's capacity increases as he begins to push his limits. Amid all the intensity, I had completed 31 courses within the scope of my master's degree. I could repeat the staff college preparatory books from start to finish a few times.

Focusing on my goal of becoming a staff officer again fueled my motivation. Even though I ran all my preparatory documents through a paper clipper two years ago, the knowledge I gained from all these years of work remained intact; they revived and consolidated as I read it.

Besides, I started struggling with an emotion I had never thought of before. The living standards and opportunities offered in the US were higher than in Turkey. Graduating with honors from the Krannert School of Management attracted the attention of many large companies.

In a short time, I received job offers from several giant companies with almost ten times my salary in Turkey and attractive opportunities.

At that time, many officers who went to the US for graduate education fled and did not return to Turkey. This situation had become so common that it was considered normal. In my case, there was also Fatih's education. Fatih has made significant progress in the last two years and had the opportunity to receive a highly professional and comprehensive education. Staying in America and working for a private company to establish a high standard of living was a dream for many. However, we chose not to be caught up in the glamor of this beautiful life and to return to our country, to our duty. I thought fleeing as a soldier was dishonorable.

The Naval Forces had sent us here with the Turkish taxpayer's money, and it was time to pay my debt by doing my best with what I had learned and the experience I had gained.

This is what a soldier's honor would require.

After the events of July 15 and what happened to us, I couldn't help but ask myself, "Was it worth it?" Let me answer honestly. Despite all the disloyalty and betrayal we had faced, I still believe it was worth it.

It was worth it.

It was worth it.

In my nearly 20 years of service, successfully fulfilling challenging duties and representing my state in almost 40 countries was the most outstanding value that would make my life meaningful.

On the other hand, there was also the tragicomic side.

In the dark period after July 15, when black and white were mixed, patriots and traitors were also incorporated.

Those who came to the US with the state's resources for their graduate education and then never returned began to shout and share posts loaded with patriotism and bravery on their social media accounts after July 15.

Dozens of people who fled resigned for money or were dishonorably discharged from the Navy previously suddenly embraced similar scenarios and said, "We resigned as a reaction to this group that took over the Turkish military," or they started to say, "they had liquidated us" and started to be treated as heroes.

Since social media users did not know the backgrounds and real stories, they regarded them as ex-officers who lived abroad but whose heart was beating for their country and favored them.

However, tens of thousands of people like me, who loved their homeland and were not lured by money, a better life, or positions for the sake of duty, were being defamed by the treacherous slanders of those lying mouths.

Fortunately, there is divine justice; the truth has a nice feature of shining out when the day comes. Fortunately, our foreheads are high, and our consciences are clear. Despite everything, there is a genuine love of homeland in our hearts that does not fade or diminish.

The List

LOVE FOR THE PROFESSION
Ankara, Turkey, 2005

It was time to say goodbye to our life in America. We came here with three suitcases and were returning with three.

We also took friendships, memories, and experiences we would remember forever. More importantly, our family of three, consisting of my wife and Fatih, has expanded, and we bought tickets for our baby, Hakan, who brings joy to our lives.

It was exciting to be back home after two years. Ahmet greeted us in Ankara. They longed to see our families and were excited to meet Hakan. Due to the risk of losing our suitcases, I took all our official documents and valuables in two backpacks with me.

The plane would first land in Istanbul, and then we had a connecting flight to Ankara—the 12-hour flight passed by taking care of Hakan and Fatih and dreaming about our life in Turkey. When we landed in Istanbul, we had less than half an hour to catch the other plane, and the airport was very crowded.

The UEFA Soccer Cup final was played in Istanbul, and those who came to watch the game flocked to the airport for their return journey. Hatice had taken Hakan, and I had taken on the responsibility of Fatih and his backpacks.

A gentleman who saw us running said, "I can help you if you want. You will miss the plane at this rate," I gave him the two bags on my shoulder without hesitation. We were both trying to catch the same plane. The gentleman helping us was leading, and in a few minutes, he disappeared into the crowd. At that time, the most important thing on our minds was to catch the plane, and we thought we'd meet on the plane anyway. We reached the domestic lines and got on the buses to the aircraft at the last moment. My eyes were looking for the gentleman who helped us, but I could not see him. I didn't want to think of a lousy possibility and was trying to stay positive. "He got on the plane with the previous bus," I thought. We were tired from running and dying to get on the plane immediately. When we got on the plane, I placed the children and started scanning the passengers from the corner of my eye. The person helping us was not on the plane.

When I asked the cabin crew if there was a passenger they were waiting for, "The boarding process is complete. We're leaving soon," he replied. I understood the gravity of the situation. I asked the cabin crew to reach airport security.

Our diplomas, Hakan's birth certificate, marriage certificate, and electronic items were in the bag I gave to this man. Worst of all, I didn't know the man's name nor pay enough attention to what he wore to describe him.

Although the pilot informed airport security but could not keep the plane waiting, he started the flight preparations. He said, "When you arrive in Ankara, you will start the lost property procedure."

The other passengers on the plane had overheard the situation, and in as little as ten minutes, almost everyone was talking about us.

"How does a person trust a stranger with his bags?"

"He should have at least taken his name or phone number."

"Who knows what valuable items they had in the bag that is making the plane wait."

"It's sad; they have two children!"

The trip to Istanbul was one of the worst trips of my life. I can't say it's the worst because we will experience worse in the coming years.

Throughout the journey, I was angry with myself, making plans for how to regain our lost documents and trying hard not to hear the comments of those around us.

Finally, we arrived in Ankara, and when we saw Ahmet at the door, we forgot everything. Leaving the children with Ahmet and Hatice, I applied to the lost and found office and started the search, although I was not hopeful. Then we arranged a room at an Officer's Club in Ankara. We bought gyro and ayran from the cafeteria. Even though we spent two excellent years in America, we missed the flavors of our own country. We were trying not to think about our lost bags and to enjoy this moment of being back home. Even though we tried to push the limits, we could not get permission for Ahmet to stay in the Officer's Club with us since he was not in the military.

The first thing I did the following day was to call the lost and found office. There were no positive developments.

Since I didn't have much hope, I decided to focus on the plans of how to start our new life.

I was appointed to the Turkish General Staff, the joint service headquarters overseeing all services in the Turkish Military. I was appointed as Promotion Strategies Development Officer to take part in the "Personnel Management System" Project, which aimed to renew and develop the personnel and promotion system of the Armed Forces.

There were only seven months left for the Naval Staff College exam.

Every officer had six chances to take this exam in their careers, starting when they were in service for seven years until their 13th year in service. Technically this was my fourth chance as I could not take the previous exams since I was in America for the last two years.

I had to focus on my exam preparation. Hatice also needed to find a job, and we needed to find a babysitter to support us. The first military housing allocations in Ankara were going to be made in August. We would have to stay in the officer's club for about three months.

Since it would be difficult for us to stay in one room with two children for a long time, we devised a temporary plan. Hatice would go to Adana to her family with the children, and I would stay in the officer's club until I was allocated military lodging.

Later in the day, we got a call from the airport. Our bags were found. The gentleman who helped us was trying to catch the Izmir flight and thought we were on the same plane. He looked for us on the plane and delivered the bags to the lost and found department when he landed in Izmir.

He also left a note and his phone number saying, "Sorry, I had to open the bag to find your name."

I was very touched when I read the note. I immediately called and conveyed my thanks, and in a somewhat embarrassing manner, I apologized to him for the dire possibilities that had crossed my mind.

There is a saying, "God first makes his loved one lose his donkey, only for him to find it later." The discovery of the bags made us so happy that the dark clouds that had descended on us for a few days had dispersed.

Before joining my new position in the Turkish General Staff, I served at the Naval Forces Headquarters for two weeks. I prepared a lengthy report containing my experiences in America and presented it to the Head of Personnel.

The professor I met before returning to Turkey and the head of the Purdue University student admission committee said they could cooperate with the Turkish Armed Forces.

And they could open an MBA program in Istanbul or Ankara if agreed. It was an incredible opportunity. It was an honor to develop good relations and leave positive impressions that resulted in such an offer. One of America's most prestigious schools made a severe offer based on our achievements. If the program were implemented, military personnel and many of our civilian citizens would be able to receive graduate education at Purdue University without even going abroad.

Considering the cost of training for the personnel sent abroad on behalf of the public, it would be possible to save millions of dollars. Even the dream of this excited me, which was reflected in my voice as I conveyed the issue to the Head of Personnel. At the end of my meeting, my enthusiasm stagnated. I responded, "Mehmet, you just came from America. I understand your excitement but focus on your mission. Let us think about these matters."

The Chief of Staff did not hesitate to throw away such a valuable opportunity that would come once in forty years, in a single moment. In the Armed Forces, many development opportunities were eroded at the idea stage because some people had many stars on their shoulders but very narrow points of view in their minds. Although it made me sad to witness this, it made me even more ambitious and fueled my determination to change such situations.

The head of the department where I worked was Admiral Abdullah Gavremoglu, whose name would be mentioned in the Ergenekon/ Sledgehammer cases and who would be arrested in the case.

There were highly successful and distinguished officers from all service branches in the project we would be working on. Commander Ozkan Toy and Lieutenant Colonel Ugur Zel had completed their doctorate in education. Our Branch Managers Colonel Mustafa Ilter and Major Ugur Sahin would become generals in the following years and, unfortunately, were victims of torture after July 15. Another sailor in the team, Commander Fehmi Turksever, would be among the officers who were purged after July 15.

This team, selected for the most comprehensive and visionary personnel system project of the Turkish Armed Forces, was working with great enthusiasm and hard work, unaware of the terrible events that would befall us a few years later.

The most significant advantage of working at the General Staff Headquarters was that although I was in the rank of Lieutenant, I had the opportunity to work with many senior generals and admirals. Before presenting a project to the Chief of the General Staff, we worked with many officers from each service branch and respective headquarters. We made presentations to the commanders at the ranks of General and

Admiral.

I had the opportunity to see how the high-level decision-making process worked. On the other hand, I was disappointed that the decision-making process of all the scientific and systematic headquarters work was stuck between the lips of a single commander. For example, to develop a new promotion model based on merit, we developed simulations cooperating with many reputable universities, such as Middle Eastern Technical University. We looked into different models in various NATO countries and completed this task, which took months of hard work.

In these efforts, we developed a new promotion system based on scientific criteria and merit instead of the old one based on time in service. Almost every officer was promoted automatically after completing their required years in a rank. In the current system, anyone could rise to the rank O-6, which is a colonel in the Army and Air Force or a captain in the Navy, as long as they remained in the profession. As a result, many high-ranking officers were in the system far above the staffing requirement.

So much so that a deputy commander with the rank of colonel was appointed to all command positions at the level of brigadier general in the Turkish Land Forces, and the headquarters were filled with officers at the rank of colonel, who should generally be assigned at the level of branch manager but were employed in ordinary headquarters officer positions.

In our new system, the promotions of officers beyond O-3 rank (Major / Lieutenant) would be based on their military performance and academic success, foreign language knowledge, physical adequacy, and staffing needs. This new system would ensure that the personnel constantly improve themselves, and the number of high-ranking personnel and related expenses would be reduced. Thus, a more trained and dynamic personnel structure would be adopted.

When we presented this project, which lasted months and was

approved by all the Service Commanders, the Deputy Chief of General Staff, General Ilker Basbug, showed a reaction that shocked everyone. He challenged us. "As long as I carry these ranks, no one should try to change the promotion system," he said. None of us could understand the reason for this reaction. What could it mean to reject the months-long work of an agency under his command as the second chief of the General Staff?

Evidence and documents that emerged within the scope of the Ergenekon/Sledgehammer cases would enable us to make sense of Basbug's reaction. This structure promoted every officer they wanted to the rank of colonel without any hindrance in the current promotion system. It filled the command echelon with admirals and generals from their team with the decisions of the Supreme Military Council, which was closed and opaque.

Since the system we developed was based on merit, the possibility of his own men rising to the top was at risk. With the comfort of being privileged, they did not want challenging assignments, did not study for exams, were sent to the headquarters, selected foreign posts, and would always be favored in the old system. We were hitting this dirty group with the new promotion system. According to the allegations in the case file, Basbug, the leader of this group, was preventing it with great panic and anger.

The future of the Turkish Armed Forces was at the hands of some people who put their personal and secret interests before the country's interests, and they could shape the decision process as they wished. It was a terrible situation for the Turkish Armed Forces.

As a young officer, I was determined to fight this mentality as long as I remained in uniform.

I would come home after busy working hours, and after a short break for food, I would start studying for the Staff College exams until 2 am.

Being apart from Hatice and the children was beginning to make things difficult for me. We decided to rent a house in Ankara, rented an apartment, and reunited as a family again. I was trying to spare time for the children on Friday and Saturday nights. After they went to sleep, I studied until five in the morning. After a short nap, I had breakfast with them around nine or ten.

The Naval Staff College exam was challenging, and we were preparing for this exam as a family. Occasionally, relatives came to support us, and then we could take a respite.

In this period, we thought everything was falling into place, but development took place that would turn our lives upside down. Fatih had his first epileptic seizure, and after many years we found ourselves in the corridors of GATA, the largest military hospital in Ankara. Despite using epilepsy drugs, the duration of the seizures was prolonged, and their severity increased.

Although we knew life was full of ups and downs, we were unprepared for this hard fall.

Fatih trembled at every seizure and fell when he got a seizure while standing. We felt helpless as we could not always be with him and could not predict the time of the seizures. Our house was on the seventh floor, and it wasn't easy to take Fatih up and down under these conditions, even with the elevator. Although we moved a few months ago, we decided to enter military lodging and moved to a first-floor flat in ORAN military lodgings. From time to time, Hatice and I would stay up until midnight, trying to figure out how to deal with this new situation. I feared going into the hospital cycle again, getting embittered, and losing my enthusiasm for life. We had baby Hakan as well as Fatih. As parents, we had to be strong and stand up. We didn't have the luxury of giving up and showing frustration.

I continued to prepare for the Staff College exams. Hatice found a job in a kindergarten and took Fatih to where she worked. We were going to hire a full-time babysitter for Hakan.

Even though I thought, "We bit off more than we could chew," we had to stand upright in facing life's difficulties.

I knew that God would help us. Many times, we have accomplished the impossible thanks to His help. In the end, His service was there. Hatice got a job as an English teacher in one of the most prestigious kindergartens in Ankara. We enrolled Fatih in the same school. During this challenging process, I decided to give up my evening study time to spend more time with the children. But I did continue to study during lunch breaks at work and while commuting to work on the bus. I looked at all the spare time left over from my work shift and children.

We looked at each day as a brand-new beginning. This prevented us from carrying the burdens of the past on our shoulders and from being crushed under these burdens.

Fatih had seizures occasionally, and our search for a cure continued unceasingly. We found ourselves in his practice wherever we heard of a promising doctor. Despite all the expenditures we made and all the methods we tried, the seizures continued. While in America, Fatih had almost reached the level of his peers in terms of development. Now he was melting before our eyes, forgetting one by one many things he had learned before. He could no longer count and distinguish colors as before.

It was like spending hours on the beach and building a sandcastle. We were trying to teach him something and make the walls of this castle, but each seizure was destroying this castle like a wave in the sea.

Witnessing this situation as parents destroyed our hopes and morale, like that castle, and melted it. We couldn't spend time with Hakan or get used to the babysitter during the day.

As if these were not enough, Hatice's school principal used Fatih's situation as an excuse and said that Hatice could not continue working if she continued bringing Fatih to school.

Why does life always force us to make the toughest decisions? Hatice said that if they would prevent Fatih from getting an education, she could not work there, and she resigned.

But as fate would have it, our tears dried once again with the opening of a new school a few streets away. Hatice was offered the English education department coordinator position at the newly opened Yıldız Kindergarten. Moreover, the school also had a 0-2 age group, so Fatih and Hakan could go to school with Hatice.

As we talked that evening, we remembered an old Turkish saying, "There is always something good in every bad."

Indeed, we lived through four seasons in one day. Just as our souls were struggling with the cold of winter, we suddenly found ourselves among spring flowers with the touch of a hand. Maybe it was the magic of life. God was giving us the following message: "Do not give up. Keep going. I am with you."

Finally, the big day had come. I was in Istanbul for the Naval Staff College exams, hoping to reap the fruits of years of work, sleepless nights, and bloodshot eyes. This tough exam lasted for four days. The first day was general culture, the second was military culture, and the third and last were tactical issues.

To succeed, it was necessary to read, understand, internalize, and engrave thousands of military documents, manuals, memoranda, directives, voluminous history, law, economics, and other books line by line in a way that would push the limits of human memory.

The tactical issue exams were the hardest part of the marathon. Each session lasted about four hours. After making and evaluating the map plotting with precision, it was necessary to make the right decision as required by the tactical situation and to write the rationale in detail.

Having active duties such as Combat Operations Center and Navigational Operations Officer on combat ships and gaining experience in many scenarios during the exercises made my job much more manageable. I could make the right decision in matters that many people had difficulty with, and I could complete the planning and explain my decision without much difficulty. This way, while preparing for this exam, I could spare more time to study for the general and military culture exams. I had the opportunity to repeat the publications that many candidates can only read once or twice, at least three or four times.

The four-day exam marathon was also a psychological test. It was difficult to sleep at night when the tiredness of going through a tough exam lasted for hours, combined with the excitement and stress of the next day.

After each exam, I would meet with Hatice, ask about the children's situation, and prepare for the next exam by refreshing my energy. Thanks to the exam, I could see my colleagues whom I had not seen for years.

Due to the rush and hectic environment of the exam, we could not spare time for long conversations, and we were satisfied with short talks to satiate our longing.

When I got on the seat of the Ankara bus at the end of the fourth day, I felt like a thousand tons of weight had been lifted off my shoulders. Despite all the difficulties, I did not give up. I worked and did my part.

Typically, only 30 of the hundreds of officers would pass the exam, and I had no choice but to wait to see how I did. When I returned to Ankara, I went on leave, and we went to our hometown. The last seven months had been very tough, and we needed a break.

The time we spent with our loved ones was like a pleasant coffee break after a tiring day. The period from December, when I took the exam, to mid-February, when the results were announced, was the longest time I've spent without studying in my life.

Like all good things, these two months passed quickly, and the day came when the exam results would be announced. I was so excited and nervous that if I could not pass the exam, I was afraid I would not find the strength to work at this pace again.

The exam results were presented to the Force Commanders and then to the Chief of General Staff in his office for final approval.

I anxiously waited for the results while I continued my daily work.

In the afternoon, the meeting room door opened during the branch meeting, and Chief of Staff Lieutenant General Servet Yoruk burst into the room, "Where is this boy?" He said.

Then he turned to me and hugged me in a way I had never seen before and said, "Well done, Lieutenant Mehmet; we just got the results of the staff college exams approved by the Chief of General Staff. Congratulations! You placed first, and I wanted to break the news to you."

I was amazed. This gesture by the Head of Personnel made me happy, motivated, and honored. The fact that I placed first attracted everyone's attention, many generals and admirals from the headquarters called me and congratulated me directly. At the first opportunity, I gave the happy news to Hatice. I also called my brothers and brother-in-law to share my joy with them. Years of hard work paid off, and the path to becoming the staff officer I had dreamed of was opened.

Being a staff officer was the first step to being one of the candidates who would shape the future command structure of the Turkish Military. Staff officers did all high-level planning in the Armed Forces and undertook critical command and headquarters duties. Passing the exam was not the end but the beginning of everything. Two years of tough staff college training awaited me.

I knew most of the others that passed the exam. From the first day, everyone was experiencing t own joy, calling each other to congratulate each other. The most senior of the officers who passed the staff college exam each year became the senior officer of that class. Lt. Commander Mustafa Kaya was the most senior in our class. He was known as "Soldier Mustafa" in his circle. He was highly disciplined and sensitive in human relations. During our two-year staff college education, he took the weight of the class on his shoulders in many matters. Together with his wife, Nese, they had taken the weight of occasional problems and responsibilities on their own to maintain a balance between faculty members and students many times.

Our class of thirty had a diverse structure. It was the first time a female officer had passed the exam. Lieutenant Yasemin, the first female staff officer, would make history again by graduating at the top of our Naval Staff College class.

Selami, Hakan, İsa, and Rahim, my classmates with whom I studied at the Naval Academy, also passed the exams, and we would be classmates at the staff college. I was looking forward to spending two more years with them.

I knew everyone who passed the exam was an extraordinary person; they all were very successful in their service and had the potential to do great things. I was very excited to be among these intelligent and well-trained officers.

There is a lie that the Erdogan regime frequently resorted to after July 15. They claim that after 2000, "officers affiliated with the Gulen group received support to pass the Staff College exams, they were unqualified, but they were provided the exam questions beforehand to qualify."

This was such vile slander!

It was possible to refute this slander even by looking at the officers in our class.

For example, Lt. Commander Mustafa, Lt. Ozgur, and Lt. Savas would be promoted to Admiral by this regime, although they graduated with us from the staff college simultaneously.

As for the issue of merit, though with deep indignation, I couldn't help laughing.

Many of us had completed our graduate education with honors at home and abroad. I do not want to bore you by mentioning the names of each one by one; however, especially young officers such as Hasim, Meftun, Ozer, Bekir, and Nevzat were the best and brightest officers in their classes and the best performers in their units.

I briefly explained how we studied for this exam in the previous pages. However, let me end this issue by giving an example.

The dimples that formed under my eyes from working overtime during the day and studying for the exam at night are still in place even though I am at this age. Based on these dirty slanders, 27 officers from this class, excluding those linked to Eurasian/privileged cliques, were dismissed through the July 15 plot.

The dirty plans of the regime wasted years of effort, suffering, great sacrifices, and big dreams.

The regime, which plowed into its Armed Forces like an elephant plunging into a glassware shop, destroyed everything and closed the Military Academies, which had a 150-year history and graduated many valuable military leaders, diplomats, and presidents, including Mustafa Kemal Ataturk, the founder of the Turkish Republic. The destruction was terrible.

Our people could not see this terrible destruction created by the regime, as they were deceived by tons of lies and slanders.

LIFE IS THE SUM OF HUMAN CHOICES
Istanbul, Turkey, 2006

This time our journey was from Ankara to Istanbul for training at the Naval Staff College. Ankara was a city where new adventures began for us. Our previous adventure started in Ankara and resulted in sailing to the United States for a master's degree; this time ended with our trip to Istanbul for staff officer training.

We moved to the military lodgings in the academy campus in Yenilevent, Istanbul. I had received orders from the Superintendent of the Staff College and faculty members who started to meet with us. They all advised me to be ready for an intense and challenging academic tempo, and expectations were very high as I had passed the exam in the first place. I knew that the competition among the officers at the staff college was also a challenge due to the prestige and importance of finishing this education at the top of your class. In the past years, there were situations where this competition had turned into mutual hatred and intolerance. The faculty members took advantage of this competition. They tested their limits by assigning more complex tasks to officers with the potential and desire to graduate on top of the class.

Due to Fatih's health condition, I was worried about how I would cope with the hectic pace of two years. On the other hand, my success in my career and the performance expected of me by the faculty were causing my life-long desire for success to spiral out of control. At the beginning of this education process, I struggled with not wanting to meet expectations and found it inappropriate. I didn't want to be passive, so I started to take on challenging tasks from day one. But

Fatih's seizures had become uncontrollable, and he had ongoing crises. Hatice had started working in a kindergarten in Tarabya, and we had set up a living arrangement where she would take Fatih with her. For Hakan, we hired a babysitter.

The Staff College education targeted not only the military and academic development of the officers but also their social and civil development as part of the education process. We would host social events and entertain guests, including the faculty members, in our homes. Because of this, Hatice and I needed to renew most of our furniture and spent the last money we had.

Even though we both worked, we could only make ends meet if we had additional health expenses, caregiver fees, and social expenses. We kept it secret but tried to complete the first month through our credit cards.

In the Staff College training, each officer is assigned a consultant faculty member who would be primarily responsible for developing each staff officer candidate and his family.

Captain Alaattin Sevim was our consultant faculty member. We never really got along with each other. While I was in graduate school in the US, Captain Alaattin was the Turkish Naval Attaché in Washington. I reported him as my immediate superior during my two years of education. Although I was on the honor list for three terms, he did not appreciate me and did not want my achievements to be recognized. He would have notified our superiors with praise and admiration if I were part of his elite groups, but I was not. This did not surprise me because I had experienced this in many similar situations.

This time, I was in front of him as the best performer in the exam at the Naval Staff College. His demeanor clearly showed that he didn't want to accept this fact. He was searching for my mistake at every opportunity. Because of this, I tried to keep him from knowing about any of my difficulties, even though he was my advisor.

When Fatih fell into a coma after a seizure, I would wait by his side until the morning and go to school early for my classes. It was a complicated process for us.

"Did I do the right thing by taking on this burden?" I was thinking. I was forcing myself not to give up. At such moments, my classmates came to my rescue, giving me a shoulder to rest on and morale to keep me up.

It is said that "Life is the sum of human choices." This was also my choice; I had chosen the most arduous path to do my job best, making my wife and family a part of this difficult choice. We were already beginning to face the dire consequences of our choice. When we were in America, the days of happy conversations with Hatice were replaced with pessimism.

As Fatih's health deteriorated, we questioned the situation we were in. On Eid morning, while dressing Fatih in his clothes, he had a heavy seizure, and we started to cry loudly.

Despair and loneliness had taken over us completely. At that moment, Hakan, who was not even two years old, came to us wearing his holiday clothes in the wrong way! Seeing Hakan like this instantly relieved our tears, and the sadness that overwhelmed us brought a bright smile to our faces. It was as if God had given more than enough to Hakan from what He had taken from Fatih. Despite his young age, Hakan became our source of life with his intelligence, skill, and cute actions.

We entered Eid with Fatih in one lap and Hakan in the other, hugging each other tightly for minutes. Later a close friend of ours, Sevim, came to visit. Although we met with Sevim in Istanbul when we started our education, we became very close, and she would come to our rescue many times. To experience the joy of the holidays with her dispersed the dark clouds inside us.

Sevim was living in her house in Taksim, not too far from the campus, and we visited her from time to time, trying to get away from the dreary atmosphere of the Staff College. Even though our days were difficult, we continued to stand up despite all the problems.

We took graduate-level courses in military specialization, international relations, security, and defense policies. However, it was almost impossible to fulfill the duties the faculty members had given us properly. It was as if they were putting us through an endurance test.

The long and quiet nights in which the academy lodgings and households fell asleep had become my best friend, and I got into the habit of sleeping only for three or four hours each night.

We ended the last days of 2006 with a pain that will never leave my mind.

My Naval Academy Nurettin, Cevdet, and Cemal classmates were already in their second year of education at the Naval Staff College. I knew all three well and became close friends when I entered the Naval Academy 14 years ago. Nurettin and Cemal were like a walking library. During the Naval Academy years, they would finish a few books every week, go to French courses on the weekends, and, more importantly, they would never fail to have a smile on their faces and kindness in their language and demeanor.

Years later, they passed the Staff College exam in the same year. Cemal was known for his generous personality and for dribbling the ball outside the playing field whenever he received it during football matches.

During our single years in Golcuk, Cemal and I rented a house. Although we met several times a month due to the long and frequent deployments, we were roommates for about a year.

The first term of the Academy was over, and we had a short vacation. I woke up in the morning with a phone call. It was Hakan. "We lost Cevdet. Come to the lodging if you want," he said in a sad and exhausted voice.

Before I could ask, "What do you mean 'We lost Cevdet!'" He hung up.

I informed Hatice and ran out of the house.

The distance between our lodgings was a few minutes by car.

That short road was longer than ever, and dozens of questions crossed my mind.

A few more cars were heading in the same direction. They received the same sad news. When I arrived in front of the lodging, I saw Hakan, Selami, and Nurettin at the door.

We greeted each other with tearful eyes and hugged each other.

Cevdet had a heart attack.

How could a young and healthy officer in his thirties suffer from a heart attack?

As the famous Turkish Folk Poet Yunus Emre says, "In this world, my heart burns, and I bury myself for those who died bravely. It's like the sky reaped its crops."

He had a whole life ahead of him, a beautiful daughter to raise. He and his wife had built a home that everyone looked up to with envy, and they made us feel the love and sincerity that surrounded us when we got together.

I lost a brother in my arms and a longtime friend; it hurt more than losing someone from my family. Cevdet put on the Navy whites at 13 when he first entered the Naval High School and sailed away to eternity as a young Lieutenant.

The pain of losing a friend was heartbreaking. I knew from my own experience what struggles Cevdet had been through, although he always had a smile. Preparing for the Staff College exams, keeping up with the hectic pace of the school, exams, presentations, additional duties given by the faculty, and the stress of the military environment wore out his heart.

He had served on submarines for many years. After overcoming long and complex tasks, underwater, he passed away under all the burden of the Staff College.

At daybreak, his house was filled with dozens of cars. Officers and faculty members from the Land, Air, and Naval Staff Colleges crowded the lodge's garden.

Rear Admiral Tayfun Uraz, Superintendent of the Naval Staff College, attributed Cevdet's heart attack to smoking. He did not blame himself by ignoring the burden and stress he put on students.

Cevdet was no longer with us, and our duty was to support his wife as much as possible while sending him off on his last journey. As classmates, we wanted to attend the funeral in his hometown of Gaziantep and fulfill our previous duty. Admiral Tayfun inexplicably refused our request.

His excuse was that the academic year was still ongoing. What an inhumane point of view this was! An officer, a commander, should set an example for everyone with his human values. How could we be motivated in a system that did not allow us to fulfill our most basic human duty?

Despite our insistence, only Cemal and Nurettin were allowed to attend the burial ceremony in Gaziantep, and we said goodbye to our friend at GATA Haydarpasa Hospital.

Cevdet's death opened the door to a period in which I once again questioned the meaning of life. For the remaining one and a half years of the Academy, every time I passed in front of his lodging, my eyes darted to his apartment with the dream that he would greet me from the balcony. There was a solution to everything, but all mortals were helpless in the face of death.

Yahya Kemal Beyatli, a well-known Turkish poet, summed up his desperation in the face of death in his poem 'Silent Ship':

"It's time to weigh anchor and set sail to the unknown.

She sails silently as if she has no passengers onboard.

Neither a handkerchief nor an arm waves goodbye.

This journey saddens those staying at the pier,

Eyes looking at the black horizon for days are moist.

Desperate hearts. This is one of many ships that sailed away.

Nor is this the last morning of a life of anger.

The lovers in the world wait in vain.

They do not know that those they love who are gone will not return.

Many who passed on are happy in their new place.

Many years have passed; no one has yet returned from this cruise."

As soon as the first year of the Academy was completed, we found ourselves at the peak of the Taurus Mountains in Hatice's father's home. My mother-in-law was as happy as a child at our arrival. We were so in need of such warm attention and support. While Fatih and Hakan spent time with their grandparents, we took long walks on the summits of the Taurus Mountains, just as we did during our engagement days. We were resting our souls. Our most incredible luxury was to buy the warm fresh bread from the village bakery before anyone woke up and to eat it with the cheese, we bought from the grocery store. When we returned home, my mother-in-law greeted us with a big smile, and my father-in-law said, "Come on, tea is ready!" He was inviting us to the table.

If we knew we would live this routine for years, we would never say 'no.' Being away from home wore on both of us. Even though we tried to carry the burdens we bore, our bodies and souls were worn out over time.

We were successfully climbing the professional career ladder, but the price we paid was getting heavier daily.

When a tree falls, he who planted it and raised it feels the most pain. The regime had knocked down tens of thousands of trees that had grown in decades with the treacherous trap it set on July 15. My life was just one of them. Maybe many of them had reached this level by sacrificing their years under much more difficult conditions than us.

The deviousness of the regime must have consequences; it has wasted the hard work of so many and significantly violated people's rights. I wish to see in my lifetime the perpetrators of this persecution pay the price for what they did.

The 20-day summer vacation in the Taurus Mountains was what we needed the most. Fatih's tiebreaker was relatively reduced during our break, and Hakan spent much time with his uncles and aunts. I also went to see my mother and visited my father in Yahyali. Since Ramazan and Emrah were on their summer vacation, I also had the opportunity to see them. Every time we went to Yahyali, I did not neglect to visit the graves of my grandmother and grandfather.

It was impossible to forget my grandmother's importance to me. I grew up in these lands, and although I had a difficult time in harsh conditions, many people I knew were part of my childhood memories. Even though Hatice and I were discussing where we should spend our vacation, visiting these places was a matter of fidelity for me. I did whatever I needed to convince her, and we stayed in my hometown for at least a few days.

The vacation was over in the blink of an eye, and the second year of the Staff College training had begun. Hatice left the school in Tarabya and started working in a kindergarten in Etiler, a district in Istanbul where many celebrities lived. This time, both Fatih and Hakan could go to her school. Thus, we didn't need a babysitter anymore.

At Hatice's new school, we had the opportunity to become familiar with an entirely different lifestyle we had not been exposed to before. The children or relatives of many celebrities were among the school's students. Sibel Tuzun's daughter and Sezen Aksu's niece, famous Turkish singers, attended the school. Our acquaintance with Sibel Tuzun turned into a friendly relationship. We started to meet as a family and made house visits to each other. Our conversations with Ms. Sibel revolved around "how difficult it is to raise a child in Turkey under these conditions." The footsteps of some adverse developments that would arouse concern were beginning to be heard in specific segments of society, who had their hearts set on a bright future.

The country was transforming slowly and almost without objection, like a frog in boiling water. Their minds, close to modern thought, were sharing their bleak predictions and anxieties about the future of our country. I thought that the Republic of Turkey had gone through many troubles until that day and that despite all the internal turmoil and military coups in the recent past, the system managed to protect itself and return to the path of civilization every time.

I soon realized how wrong my thinking was. While the forces that led the country to the darkness of July 15 were putting their long-term plans into practice step by step, we were caught up in the daily lives of our careers, where we worked day and night with the love of duty. Of course, we made the mistake of being unable to see the danger coming and not grasp its gravity while we were working breathlessly at such an intense - and partly artificial - work tempo.

Although the second year had a more intense academic pace, we had stored enough energy during the summer vacation and started the new term stronger. Although I was assigned to give many presentations and complete many challenging tasks, I made it out of each with a clear conscience. Unlike the stories we heard from previous years, a solidarity-based friendship had developed among the officers who made up our class, and no one was trying to drag each other's feet. And no one deviated into unethical ways out of greed for rank and power. Yasemin, Meftun, Ozer, Hasim, and I supported each other when necessary and avoided competitive games that would ruin our friendship.

As if the intensity in the Staff College needed to be increased, I also edited the Alesta magazine, a monthly periodical prepared by officers at the Staff College. We were preparing an average of 7-8 articles each month, and we would get the approval of the Superintendent of the Staff Colleges, a 4-star general before the journal went into print. It was a stressful as well as an enjoyable process.

One of the essential qualities of a staff officer is to conduct scientific research and to be able to blend it with military experience and knowledge. Thanks to my position in the magazine, I contributed to the work of my friends and had the opportunity to write original articles on various subjects every month.

My first article was on change management. It was one of the most critical issues in the Armed Forces. While protecting their fundamental values and principles, institutions and individuals had to renew their organizational structures and activities to the requirements of the time and keep up.

No matter how big and deep-rooted they were, institutions that could not realize and manage this change were doomed to weaken and collapse. In the case studies we conducted during my graduate education in the US, we analyzed how companies such as IBM and Kodak resisted change and collapsed over time. A few months ago, I witnessed how General İlker Basbug prevented change in the Turkish Armed Forces. With this work, I wanted to raise awareness about change management, albeit a small one.

My other article was on Mustafa Kemal Ataturk's foreign policy principles. Besides being a genius soldier, Ataturk was a well-trained statesman. After the national struggle, the foreign policy of the Republic of Turkey was shaped within the framework of the principle of "Peace at Home, Peace in the World." Additionally, in the first years of the young Republic, a policy was to not interfere in the internal affairs of neighboring states, and as the nation turned its face to Western civilization. These basic principles enabled us to become allies even with the conditions we had previously fought with and to avoid a great disaster by remaining neutral in the Second World War. As staff officers of a state marching to the future with these principles, it was essential that we understood the founding values of foreign policy and acted on this axis in our military and diplomatic representation duties.

It was not possible for people who did not internalize the fundamental values of the Republic of Turkey and its foreign policy to understand the importance of strategic partnerships such as the European Union and NATO for our country. In the article I wrote, I revealed that the basic principles of Turkish foreign policy in the Ataturk period should continue to be taken as foundational. The new regime established by Erdogan set aside the basic principles that had guided us for almost 80 years. It turned its direction from the West to authoritarian and anti-democratic regimes like Russia and Iran.

With such a dangerous and unreal strategy, foreign policy was involved in internal conflicts in many countries, from Libya to Syria. It engaged in dirty bargains with many terrorist organizations and covered its hands with the blood of tens of thousands of innocent people. The principle of unconditional sovereignty within our national borders and respect for the territorial integrity of our neighbors was shelved. Our young soldiers of this country were forced to embark on various adventures whose intention and scope were hidden from the public, and hundreds of our soldiers were sent to their deaths.

Any objection or questioning of the regime's dangerous foreign policy was prevented. The facts were obscured with a venomous smokescreen by playing with the people's feelings through the funerals of martyrs and religious values.

The morale, motivation, and operational power of the Turkish Armed Forces, the defender of peace and stability in many parts of the world under NATO and the United Nations were destroyed. The paramilitary organization called SADAT, which had connections and provided training to some terrorist organizations and gangs that were systematically given way and opportunity, and the terrorist groups, which were the subject of proxy wars, became the foreign policy and security tools of the Erdogan regime.

As we approached the end of the two-year Staff College training, two exciting processes were awaiting us. One of them is a wide-ranging war game in which the staff officer candidates will demonstrate their competence, and on the last day, the Chief of Staff and Force Commanders will participate as distinguished observers. The other was determining the first places of duty we would be appointed to as staff officers.

Within the scope of the war game, each staff candidate was given tasks at different levels and difficulties, considering their success in the two-year training. I was assigned as the Fleet Commander of the generic blue country, representing Turkey as the highest-ranking naval officer in the wargame scenario.

After days of preparation and headquarters work, the distinguished observers, attended by the Turkish Armed Forces command, came to observe. We completed our presentations before the Chief of General Staff and the Force Commanders. After my presentation, the Chief of General Staff of the time, General Yasar Buyukanit, said, "Lieutenant, that was a nice presentation, thank you," and asked the following questions, "How many guided missiles are left in your inventory at the moment, and do you have any additional guided missile requests as the Fleet Commander?" It was not the expected question, and I had not prepared the answer beforehand. There was a short silence, and the distinguished observer delegation, consisting of nearly forty admirals and generals, and the faculty members focused their attention on my answer by looking at me.

"Sir, the guided missile stock level remaining in my inventory is six percent. As the commander leading the naval operation, if we could solve this by domestic means, I would have requested additional ammunition without thinking. However, considering the economic and international political situation, we must decide on procuring guided missiles worth millions of dollars from abroad. This requires a separate situational reasoning process at the political-strategic level," I replied.

Upon my response, General Buyukanit said, "Well done! I got exactly the answer I wanted to hear." He confirmed me, and the tense waiting in the hall gave way to relaxation. While the commanders were leaving the theater, Naval Forces Commander Admiral Metin Atac congratulated me and expressed his satisfaction.

I would later learn that before the distinguished guests came to our wargame headquarters, they had discussed the need for national guided missiles, and I gave an answer confirming their conclusion.

Our success and effort, which was personally appreciated by the Chief of the General Staff and the Commander of the Naval Forces, was ignored by the Superintendent of Naval Staff College. It was a situation I frequently encountered in my professional career, and I was not surprised. Crumbs of success of a particularly privileged group were brought to the fore; the efforts and achievements of those other than them were consciously ignored.

During the war game, we also learned our following appointments after graduating from the Staff College. I decided to return to the ships and was assigned to the TCG Giresun frigate as Combat Operations Officer. TCG Giresun was stationed in Marmaris, so I would return to Marmaris, where I said goodbye to TCG Kocatepe years ago. The wargame protocol and my appointment had been concluded as I had hoped.

The second year of the Staff College went better than we expected as we got used to the slow pace and dynamics of the academic and social environment. As a result, I finished the Naval Staff College in second place and graduated with honors.

The first female officer to attend the Naval Staff College, Lieutenant Yasemin, graduated on top of the class and made another mark in history. Lieutenant Meftun finished third. The graduation ceremony had brought significant names together in the same frame. As the officers who ranked highest from all three Land, Naval, and Air Staff Colleges, we received our diplomas from the hands of the statesmen.

President Abdullah Gul presented Lieutenant Yasemin's diploma, and Speaker of the Assembly Koksal Toptan presented my diploma. Meftun's was given by Prime Minister Recep Tayyip Erdogan. This ceremony meant acknowledging and appreciating our achievements at the highest level of the state.

However, after July 15, all three of us would suffer the same fate and be dismissed from the Navy. We would pay the price of success by being declared a traitor by the genocide lists published in the middle of the night and saying goodbye to our uniforms for which we had sacrificed our years.

Who was the loser?

Was it us, soldiers of this country for which we are ready to give our lives, or the Turkish people, who had paid with their taxes for all our education and training for many years?

Since raising a well-educated and qualified generation is the most complex and costly job in the world; however, in Turkey, well-qualified and trained hundreds of thousands of people from all professions were purged from service. Merit was replaced by nepotism, and eventually, the country and nation would undoubtedly be the ones to lose in the end. In the following years, the catastrophic collapse in all fields, especially in the economy and law, would fully justify this thought.

NEVER-ENDING DEPLOYMENTS

Aksaz, Turkey, 2008

Two weeks after the Naval Staff College graduation ceremony, I reported to frigate TCG Giresun as my new assignment in Aksaz., Marmaris. TCG Giresun was built in the US in 1981 as a Perry-class frigate and was transferred to the Turkish Naval Forces in 1998. The ship was about 140 meters long and had a crew of over 200.

I received two years of early promotion after the Staff College education; I was promoted to staff Lt. Commander in the month I joined the ship. I was the fourth senior officer on board, after the commander, executive officer, and chief engineer. As a Combat Operations Officer, I was responsible for the ship's operations, communications, weapons, and training activities.

The Commander of the Ship was Captain Cenk Dalkanat, and Commander Murat Sirzai was the second in command as the Executive Officer. Captain Cenk was an extremely authoritarian officer, and his relationship with the personnel was task oriented. His attitude towards young officers was extremely harsh.

The commander had problems with the previous Combat Operations Officer Lt. Commander Ramazan Ozoglu. While handing over the task, Lt. Commander Ramazan needed to say, "May God make it easy for you. I hope you realize how difficult he is to work with."

I had already worked with officers like Captain Cenk with a management style many would explain as "impossible to work with." Ferda Narinc, Sinan Ertugrul, Sadi Unsal, and Hasan Hosgit were the first to come to mind. I established a successful work-oriented relationship with all of them except Admiral Hasan. The biggest experience I had while working with these people was that if you focus on your job, it is possible to remove the harshness or disagreement of the supervisor from getting in the way.

I previously worked on Knox-class frigates; I was now assigned to one of the critical billets on a relatively modern Perry-class frigate. While there were many similarities as both classes were US-made, my new ship was more recent and had advanced weapons and gas turbines as a propulsion system. For this reason, I would prioritize learning the technical features and maneuvering of the ship and start working to create a team spirit in my department, which had 70 people.

In my first meetings with the captain, I asked him about his priorities and if he wanted me to focus on anything immediately. My professional and academic achievements supported my self-confidence and strengthened me when I started my job. I developed my relationship with the captain not with the fear and shyness of "what will the commander say" but within the framework of the search for "what and how we can do to work best with the commander."

Serving on a warship had its challenges. It was staffed 24 hours a day, seven days a week. It almost resembled a small town with its bakery, barber, tailor, cook, infirmary, police force, mess halls, dormitories, laundry, and cafeteria.

The first week was busy. I spent time getting to know the personnel, observing the operation, and reading the relevant documents. Since our furniture had yet to arrive, we stayed in the navy lodging in Aksaz. We would go to Marmaris with Hatice and the kids in the evenings. Aksaz Naval Base was about 20 minutes away from Marmaris downtown. It was a fascinating place where hundreds of thousands of tourists flocked yearly with its long beaches, rows of restaurants, marina, and unique sea. It was like a paradise where people would want to spend their whole life. For us sailors, lengthy deployments and strict life based on the rules required by the military environment grayed out this colorful picture.

In all this turmoil, Hatice and I were trying to catch the beauties of life with the approach of "every moment is valuable, and every moment spent in happiness is the happiness we may never find again." On the weekend we were at the port, we discovered a new village breakfast place and found ways to step out of the grayness of the lodging at every opportunity.

Since TCG Giresun had just left the shipyard period, intense operational readiness preparations and activities were ahead of us. We had to move to the house as soon as possible and arrange the children's school and Hatice's job. We got an apartment on the third floor at the first military housing meeting without being too picky. Since I couldn't get any leave time, my classmate Murat helped to ship our furniture from Istanbul, and we hurriedly moved into our house over the weekend. Hatice made a list of schools in Marmaris and quickly started job applications.

We would go on our first deployment in two weeks, and after a long break, my wife would be alone again with Hakan and Fatih.

Did I make a mistake by asking for a ship assignment?

We already had a difficult life, and extended deployment periods at sea would make this situation even more difficult.

The same anxiety gripped Hatice, and we started to look for formulas to make it easier. The easiest solution was family support. My mother and mother-in-law had children who went to school and had regular schedules. Brothers who could support us were studying at the university. The ship's tempo was increasing daily as I struggled to find ways to help my family.

In addition to my responsibilities, I made the operational plans ordered by our commodore, Captain Safak Yurekli. Since most of the ships of the Turkish Fleet were stationed in Golcuk, the number of staff officers was four or five times more than in Aksaz. Despite this, the Northern Task Group Command in Golcuk and the Southern Task Group Command in Aksaz had almost the same operational tempo and workload. The staff officers drafted the operational and training planning, so I became the sought-after person in all the planning activities of the Southern Task Group. This brought an exhausting work schedule, and I regularly worked late, even on weekends.

The ships already had long-term deployments, and it was necessary to reduce the activities during the port periods to allow the personnel to spend time with their families. However, this was never the case for the officers, especially the staff officers. Commodore duties were among the best billets to be promoted to admiral. Hence, commodores often needed to consider the intensity and difficulty of the job and the staff's struggles. They continued to take on additional duties, devoting intense staff activities such as planning and preparing orders to their subordinates.

The year I took office, Captain Cem Cakmak, the previous commodore, was promoted to one-star admiral and became the Southern Task Group Commander. Our commodore Captain Safak also intended to follow the same career path. However, promotion from captain to admiral was not only based on career success but also on political connections. The Supreme Military Council, known as YAS, convenes annually, and five or six officers are generally promoted to rear admiral among hundreds of qualified captains. However, since the process behind the YAS decisions was kept secret, it needed to be known who was promoted according to what criteria and what was discussed at the council. This secrecy was a unique opportunity for those shaping the Armed Forces leadership. They could easily use the opportunity to promote any officer they wanted, to retire due to age limit or non-cadre, as they saw appropriate. It was widespread for a front-ranking officer to retire while those in the fortieth and fiftieth rank were promoted.

That year, a few days before the Supreme Military Council, a momentous event involving TCG Giresun occurred before I had joined the ship. TCG Giresun and TCG Gemlik collided due to a wrong maneuver while performing backup training under the command of Cem Cakmak, the commodore at the time. As a result of this accident, TCG

Giresun's bow was severely damaged. It was a massive shipwreck, and the repair process had to be immediately started by reporting it to the higher authorities. The commander of TCG Giresun was Captain Cenk Dalkanat, and the commander of TCG Gemlik was Captain Berker Emre Tok.

For an unknown reason, the incident message and casualty report system was not sent, and the relevant authorities in chain-of-command were not involved in the process. The two ships were quickly towed to Aksaz Port, and all the facilities of Golcuk Shipyard and Aksaz Repair Support Command were mobilized. The ships were repaired before the council meeting. The footage and records of the accident were hidden in the commander's safe, the password of which only Captain Cenk knew. An incident that required an administrative and judicial investigation was meticulously covered up. At the same time, Cem Cakmak was promoted to the rank of one-star admiral, and the ship's commanders continued their duties.

Since we did not know the power, will, and motivations of the decision-makers behind the events, there needed to be more information to question and make sense of what happened. Looking back, I now realize certain people were protected in the Navy by an invisible and robust mechanism. The path of the privileged was cleared, and any obstacles that might cause them to stumble were removed at the expense of lawlessness. The system was not based on merit. And "orphan" officers of the system, like me, would be used in complex tasks up to the rank of captain but would most likely never be promoted to admiral. It felt like the system used us as steppingstones for its privileged children, so they could rise on our shoulders by using our intellect and hard work.

Several months had passed since I was first assigned as Principal Warfare Officer, and I had already proven myself onboard the ship at the Commodore headquarters and the Southern Task Group.

During this time, we arranged Fatih's special education program and enrolled him in the school in the military lodging. Hatice started a job in a kindergarten in Marmaris, and we were finally able to have somewhat of a stable life.

After a while, during a parent-teacher meeting with Fatih's teacher, he said, "Some parents do not want Fatih to be in the same class with their children and that his disability affects the psychology of other children negatively." What a pity that my colleagues, with whom I worked, and their spouses, with whom we became neighbors and destined friendships, disregarded Fatih's right to education without having the courage to talk to us!

We were experiencing the hardships of raising a disabled child in Turkey. This experience showed how brutal and cruel the following years would be.

There were long deployments and a busy work schedule ahead of me. My role covered critical functions on the ship, and my daily workload increased.

While we were considering handling being away from home for a couple of weeks for exercises and training, TCG Giresun was assigned to participate in international efforts to combat piracy in the Indian Ocean. It was a task that would take four and a half months.

When I heard the news, I felt the honor and joy of being one of the first sailors to go on such a critical mission and the sadness of going on a long deployment, leaving Hatice and the children alone. "Navy life is truly a single man's profession!" I thought to myself. While we were thinking about how to escape this difficult situation, my mother-in-law came to our rescue, and Hatice's siblings, Muhammed and Habibe, decided to change their whole routine and move to our house for six months, even though they were in school. It was a great sacrifice.

Working in Marmaris and living there as a family must have seemed attractive to many. However, the Navy was one of the most challenging professions in the world, requiring your family to make sacrifices with you wherever you were. The sacrifices of my friends in the Army or the Air Force were no less; they had to leave their spouses and children for periods ranging from six months to two years and went on domestic and foreign assignments to fight terrorism. Their tasks were riskier than ours. It must have been tough for those who left and stayed behind to work in geography, where news of martyrs came every week and sometimes every day! Despite all the longing, danger, and hardship, the emotions, love of the homeland and the military, and our core values kept people like us in these positions.

The Counter Piracy Operations would be a first in the Turkish Naval Forces, and we would be navigating in unfamiliar waters. Hence, this historical mission's navigation and operational planning were quite intense. On the one hand, we were trying to prepare the ship logistically and technically; on the other hand, we were hosting inspections and visits by senior commanders such as the Commander of Turkish Naval Forces, the Fleet Commander, and the Chief of General Staff.

While preparing for our mission, we examined in detail the port characteristics in the operation area, the pirates' tactics, the Coalition Force's command structure in the region, and many issues related to the operation. Since these activities required an advanced level of English, a significant part of the preparations was on my shoulders.

I was relieved when my mother-in-law arrived. After living abroad for many years, Hatice was happy to be with her mother and siblings, forgetting my absence.

After months of preparation, the day of the deployment came. After the farewell ceremony broadcast on national TV in Aksaz Port, we hugged our spouses and children, said, "You are entrusted in God," and threw the ropes off. We took a last look at Aksaz Port and began our route to the Suez Canal.

The Suez Canal crossing was a grueling course that took about a day. Although the Egyptian pilots, experts in navigating the canal, were on board, there was a lot of anxiety and tension in this first canal crossing. We were caught in a severe sandstorm in Crocodile Lake, the middle of the canal transit.

During the storm, which lasted for hours, we had to anchor and wait for the storm to pass, but the ship dragged anchor several times, and the entire crew constantly waited at the maneuvering points. The storm we experienced at the beginning of a four-month-long deployment tired us all, and the ship's deck was filled with sand. Fortunately, the weapons and systems were not severely damaged, and after a three-day underway period, we could pass through the Bab al-Mandab Strait and enter the Port of Djibouti.

Although Djibouti was a small and poor country, it was a strategic port state connecting the Indian Ocean and the Red Sea. While the country could be prosperous with the revenues obtained from the maritime sector and military bases, bribery and corruption in this country prevented the equal distribution of resources to the people, as in many other countries. The streets were covered with dust, just like in the documentaries, and people were emaciated from drought and malnutrition.

Despite the misery, the natural and sincere smiles in the eyes of the children on the street surprised me. A weed called 'kat,' which has a narcotic effect, was sold on every street corner, and no one questioned the misery they were in due to the widespread use of the herb.

Djibouti was home to the military bases of the United States and France. High-level visitors to the city benefited from the social facilities at the headquarters. Kempinski Hotel offered a luxury service to foreigners and the local elite of the country. This state of Djibouti was quite exemplary. It was like how in Turkey, the foreign tourists visiting could have beautiful holidays in five-star hotels, but the people struggled to stay alive. The unjust order and the personal interests of those who ruled the state enslaved the people to their homeland.

After departing Djibouti, we stayed at sea for about ten days and collaborated with ships from many Navies in the operation area. We participated in joint exercises and operations with the vessels of NATO member countries. In this mission, we were in the same operational environment with the ships of Australia, Japan, South Korea, India, China, and the regional countries. It was an invaluable experience. I wanted to contribute to strengthening relations with these countries and having the opportunity to observe their peculiarities.

We provided advisory and protection to the Turkish merchant ships in the area and the Gulf of Aden, where piracy activity was intense. Witnessing the joy of the crew on Turkish merchant ships who saw the warship of their country thousands of miles away relieved our tiredness and longing, and an indescribable pride replaced these feelings. Our duty was difficult, the conditions were harsh, and the hope for home was hard. Still, it was such an honorable duty to protect the interests of our country and, at the same time, contribute to international peace and stability. The love of duty and the responsibility of representing our country made it easier for us to overcome these difficulties.

As the first month passed, Admiral Metin Atac, the Commander of Turkish Naval Forces, visited the ship with a crowded press corp. It was critical to transfer such a large protocol group on the boat off the coast of Djibouti and ensure their safety. The coordination of this task fell on me.

After meeting with the US officials at the Djibouti base, we planned helicopter transfers and ensured the guests were transferred to the ship without disruption. We had a long working history with Admiral Metin Atac, and I briefed him with a comprehensive presentation on press and public relations.

When he came to the ship, we had the opportunity to meet with him briefly. He asked about Fatih's condition. He forwarded the letter he brought from my wife and children to me as he did with other personnel. This high-level visit to the ship by a four-star admiral, his way of caring for the personnel and bringing greetings and letters from their families motivated the whole crew.

After the visit, press members reported about life onboard the ship and the operations. TCG Giresun was featured frequently in the news, and the public regarded us as heroes. One reporter focused on my successes in the planning and execution of this mission. He put "The Fearful Nightmare of the Pirates, Commander Mehmet" as the title of his article and elaborated on the sacrifices of our heroic shipmates onboard throughout the story.

Yes, there was heroism displayed on the deployment. The heroism was displayed by shipmates who showed their sacrifice, even with the risk of death. A hero is not born; one is made a hero. **A hero is always a hero** with honor, dignity, courage, and a stance against injustice. Slander's lies and being unjustly demoted from his profession do not diminish one's heroism; on the contrary, it crowns one's heroism with an upright stance against injustice and oppression. Even though the heroes of yesterday are in exile and prison, they will, **one day**, certainly take their place on the stage of history as the heroes of today and tomorrow. In the reporting, the reporter defined heroism through the story, but each day, it is up to me to explain the real heroes through my own story.

During the visit of Admiral Metin Atac, he said that they were planning a port visit to Kenya and Tanzania, and the necessary permits had been obtained. A sweet rush and curiosity arose on the ship. It was our first time crossing the equator into the southern hemisphere. The visit schedule required me to work hard as the officer in charge of the ship's general operations. We planned the operations and intelligence studies in detail with the navigation officer on many issues, such as port characteristics, current situation, and tide calculation.

The longing inside us for a home increased daily, and the burden on our spouses' shoulders was heavier. I talked with Hatice by satellite phone. When I was at sea, I used to write letters and send them via e-mail as soon as I got to the port and got an internet connection.

Since there was more than 250 crew on board, everyone was limited to a 3-minute phone time, and most of the time, the words were stuck in our mouths. Fatih and Hakan were growing up without me, and maybe they were angry with me because they were too young to understand where their father was going. Hatice questioned the extended mission thoroughly and said, "You are a good officer but not a good father," as she slammed this fact on my face with all her coldness. On the one hand, I was proud of the importance and sanctity of my duty, and on the other hand, I felt guilty for the longing I inflicted on my wife and children. Every time I tried to suppress this feeling by saying, "military profession is a profession of sacrifice."

A sailor should know how to bury the storms inside him into his heart. My staff should always see me as strong. I was suppressing the batteries inside me at night when no one would see them, accompanied by a cup of tea and in the light of the stars that stretched as far as the eye could see. I listened to the staff's troubles, comforted them – even though I was in the same situation – gave advice, and reminded them that they should be proud of what they are doing.

We had changed our route to the southern hemisphere for port visits in Kenya and Tanzania. Somalia was a relatively large country, with thousands of miles of coastline from the Gulf of Aden to Kenya. We surveyed the piracy camps and gathered comprehensive intelligence. Before the equator crossing, we planned a reconnaissance helicopter operation. I was included in the flight crew in this operation, and I was among the first Turkish Navy personnel to cross the equator with a helicopter.

At the end of the proud and exciting transit, we arrived at Mombasa Port. Mombasa was Kenya's largest port city. Of course, we could take advantage of the opportunity to visit Kenya on a safari. I arranged it with a local tourism agency and took around 100 crew members on a safari. Although the ship's commander, Captain Cenk, did not like this activity, he probably permitted it because he wanted to avoid conflict with me who planned every stage of the operation to the minor details. We had a wonderful day on the safari, which we had only seen in movies until that day.

When I returned to the port, I first talked to Hatice online. I excitedly told her about our experiences and said, "I want to come here with you one day." I had always felt this emptiness when I did something fun or exciting without my family.

I compensated for this by taking my wife and children on the subsequent scheduled port visits. After that day, I had my family come to the ports we visited during this deployment, and this would become a routine for us in the future. Hatice joined me in our port visits to Maldives, Oman, Germany, Belgium, the Netherlands, and Cyprus.

After our two-day visit to Mombasa Port, we visited Tanzania. Our ambassador welcomed us and hosted us in his private residence. Although it is not very well known, we saw that the real safari destination was Tanzania. About ninety percent of the famous Serengeti Valley was in Tanzania. We made official visits to these lands some had yet to hear of. We gave training on combating piracy to the countries of the region. We were greeted with great love and excitement at every port; once again, we said, "I'm glad I took part in this operation."

Toward the end of the deployment, an unprecedented sequence of events unfolded in Turkey. Almost every day, we would hear news about the arrests of many officers, admirals, and generals within the scope of the Ergenekon trials. Alleged members had been indicted on charges of plotting a military coup, among other things, by assassinating critical leaders to topple the government. The high-rank military personnel was accused of forming a secret organization within the Armed Forces. Although we tried to understand the developments as much as we could observe, we needed help interpreting these events.

For the first time in Turkey, mighty admirals and generals were questioned. While the cases were loudly supported by the prominent figures of the AKP regime and liberal intellectuals, the prosecutors who carried out investigations and prosecutions were hailed as heroes. Recep Tayyip Erdogan, the prime minister at the time, self-declared himself as the prosecutor of these trials to show how much importance and support he gave to these allegations. It was reflected in the press that he allocated official armored vehicles to the prosecutors of this trial. The allegations were grave yet so frightening.

It was claimed that some senior officers, bureaucrats, and civilians in many state units aimed to destroy the constitutional order and democratic functioning. It was told that many unsolved murders, which stand as a stain on Turkey's recent history, were committed by this organization and that the organization brought its members to high-level and critical positions in many state institutions.

These striking developments, also closely related to the Turkish Naval Forces, caused uneasiness among the ship's crew, and everyone followed the news with great curiosity.

Captain Cenk was in a different mood. One day, he summoned the Executive Officer Commander Murat Sirzai and me to his cabin and made an uneasy assessment of the case. It was as if he was confessing his sins. He would later be arrested as part of the Sledgehammer case.

We returned to Turkey in June 2009 amid the waves of the storm. We had completed our four-and-a-half-month deployment and returned to Aksaz Port without an incident. In the port, I hugged my wife, Hakan, and Fatih for minutes and tried to relieve the pain of the days of longing.

After the deployment, we visited our hometown and saw many relatives, spouses, and friends. The conversations about the deployment and the things they wonder about piracy would soon revert to the Sledgehammer-Ergenekon cases. Questions like "Are you okay? You didn't get involved in these groups, did you?" were asked with an uneasy tone.

Using the Seledgehammer-Ergenekon cases, the AKP regime made the Armed Forces questionable in the eyes of the public. Some people we know to be AKP members would state, "You see how we brought the military to its knees?" They were intoxicated with victory and kept talking about the Ergenekon-Sledgehammer cases. It also revealed a terrible truth. Erdogan consciously managed this process, and he could negotiate with the 'deep state,' which was a problem for him. As many people who played an active role in the process admit, behind closed doors, Erdogan and the deep Eurasian cliques agreed to a bargain in which these cases were put forward as leverage.

Dogu Perincek, the leader of the ultranationalist Vatan Party, whose relationship with the deep state is well known to the public, would state in an interview that they had given the regime the list of officers supposedly linked to the Gulen group. Those whose names were mentioned on the list were ordinary citizens who did not belong to any clan of the deep state or any privileged and elitist class. Not being one of them was enough to be labeled.

The role that fell to the Eurasian deep state was to play victimized patriotic soldiers. On the other hand, Erdogan would leave the negotiating table, having had the opportunity to destroy people who would never obey him and establish absolute authority over the Armed Forces. As a matter of fact, at the end of the cases, Erdogan said, "I was deceived." He would make a 180-degree turn by saying that those imprisoned in the Ergenekon and Sledgehammer cases would be released, brought to critical positions, and rewarded with heavy compensation.

Another effect of the Ergenekon-Sledgehammer cases was the increase in workload due to vacancies in various positions throughout the Navy. In addition to my ship duties, I acted as the Southern Task Group Operations Branch Manager and Chief of Staff. It was like that with almost everyone. Many officers involved in these trials did not come to work, and the staff officers did a critical or heavy job on duty. Our aim was not to weaken the Armed Forces and not to allow the slightest vulnerability, no matter what. All planned operations were carried out successfully during the periods when it was said that "Experienced commanders and personnel were purged, the Armed Forces lost their effectiveness."

However, the Naval Forces continued its operation to combat piracy, and for the first time, with five warships. It completed the operation covering the African continent, from Gibraltar to the Atlantic Ocean, from the Cape of Good Hope to the Red Sea. Circumnavigating the African continent, the Turkish Task Group visited 24 African countries, 19 of which were for the first time. Turkey was represented at the highest level, and this deployment was a bookcase example of utilizing the Navy as a peaceful foreign policy tool. This selfless and well-equipped personnel, who shouldered the heavy burden of duty during these rough times, would later be declared 'terrorists' and purged from the Navy after July 15.

I participated in three deployments in the Indian Ocean, two as a Combat Operations Officer and the other as the Executive Officer. We would later find out that those who introduced themselves as heroes and were promoted by the regime had done everything possible to avoid complex tasks and spent their time planning the July 15 betrayal scenario instead of the Armed Forces' success.

One of the things that upset me was that, at that time, we were highly tolerant and naive toward these people. We would eat, drink and joke with these people and help them when needed, but in the meantime, they were plotting these treacherous plans behind our backs. We never stopped showing them respect due to our military decency, even when they were being tried and there seemed to be compelling evidence against them. We provided every support until the judicial process was completed.

A high-ranking officer, dismissed after July 15, explained the support he gave to the wife and daughter of an admiral detained in the Ergenekon case. He stated that they rushed to help the family with their smallest requests and needs and were with them every day not to make them feel lonely. They gave them both financial and moral support. After July 15, he said they were surprised that the people they supported were the first to declare them terrorists.

Afterward, I read countless similar stories on social media. It turns out that the traitors seemed friendly until they achieved their goals, and when they got the chance, they betrayed their brother-in-arms, one of the most sacred bonds in the world, without even blinking.

In the midst of these Ergenekon and Sledgehammer trials, I was assigned as the Executive Officer onboard TCG Giresun ship in 2011. The Commander of the Ship was Captain Ramazan Ozogul. During this period, we worked together; he was also under judicial investigation within the scope of an espionage case. Again, I displayed a fair amount of respect during my duty. Since he was primarily busy preparing his defense for the case, I was technically acting both as the Executive Officer and as the ship's Commander. He would explain that he was mentally ill and did not understand why he was still being held in command of the ship, so much so that he did not leave his cabin when the inspection team came to the ship before the operational inspection. "I don't care if the ship passes the inspection. I don't want to go out for any deployment," he said. It is a tradition in the Navy for the ship commander to "conn" the ship by giving the first orders to get underway, and then he transfers the "conn" to a junior officer. "Commander," I said, "Come to the bridge, and after you give me the command, you can go down to your cabin again," convinced the Captain.

The Turkish Navy had only 16 frigates at the time, and being the commander of a frigate was seen as one of the best honors in the Navy. However, the attitude of Captain Ramazan was such a shame; his ship was trying to pass inspection despite the attitude of its commander. Although it was a dire situation, we managed to pass the inspection at the end of the day.

Unfortunately, Captain Ramazan would be promoted to admiral after July 15. This promotion, only by itself, was an excellent example of the dire situation of the promotion system in the Turkish Armed Forces and Naval Forces after July 15th. Merit was trampled on, and the billets, once occupied by the Turkish homeland's well-equipped, hardworking, and selfless sons, were now taken by inadequate, selfish, and short-sighted people who aligned themselves with the Erdogan regime.

The following years were difficult in every sense. Before my second

Indian Ocean deployment, my mother-in-law passed away from cancer. She was the biggest supporter of our family, and she was with us in our difficult times. From the first day, she treated me like her son, and there was never any problem. Losing my mother-in-law after long deployments and endless tasks were hard for all of us. And Hatice blamed me and my profession because she had only been able to visit her mother a few times during her fight against cancer.

In this period, when everything became inextricable, I found the solution by moving o Adana, my wife's home city. This way, my wife could support her father and siblings. She would be with others while I was on deployment. I was embarking on my second piracy mission under harsh conditions. I had mixed, heavy emotions but had to keep my sense of duty and carry out my task with the usual seriousness.

The second Suez Canal crossing was easier than the first. We reached Djibouti Port with the self-confidence and experience gained from the previous mission. This deployment, unlike the first, would last six months. When we got to the port, I received the news that Fatih had a seizure and was in danger. The Commander of the Frigate, Captain Murat Sirzai, gave this news to me personally. He was one of the bravest and most honest people I know. I told him I wanted to coordinate with the Naval Forces and return to Turkey. Captain Murat approved my request without hesitation. After completing the flight procedures, I made the most challenging journey from Djibouti, Ethiopia, to Istanbul.

"What if we lose Fatih!" I feared. "I can never forgive myself if something like this happens," I thought throughout the journey.

I always left them alone because of my strict sense of duty, love of the Navy, and job. I had never left them needy, and I had never left them hungry, but I wasn't with them right now. I couldn't sleep during the flight. My soul was bent in anxiety as my knees bent uneasily in the narrow space before me.

Thankfully, Fatih had managed to survive after this heavy seizure. After ten short days, I rejoined the ship as there was no new assignment.

I contacted the human resource department of the Navy and informed them that I wanted to take a break from the ship's duties and that my wife and children needed me. I aimed to get my family to a calm harbor amid harsh storms.

After serving as a combat operations officer onboard a frigate, it was routine to have a shore duty either at headquarters or to receive education at the Command College in Turkey and abroad. On the other hand, I could not understand why I was persistently kept onboard ships, having spent almost all three years on intense operational tempo. My request to be assigned shore duty where I could support my family still needs to be answered. I would consecutively serve as Combat Operations Officer, Executive Officer, and finally, as the Commander onboard TCG Giresun.

However, life threw some attractive opportunities our way during these times of struggle. While on my second counter-piracy mission, the operating area was expanded to the east and south, and the Maldives were included in the port plans.

I had made my decision. I would bring my wife to the Maldives at any cost. It was planned to be a four-day port visit. It was a unique opportunity to renew our tired relationship. When I told Hatice the news, she was happy beyond explanation. In our conversations, her reproaches of me were replaced by "Which outfit should I wear? What dessert should I bring for you?" There was a sweet flurry of preparation for the port visit.

I reaffirmed life's lesson repeatedly: "If conditions are not going the way you want, change them!" I met Hatice in the Maldives and had our second honeymoon.

Maldives was like a paradise on earth. Another officer on the ship had brought his wife. Most of our friends would say, "Why do you spend so much money? Just be patient a little longer!" They would never understand Navy life and its impact on families and relationships. Even so, it was one of the best decisions I've made. Maldives became the place where we smiled at life again.

My mother was taking care of the children. Hatice and I were talking to our children on the phone at the end of each day. We were fulfilling our longing for one another and our children. After this experience, we met with Hatice and the children more frequently during port visits. Maintaining this situation wasn't easy financially, but it was the only way to keep my family afloat, and it was worth it.

At this stage of my career, I was rewarded with certificates of appreciation by commanders from different countries, not only in the fight against piracy but also in many missions I participated in. Vice Admiral George Zambellas from the United Kingdom, who came to visit TCG Giresun, sent a letter stating that they were highly pleased with their visit and that our ship performed its duties at the highest level.

The third anti-piracy mission was of particular significance. Our ship was carrying the headquarters of the NATO Naval Task Force under the command of a Turkish admiral. In addition to foreign personnel, the most successful officers of the Turkish Naval Forces, such as Lt. Commander Meftun Metin and Lt. Commander Mehmet Elyurek, were assigned onboard as part of the mission. Rear Admiral Sinan Azmi Tosun was fulfilling a historical task as the first Turkish admiral of a NATO operational mission.

After Operation Ocean Shield, which was effectively carried out during his command, the piracy activities in the Indian Ocean declined to the lowest level, and the cooperation between regional countries and NATO increased to a high level. I learned a lot from Admiral Sinan during my tenure. We sent the projects we believe will carry the Turkish Naval Forces forward with comprehensive reports to the headquarters. I have to say regretfully that this well-decorated admiral, who would be revered as a hero in any other Navy, was dismissed from the Turkish Navy and put behind bars for participating in the coup attempt, even though he was on leave during the July 15 plot.

Operational and international missions gave me a unique experience.

I planned many multi-national operations and represented the Turkish Navy in numerous international exercises. Because of my experience, I was assigned to the French Naval Task Group Headquarters under NATO Command for one month. The French Rear Admiral appreciated my diligence in my duties and conveyed a letter of appreciation to the Naval Forces led by Captain Ismail Budanur.

Following this experience, I was tasked with planning the "Sea of Friendship" exercises, which would be held for the first time after years of tension with Egypt. I had planned the first activities in Aksaz Marmaris and the second in Alexandria, Egypt. Planning and carrying out such a historical and essential exercise had a different meaning. The two countries, whose maritime continental shelves border each other and have historical ties in the Mediterranean, would conduct mutual comprehensive exercises and training at a high level for the first time. By planning these two joint exercises, I acted as diplomat in addition to my title of naval officer. I served my state in the field of security diplomacy within the scope of the pursuit of our national interests and in foreign policy and the execution of staff activities. I was proud of this accomplishment.

After these successes, I was selected as the "Personnel of the Year" by the Naval Forces Commander. It was not only my success, but my wife's, my children's, and our family's joint success to come out of the assigned tasks with great success while going through heavy and challenging times. We endured every challenge, hugged each other tightly, and did not give up in difficult conditions.

Unfortunately, these accomplishments and even our disabled child would be used against me during my dismissal from the Navy. The regime created a weapon of genocide known as the "fetometer" which laid out criteria for discharge from duty after July 15th. Having a disabled child, being successful in your job, being fluent in a foreign language, serving in a foreign or NATO post, and many other criteria were used to purge thousands of well-qualified personnel from the Navy. Other service branches and government agencies later adopted these tools. How could all moral and human notions be so upside down, so corrupt? Liars, swindlers, plotters, and slackers were declared heroes overnight, and those who did their duty by devoting their hearts to this Nation day and night were declared terrorists.

Tens of thousands of people, who had sacrificed their youth and the best years of their lives for the sake of performing their duties in the best way, were put aside, and the fate of the country was entrusted to the incompetent, selfish, and greedy people who were placed in office. In a society with no merit, there could not be a more natural outcome than everything getting worse, and this was precisely what happened in Turkey day by day. The regime contributed to the economy's collapse, foreign policy, defense, security, education, health, social order, and tranquility. And most of the population listened to these stories like lullabies and were put to sleep with fairy tales.

After 21 years of military education and career, including at the Naval Academy and the Staff College, I was appointed as the commander of TCG Giresun in February 2013. I was the youngest officer ever appointed to command a frigate. Due to my professional and academic achievements, I was promoted early. While most of my classmates were still in the rank of lieutenant and some of them in the rank of Lt. Commander, I became the commander of one of the best frigates of the Turkish Naval Forces at the rank of commander.

Even in the best conditions, commanding a frigate required more than twenty years of training and professional experience. This period they exceeded thirty years for an officer who started his career at Naval High School and did not have an early promotion. Because as the frigate commander, you were primarily responsible for the prestige and deterrence of the entire Armed Forces. The lives of nearly two hundred and fifty crew members depended on your decisions and how you performed. The decisions you made had an effect that could lead your country to war. The prudent decisions the naval commanders took during many crises, both in the Eastern Mediterranean and the Aegean, prevented us from being dragged into the war.

When I reflect on the hundreds of thousands of personnel who were dismissed after July 15, it is possible that the regime tried to destroy the experience, education, and knowledge that the Republic of Turkey had trained laboriously for many decades. If we could calculate the tangible value of the wasted savings, we would encounter a price that could reach or even exceed the current annual GDP of the country. The future of a country is its well-educated generations. This regime was trying to destroy this future explicitly in front of the eyes of the public.

The famous Turkish saying "the fire burns where it falls" was true. Only the firsthand victims of this cruel regime tried to raise their voices, but they were shot down immediately, and those who did not get burned by the fire were all silent. When the economy sank, the regime started to roll over many other sections of the society like a cylinder, the number of those who cried out, "We are burning!" began to increase. However, the fires, which were not intervened, spread all around and raged out of control.

Those who watched the fire of injustice and cruelty that pierced the lungs of the innocent and their families after July 15 would find themselves in a bottomless pit that no one could hear, even if they raised their voices.

On the first day of my command of the ship, I sent a letter to the families of all the personnel, stating that their spouses and children were entrusted to me and that they should be proud of their heroism. I aimed to make TCG Giresun as combat ready warship in any categories including motivation and happiness of the crew. In doing so, I would put crew morale, health, and family order first among my priorities. The first order I gave to my Executive Officer, Lt. Commander Hasim Turker, was not to work overtime in any way while the ship was in Aksaz, our home base.

The staff spent almost nine months of the year on deployments and deserved every penny they earned. While we were in the port, I wanted to extend the time the person could spend with their families.

During the port periods, I gave orders to ensure every sailor could use their annual leave and to provide additional leave to the personnel celebrating special days such as wedding anniversaries and birthdays. I told Lt. Commander Hasim never to wait for me; if I stayed overtime, leave work when appropriate.

It was almost an unwritten rule or custom in the Turkish Navy that the personnel were called to the ship on the weekend before inspections and essential activities. But I always believed this practice was counterproductive and that forcing the personnel to do their job under these conditions would harm their motivation more than reasonable. This would also adversely affect their combat power.

As part of an inspection, the delegation from Yildizlar Surface Training Center came to my ship. My crew were devoted and prepared, and as the ship's commander, I had already earned my appreciation. As an officer who had served on frigates and had undergone numerous inspections, I knew my ship would pass the check. At the time, the Armed Forces had been drawn to such a political and sectarian conflict that the person, who was at the head of the delegation and tried as a defendant in the Ergenekon - Sledgehammer cases, was acting with a motivated hatred. The Southern Task Group Commander was Rear Admiral Faruk Harmancik, and the Commodore of the Fourth Destroyer Flotilla, to which my ship was attached, was Captain Namik Alper. They were both brilliant and hardworking officers who had devoted years to their profession. The delegation was looking for an opportunity to find the mistake of these commanders. They wanted to reflect the Southern Task Group Commander as a failure and shine the star of the Northern Task Group Commander, Iskender Yildirim, who was also under a judicial investigation. The delegation's attitude became apparent after getting underway as part of the inspection. Despite the extraordinary performance and reactions of the personnel, they prepared a report showing the failed at damage control and surface warfare. This meant we failed the combat readiness inspection.

They expected that I would keep the personnel onboard even over the weekend as a punishment and would make them prepare for re-inspection. I told the head of the inspection team that, as the ship's commander, I was responsible for this outcome and that they could re-inspect at any time. "Will the crew stay on board?" He asked. "No, they will not. Besides, this is my decision, not yours!" I replied. The delegation had put its intentions into practice but had to leave without getting what it wanted. They had left the ship without inspecting it but understood that I would not keep personnel on board. They expected me to demotivate my already exhausted crew by acting with panic and anger.

After the delegation left, I ordered the crew to assemble. As their commander, I said, "In my opinion, we passed the inspection successfully, and personnel other than those on shift duty should go to their homes and spend time with their families." I added, "There will be a second inspection, but I don't want any preparations on board during the weekend."

While waiting for me to get angry because we didn't pass the inspection, they were surprised by my words. When I said, "I am proud of every one of you," they loudly shouted from the bottom of their hearts, "Thank you!" Then I reported the situation to the Southern Task Group Commander Admiral Faruk. Admiral Faruk said he "expected such a situation" and stood by my decision, which surprised and pleased me.

The next day, I summoned the Executive Officer. I ordered him to issue a certificate of appreciation to the crew for their success and hard work during the inspection without any exception. The view I watched while the Executive Officer handed out the certificates of appreciation was worth seeing. The crew congratulated each other with pride and joy as if they had been united like never before and had received the most important award of their lives.

When the inspection committee arrived the following week, they were surprised to find a crew with high energy and vigor who carried out every task with great perseverance and determination. Despite high motivation and dedicated efforts, they had no choice but to register that we successfully passed the inspection. They had gone as they had come, and my crew had returned to port triumphantly.

My responsibilities as a ship commander were different from all other experiences I had to date. It carried a heavy burden but came with great personal satisfaction. It was as if I had a load of 4000 tons, and this responsibility continued 24 hours a day, seven days a week. I believed that the way to lighten my burden was to train the personnel well and to trust them. I sought to convert this belief into a fixed motto at every opportunity. During one at-sea period, I asked my Navigation Officer to prepare a schedule, with each officer taking turns in command, regardless of their billet. I saw the ship's course as an opportunity, gave the order to all the officers, especially the Executive Officer, and tried to convey my experience of navigation, operations, and ship maneuvering that I had learned for years.

After the cruise, we assessed the situation and discussed the lessons learned. My ship had been the flagship of the Southern Task Group Command, and our success was crowned with the honor of carrying the flag of the Commender of Fleet, Southern Task Group and Western Task Group.

When we came to the sixth month of my command onboard TCG Giresun, I had trained a team that I could entrust the ship with my eyes closed. The Executive Officer, Chief Engineer Officer, and department heads prepared the ship diligently and deliberately.

I took every opportunity to spend more time with the crew. I had dinner with junior and senior enlisted personnel and the draftees weekly. I offer coffee to my staff in my cabin whenever possible. Another navy custom was to exchange caps, mugs, and t-shirts as gifts and collect them as a collection. Many sailors displayed these gifts in visible parts of their rooms. I preferred to present the assistance I received to the crew members on duty or perform well. The sailor chosen by the shift supervisor would come to my cabin with the officer on duty. The meetings that initially felt uneasy with the effect of military discipline and respect turned into sincerity. Each contributed to many works, such as the ship's maintenance, cleaning, and preparation. As the ship's commander, I was giving the gifts presented to me to those who truly deserved them. On the last day of my assignment, I left the ship with a one-piece collection, the command ballcap I wore that day.

One incident completely changed our lives in the second year of my ship's command. Hatice had started at Girne American University to complete her degree in early childhood education. Since the journey between Adana and Cyprus is 30 minutes by plane, Hatice would go to Cyprus once a week, and my mother or my wife's siblings would take care of the children. My phone rang one cold February evening when I was returning from exercise. My wife was hit by a vehicle in Cyprus and hospitalized. She had a skull fracture and was in serious condition.

I reported the situation to my superiors and left for Dalaman Airport. To be able to leave the garrison as a ship commander, a proxy order had to be issued to another ship commander. The Southern Task Group Commander and the Commodore said they would take care of the proxy assignment, and I should get to my wife as soon as possible to take care of her. Admiral Veysel, the Fleet Commander at the time, stated that he reached out to the authorities in Cyprus, and they would provide the necessary support. The support of my superiors during challenging times was so precious that I would never forget it.

From time to time, I can't help but think, "I wish Admiral Veysel had not taken part in the betrayal of July 15." I had hosted him on my ship many times, and he left extremely satisfied each time. He would point out the value of trained personnel in his speeches. However, fate had made him part of a betrayal that would lead to the slaughter of thousands of trained personnel. The flight to Cyprus reminded me of my return trip from Africa two years ago for Fatih. I couldn't hold back my tears when I reached Cyprus and saw my wife after a journey where minutes seemed like hours. Commanding a giant warship and struggling with many storms, I was caught in tears. Doctors said that the risk of cerebral hemorrhage continued, and they would keep Hatice under observation for a while. The next day, my phone rang constantly. Many of my friends and commanders were calling to convey their best wishes.

The hospital process in Cyprus took two weeks. When Hatice was able to get out of her hospital bed, she had difficulty balancing. She also lost a great deal of her sense of smell. Life continued to bring us all kinds of surprises and tests. Thankfully she was alive; God helped her recover quickly.

After this incident, I was appointed to the Naval Staff College in Istanbul as an instructor with an interim assignment order from the Naval Forces. I handed over the ship's command to the Executive Officer, Lt. Commander Hasim.

Our acquaintance with him started 22 years ago while searching for a book in the Akmar passage in Kadikoy. That day he handed the command of the ship a sacred duty. Hasim was an exemplary officer in every aspect. He is well-trained, both professionally and academically. I did not doubt that he would excel as the ship's commander. He proved this by passing the ship command qualification exam in the first test. It was an honor and a pleasure to hand over command to such a fine naval officer.

On February 08, 2014, my ship departed for Famagusta Port, Cyprus. The handover command ceremony was held in the port I had visited many times. My brother-in-law Ahmet attended the ceremony with my son Hakan. Hatice was still in the hospital, and Fatih stayed with my mother.

I did expect that saying farewell to my ship would have been such a sad moment. I served for years and served with so many valuable personnel. That day, the sea was calm and serene; I felt like it understood me. I commanded the ship off the coast of Famagusta for the last time and said goodbye to my crew, one by one, at the handover ceremony.

I still have a hard time describing the feelings inside me. The naval mission that set me apart from my loved ones also helped me grow as a sailor and diplomat. A part of my heart will always remain in TCG Giresun, even if a significant burden was lifted from my shoulders.

RISING STARS

Istanbul, Turkey, 2014

I completed my ship commander duty without any incidents and reported to my next assignment at the Naval Staff College in Istanbul. Soon after my arrival in March 2014, I learned that my follow-on assignment would be as the Personnel Education and Training Branch Manager at the NATO Transformation Command in Norfolk, VA. That job would begin in July 2015, so I only had 16 months to cherish my time as a lecturer at the Naval Staff College.

At the same time, I learned I was assigned to the four-and-a-half-month-long Turkish Military Command College, a joint staff college in which staff officers from every military branch received strategic-level military and political education. However, the training had already started two weeks earlier. The school dean was unwilling to accept me because I missed the first two weeks of the course. But this was just another challenge ahead of me.

Lt. Commander Selami, a close classmate from the Naval Academy, worked in the Personnel Assignment Branch and was responsible for Command College training assignments. Selami would later tell me that he convinced the Dean by assuring him I would catch up quickly.

On the first day I started my education at the Command College in Istanbul, I reported to the Dean, Captain Cengiz. At the same time, my wife was transferred to Adana, and she still could not stand up on her own. Therefore, my mother, aunt, and father-in-law supported us. I told Captain Cengiz about my wife's situation and stated that I had to go to Adana every weekend and wanted to take leave on Fridays. I

243

arrived two weeks late, yet I requested one-day off-garrison leave every week. Captain Cengiz was not excited about the situation, but he did not refuse my request after learning the details of my wife's health.

My job was to focus on my courses with total concentration. Four days a week, I would go to Adana on Thursday evenings and support my family. Then I'd be back at school in Istanbul on Monday morning. The good news is that I would be with the children for three days, caring for my wife and helping her recover.

Command College was an institution under the Turkish Military Academies. Command and staff officers from the Land, Naval, Air Force, Gendarmerie, and Coast Guard receive strategic-level training there. The class of seventy-six consisted of very bright and successful officers. We all learned a lot from each other during our education at Command College. Although there were differences of opinion from time to time due to military service branch cultures and priorities, we were all striving for a common goal, a solid and ready Turkish Armed Forces.

Future generals, admirals, and high-level government officials would emerge from this group. Of course, we were unaware of the plot against the most distinguished officers of the Turkish Armed Forces on July 15, 2016. The curriculum was the best offered and equivalent to high-level military training in other countries. It was intense, informative, and very challenging at the same time. On average, the officers in training had 20-25 years of professional experience, and all had their master's degrees from prestigious universities worldwide. Some of them had even completed their PhDs. We all had participated in international missions and had been exposed to NATO, the UN, and many other multi-national working environments. As a result, someone or a couple of officers could pass as a Subject Matter Expert in almost every course or subject we dealt with during this training. Collectively sharing our experience and knowledge broadened our views and immensely improved our education.

High-level government officials from the Ministry of Foreign Affairs also lectured about Turkish foreign policy. They would be surprised to see that at least one officer serving in the country was in discussion. The lecturers usually acted as mere moderators, and the exclusivity of the regular group enabled high-level talks and sharing on every subject. Even if it was for a short time, the training allowed me to make friends with distinguished officers of all military branches and to benefit from their experiences.

Although I spent my time on the road on the weekends, it did not disturb my studies. I completed homework and presentation tasks and reviewed the notes of the lessons I missed on Fridays. The lodging was limited at the Military Academies Command, so students had to share a double bedroom. My first roommate was Lt. Commander Savas Bilican, who became one of the regime's "golden boys" after July 15. He also had his master's degree in the United States, and we graduated from the Naval Staff College in the same year. We had a collegial relationship based on mutual respect. When he was questioned about the Ergenekon and Sledgehammer cases, we met several times and exchanged ideas. His English was better than most because he graduated from Naval High School.

Although we graduated from the same schools, received staff officer training simultaneously, and went through similar professional and academic processes, the so-called "fetometer" criteria declared him a hero and me a traitor.

This is what this situation looked like. Two vehicles are traveling at the same speed in traffic. The police salute one of the vehicles and say, "Your car is very fast. Congratulations. Enjoy the road." On the other hand, the second vehicle's driver not only has a fine imposed on him but also has his car, driver's license, and belongings confiscated and is imprisoned after unnecessary treatment. When describing such a contradictory situation, a tragicomic image emerges. Those who did not think about anything other than their interests were dressed as the most valiant patriots in the offices they usurped after July 15, while those who risked or gave their lives in the fight against terrorism, piracy, and criminals in heavy duties were declared traitors. Most of the population, blinded by the regime's intense propaganda, viewed black as white and white as black.

The corruption and lawlessness of the Erdogan regime, and the damage it caused to the country, had already been exposed by the Gezi Protest in May 2023 and the police operations on 17-25 December 2013. The government tried to shut both down hastily, without success.

A group of activists started to protest the government's plan to demolish the Istanbul Gezi Park to build barracks that would have shopping centers. The excessive use of police forces sparked mass demonstration. Millions of people took the streets. These protests turned into big movement demanding democratic rights and freedoms. Regarding 17-25 December operations, dirty groups, including ministers, children of ministers, businesspeople, and bureaucrats, committed the most egregious corruption in the history of Turkey by using state apparatus. Some businesspeople took billion-dollar tenders with bribes to politicians and bureaucrats, and the forming extended to Erdogan and his family. The day the investigation turned into a police operation; Erdogan instructed his son to hide the money they had stolen. A businessman talked about they stole state property, gave tenders, and how Erdogan received commissions from them.

The most important recordings, which revealed corruption, were the speeches of Egemen Bagis, one of the ministers of the regime. In his remarks, he said he shared verses from the Qur'an every Friday on his social media account to deceive the public. This meeting exposed how hypocritical the regime was and how the people's values were abused. On the one hand, rulers acted as the spokespersons of spirit matter lues with nationalist-conservative rhetoric. On the other hand, they led a life full of luxury, corruption, and lies.

Despite the thousands of folders of evidence obtained within the scope of the investigations, the prosecutors who carried out the investigations and the police officers who carried out the red-handed operations were arrested with the alleged coup attempt, and the criminals were released. This was when the thieves were released, and the police were declared guilty. Tens of thousands of police officers and bureaucrats were dismissed from their posts and sent into exile. The self-preservation reflex of the theft and corruption order had descended on the country like a dark cloud.

Even though I tried to stay away from politics as a soldier, the situation in the country worried me a lot. Most of all, I had a hard time understanding the silence of the people and the indifferent support they gave the regime. Corruption, revealed with the evidence, impoverished everyone daily, except for a small group who took part in the theft wheel. A handful of thieves were plundering the future of our children.

In the midst of these storms, a development made us smile at the beginning of May 2014. Hatice could stand up on her own, and her balance problem was almost gone. Although her sense of taste was not restored, she could now meet her basic needs. Encouraged by these developments, I decided to take her on a foreign trip organized within the scope of education. The training program included a cultural trip to a foreign country, and our class would visit Austria.

The officers made official visits and contacts during the trip, while the spouses made social and cultural tours. As part of the visit, we studied the unsuccessful siege of Vienna by the Ottoman Empire on a high place overlooking Vienna. Vienna, by the Danube River, was a wonderful city. It was a fascinating experience to see this beautiful city from the hill we were on. Maybe our ancestors were once watching this city, which they came to besiege, from our current observation point. On the other hand, we were analyzing that historical siege from the same issue with our Austrian colleagues. Much water has flowed under the bridge over the centuries, and time has turned from taking each other's lands to learning from each other on the way to ensuring regional peace and stability.

An essential feature of Austria was that it had the status of a neutral country. As a country that declared neutrality in 1948, it used its resources to increase the welfare of the country by minimizing military expenditures, and they were successful. They were among the top twenty countries in national income and were at the top of the happiness and life indexes.

I asked my Austrian colleague, "How can a warlike society that builds empires adopt and maintain its neutral state status?" My colleague stated that their experiences in the Second World War taught them a lot and that the people refused to pay another heavy price to be strong.

As states increased their defense spending, they had to reduce investments in other areas. Germany and Japan were other examples where we observed successful results of prioritization between security and welfare. After the Second World War, the military expenditures of the two countries were restricted. In the years when many states increased their military spending during the Cold War, these two countries focused on economic development and increasing the welfare of the people. Among these heavily damaged countries, Japan had made significant progress as the third-largest economy in the world and Germany as the fourth-largest economy. These examples showed that it would be much more beneficial for states to form alliances with other nations based on democracy and freedoms, thus providing an effective deterrence rather than trying to create and maintain substantial military forces based on unrealistic threat perceptions. NATO is one of the excellent examples of this alliance.

After the trip abroad, final exams and thesis presentations were complete. I managed to graduate first in the class. In my speech at the graduation ceremony, I expressed my pride in representing a distinguished group. My education was a period where unforgettable friendships were made. After the graduation ceremony, we said goodbye to our brothers-in-arms and dispersed to our following assignments. We moved our home to Istanbul, about one hour from Tuzla, and settled in military housing close to the Military Academies campus. The Military

Academies and the accommodation were in a unique location between Levent and Maslak, on the north side of Istanbul. The campus area was the only green area left in the middle of dozens of skyscrapers in the city. There were various fruit trees, from apples to walnuts, figs to plums. In the middle of Istanbul, we heard birds instead of the city's noise.

This assignment allowed me to spend time with my wife and children after years of sea duty. At every opportunity, together with Fatih and Hakan, we would explore the outdoors and enjoy fruit picking from tree branches. Every time I saw a fruit tree, I felt a childish joy enlightened in me. Hatice couldn't help but laugh, "I don't know if we came for the children or you." There was a huge walnut tree in the middle of our lodgings, on the sidewalk of the stop for the municipal buses.

One of the difficulties of a military environment was that it was impossible to always act as your heart desired, probably due to the weight of our ranks and responsibilities. I was sure many people wanted to go to the walnut tree and pick fresh walnuts. However, because everyone was worried, "What will people say if they see me," the beautiful walnuts remained on the branch. Yet I was determined. I kept saying to Hatice, "The season will pass. If I don't pick a few walnuts from the tree, I will regret it for the rest of my life." I waited for a small sign of her approval to act with childlike excitement. She stopped me each time, reminding me that "If anyone sees you, what will they say about the well-respected captain climbing onto a walnut tree?"

One evening, I took Hakan and went up the tree. We filled our pockets with walnuts that I had been eyeing for months. When we got home, there was nothing that could describe our joy. We entered the house triumphantly as if we had accomplished a remarkable feat.

Over time, we soldiers got used to imprisoning ourselves in specific patterns without realizing it. Yes, I was a soldier and an officer, but above all, I was a man and a father. Our relationships and life have become dull because rules imprison us. As a lecturer, the first lesson I would give to the staff officers, who will form the command echelon of the future, was, "Break unnecessary stereotypes in our lives. Be a good soldier and a good person."

Nearly one hundred staff officer candidates were studying at the Naval Staff College, which offered a postgraduate program and staff training to rigorously selected naval officers. A consultant lecturer was assigned to each class. It was an honorable task but a heavy responsibility at the same time as a lecturer. It required playing an extremely critical role in the education, professional, and academic development of brilliant minds who would form the future leadership of the Turkish Navy.

With this awareness, I volunteered to be the second-year class advisor. I would be closer to my students and could share my experiences with them. My wife would advise their spouses and convey her knowledge and experience in protocol matters, including representation duties. As students at the Staff College, we needed help establishing a close relationship with our advisor faculty members. We could not need the strict official wall that would prevent the transfer of experiences that are impossible with formal education.

While undertaking this task, I aimed to establish a sincere friendship based on trust and respect, where every officer I consulted could approach me whenever they wanted. We began developing relationships by hosting the senior officer of the class, Lieutenant Atıf, and his wife, Zuhal, at our house for Sunday breakfast. I aimed to show them that putting distance between us would make communication difficult—the respect required by military courtesy impedes our academic endeavors. Our breakfast with Lieutenant Atıf and his wife would become a friendship lasting many years.

The officers in the class were very well trained. We witnessed them having professional dexterity and admirable talents in class and social activities on weekends. Most of the officers in this class excelled in more than one field of art, music, and sports, as well as military and academic achievements. Some painted professionally; some played the Turkish instrument saz, guitar, or violin and composed their compositions;

and some made beautiful ship models. One of the officers had a stamp collection. The spouses of these officers were also well-educated and social people, well-equipped to match the officers. Each one of them shone like a rising star with their spouse.

Unfortunately, many officers involved in Ergenekon and Sledgehammer cases would spread baseless rumors at every opportunity and say, "The old education quality is no longer present in the Staff College. Recent staff officers are very inadequate." These statements were not only far from the truth but also purposeful and had malicious intent. Some of these officers were also lecturers at the Staff College, which was a remarkable and worthy contradiction. These people were both occupying those positions and trying to slander these brilliant officers instead of correcting the so-called or claimed deficiencies they identified.

Their motivation was clear. They were trying to create a perception that would reverse the difference in quality by slandering the young officers who had successfully earned the right to be Staff Officers and shape the future of the Turkish Navy. In the old system, the privileged small group was used to get into the Staff Colleges without any competition or even without making any effort. They were frustrated that these well-qualified young officers were filling the ranks, and this privileged group had no free ride.

These very same people would call the students to duty from their homes to the Academy buildings on the night of July 15, and they would then torture the students at the Army and Air Force Staff Colleges until the morning.

Those who treated the most distinguished Armed Forces officers this way were in a desperate betrayal. These people fit Gazi Mustafa Kemal Ataturk's definition of "heedless, heresy and even treacherous," and history would one day hold them accountable for this betrayal.

Names such as Ramazan Ozogul, Burak Akcay, Erdinc Altiner, Aydin Sezenler, and Aykut Manioglu were lecturers at the Naval Staff

College and would be promoted to the rank of admiral by the regime in return for their betrayal.

We were trying to raise our students in the best possible way, unaware of the great trap set on the honorable sons of the country who would not sacrifice the honor of their uniform to their blind ideologies, their interests, or bargain for blackmail materials. We believed that showcasing the talents of these officers and their spouses to the senior officers at the Staff Colleges and the Commander of the Military Academies would best serve their interests. In this context, Hatice and I, together with Lt. Commander Orhan Caylak, who was the advisor of the first-year class, and his spouse, Lt. Commander Hacer, organized an exhibition that our students and their spouses prepared with a great deal of effort and perhaps left their mark on the history of the Staff College.

The Commander of the Military Academies, Abdullah Recep, a four-star general, originally planned to join this exhibit only for the opening. He was so impressed by what he saw that he stayed there for more than three hours, chatting with the student officers and their wives one by one. In addition to giving a mini concert with the music group they formed among themselves, the students exhibited their works consisting of nearly a thousand photographs, paintings, models, and collections. This event was one of the best answers to the group of Ergenekon and Sledgehammer officers who tried to slander and smear these well-accomplished staff officer candidates at every opportunity. Contrary to the perception they attempted to create with gossip, more talented, successful, well-equipped, and modern staff officers were being trained at the Staff Colleges.

The Staff Colleges had always been the alma mater of many visionaries, pioneers, and leaders in the modern Turkish Republic, including the founder of the Republic, Mustafa Kemal Ataturk. Hence, the Erdogan regime saw the closure of these historical institutions as a pre-requisite to the brutal destruction project he undertook to reshape the Turkish Armed Forces after July 15.

The regime had also labeled almost all the recent graduates of the Staff Colleges as terrorists and purged them from the military at once by baseless and illegal decree laws. This paved the way for many under-qualified people, who were deemed to be loyal to the regime, to become admirals or generals in the following years. Those who were promoted to the ranks of admiral and general in the next years knew very well that they couldn't compete against the qualified, well-trained, capable, and equipped staff officers, so they jumped onboard with the regime to slander and stab their comrades in their backs.

After the exhibition, the Superintendent of the Naval Staff College, Rear Admiral Tayyar, organized several events, and dozens of people, including senior admirals and their spouses, attended these events. The admiral's wife complimented the spouses of these officers with nice words despite what was witnessed. These gentlemen and ladies, who participated in the circumstances, who could not hide their admiration and congratulated the future leaders and their spouses with kind words, would prefer to watch in silence, some with satisfaction. At the same time, these same officers were lynched with their families after July 15. It was such a sad picture.

Reflecting on these events, I never imagined that I would have such a hard time writing about these memories. My thoughts took me back to about a year before July 15. My feelings were no different from the pain and anger of a farmer who lost his crops in a massive fire. Moreover, this fire burned thousands of young saplings watered with sweat, grown with bruised elbows, and calloused hands-on sleepless nights, which stood like beautiful flowers during their most productive age. But the fire, caused by the persecution of staff officers and the closing of military schools with a more extended Turkish Republic history, is still hot and painful for me. Of course, this pain and fire will end one day, and the year I spent with my students at the Naval Staff College will remain one of the most precious periods of my life.

My one-year term as a lecturer at the Naval Staff College was full of memories worthy of a book by itself. But I moved on, and I started doctorate program in Political Science and International Relations while in Istanbul. I took doctoral classes in the evenings, spent the weekends with my children, and took morning walks with my students whenever possible. On weekends, I would wake up at five o'clock and walk about 3 miles from Bebek Beach to Kalender Military House with those who wanted to join me without any obligations. Afterward, we rewarded ourselves with a hot bagel and a freshly brewed cup of tea while watching the beautiful Istanbul Strait.

Every day was full of adventure in the second Istanbul chapter of our family life. So much so that I am amazed at how we could handle such heavy and varied burdens. In addition to all life brought to us, life did not keep us away from bittersweet surprises. Fatih's seizures had reached uncontrollable levels, and we had to stay in the hospital several times. At a point where our souls almost drowned in despair, a doctor would come to our rescue. One of our friends recommended a doctor, so we went to his office. We had not hoped to meet someone different from the nearly twenty doctors we had visited over the year, nor did we expect to get a different result. Fatih had been suffering before our eyes for years, and this situation hurt us as parents.

After examining Fatih and his medical records, Doctor Burak Tatlı asked, "How long have these seizures been going on?" We said that Fatih had had these seizures for ten years and that we tried all sorts of medication, namely Topamax, Depoken, Kepra, and Sinakten. After looking at us, Dr. Burak shook his head and said, "You have lost all these years for nothing." He said, "None of these drugs are fully effective in Fatih's seizure type." He said that there is another drug called Banzel, which is not available in Turkey, and that this drug would immediately stop Fatih's seizures if we could get it and use it.

We could hardly believe our ears. It sounded like a miracle. The doctor gave a sample of the drug he had in his hand and said, "Start this right away. You should see a change in two days." He said it would be good if we applied to a medicine delivery unit abroad and got the medicine without wasting any time.

When we got home, the first thing we did was make Fatih drink the new medicine. We observed him every second with great excitement and hope. His forehead had hit the ground after his most recent seizure, and the scars and stitches on his face were still fresh. Our prayers were to find a cure for this affliction. As the doctor said, Fatih's seizures stopped at the end of the second day.

It was a miracle. We couldn't believe it. It was almost as if God saw our haste, answered our prayers rising from our painful hearts, and rewarded us with such a reward. Fatih's eyes looked brighter than ever. We were happier than a child.

The miracle depended on our ability to get the medicine delivered from abroad. Even though we applied to the relevant unit of the Ministry of Health, there needed to be more development. Every time we called, we received the response that they were waiting for the medication. The sample drugs we had were about to run out. Desperate, we knocked on every door we could to find a solution. However, dozens of people would get the same answer: "This medicine is not available in Turkey." Finally, a pharmacist said that this medicine was sold "under the counter" in Aksaray, and we could get it temporarily from there.

Indeed, I had found the medicine, even though a box cost half my monthly salary. When I got home, we had a feast. But the medicine package needed morning and night was only enough for three weeks. I thought of contacting my friends who were on foreign assignments in Europe.

One of my friends in the Air Force, Lieutenant Colonel Huseyin, who was on permanent duty in Germany, came to our rescue. Although I met with him during our four and a half months of Command College training in Istanbul, we had become close like brothers. He had a calm disposition and an extraordinary love for his duty. As soon as he delivered the news, "My dear Mehmet! Don't worry, I will do what is necessary and find the medicine," he hung up. Three weeks later, four boxes of medicine reached us. That's what friendship is. Despite my insistence, he did not take the money for the drugs, and he reproached me by saying, "Fatih is our son as much as yours," and I was very touched.

You can guess what happened to such a magnanimous and valiant officer after July 15. Like all well-trained, honest, and hardworking officers, he would be dismissed from his profession, which he loved so much, and he was declared a traitor. Even though he was representing his state thousands of miles away from his country on the night of July 15, he also was a victim of this treacherous trap.

The improvement in Fatih's health renewed our joy, and a separate peace filled our home. Just as I thought everything was starting to work out, I was beginning to experience severe abdominal pain. After a painful night of unbearable pain, I ended up in the emergency room of GATA Military Hospital in Istanbul. We left the house in a hurry. I thought I would be given painkillers or a serum, some tests would be done, and we would return home. However, the pain became so severe in the following hours that I had to be hospitalized.

Despite all kinds of tests and analyses, the doctors could not identify the source of the pain. Biopsies were taken because doctors suspected it could be cancer, and further tests were performed. I was not allowed to eat or drink water and was only fed with serum.

This situation damaged not only my health but also my morale. "While everything was getting better, when Fatih was starting to get better, why did this have to happen?" I growled. Dozens of visitors came to the hospital daily, and the personnel of the Naval Staff College and the Military Academies flocked to GATA.

Once again, Hatice's burden increased. She always cared for the children and supported me at every opportunity. My brother Emrah also came to Istanbul to help me. The longer I stayed in the hospital, I thought of many bad scenarios and wondered what kind of life my wife and children would have if something happened to me. This feeling consumed me. My body, which had been running for years, was tired.

The most frustrating aspect of the illness was that the cause of the pain was not found.

Thankfully, our friends did not abandon us. One of my classmates, Murat, stayed with me for two nights, and Burak Akcay stayed for one night. We had a deep friendship with Murat going back to the Naval Academy years. Burak and I were working as lecturers at the Naval Staff College. He was an ambitious and hardworking officer. He was a submarine officer and was assigned as a lecturer at the Naval Staff College due to his health problems. The night he accompanied me, even though I insisted he goes, he stayed, and we chatted all night.

I cannot describe the disappointment I felt in my heart when I heard that Burak was one of those who helped the regime in the treacherous July 15 plot. On our night at the hospital, he said that the essential thing in the world was health and family; he expected his career to suffer after his health problems began. However, as a reward for his support to the regime, he would first be assigned to a foreign post and later promoted to rear admiral. Once again, I understood that people who seemed to be friends and stayed close to us were imposters aiming to gather information about us, and they were making dark plans to implement them when the day came.

After ten days of treatment, doctors stated that the sudden deterioration in my health was most likely due to food poisoning. My pain subsided, and I was finally discharged. It felt like I was reborn. I appreciated the value of health better, but our hectic life continued from where it left off.

At the end of the year, while Hatice graduated from Istanbul Aydin University as a preschool teacher, I completed the doctoral proficiency exam. Fatih's seizures were over, and Hakan had a successful year in school and on his swim team. No matter how rough the road was, God somehow helped those who set out on the road and did not leave the efforts of his servants unrewarded. I saw this clearly as I looked at my family.

The Military Academies came to the end of the academic year, and we successfully graduated from the 2014-2015 class. Brilliant, young staff officers were appointed to their new posts, armed with cutting-edge knowledge and skills, with exceptional motivation for duty and great hopes for the future. However, this class, destined to build and lead the end of the Turkish Navy, would go down in history as the last staff officer to graduate from the Naval Staff College.

We had completed our preparations to start our new assignment in Norfolk, VA, with the peace and comfort of having a successful graduation.

On July 21, 2015, we boarded a plane from Istanbul to United States. Our dream was to represent our country in the best way during this two-year tour at the NATO Headquarters in the United States. We dreamed of returning to Turkey with a broader vision, increased knowledge, new experiences, and better motivation to serve our country, military, and navy. Like the young officers we just graduated from the Naval Staff College, our dreams would be crushed and stolen, and our two-year journey in America would be exiled for many years.

THE PHOENIX
Virginia, USA, 2017

As time passed quickly in the US, we were trying to get used to our new lives, and even though our bodies were in America, our minds and souls continued to live through the struggle for life in Turkey. Every time we came together with friends, we talked about Turkey. We hoped that something would change, the truth would come to light, and tens of thousands of innocent people would regain their freedom, families, and jobs.

The news from our homeland covered the light of hope like dark clouds, pushing us into a spiral of pessimism. The regime increased persecution, and new detentions and arrests amounted to hundreds of thousands daily. People were looking for a solution to leave their country where they were born and raised and served for many years. However, that scary journey to the unknown was also thorny without being able to say goodbye to your loved ones by stuffing your entire life and dreams in a backpack.

Some lives were ended by drowning in the cold waters of the Maritsa, and others in the dark waters of the Aegean. Not a day passed without news of death or the cry of people who were caught trying to cross the border and were subjected to various tortures. Was human life really this invaluable? All the suffering, years of effort, and hopes were destroyed by a mad regime that sought nothing but its interests. Saplings that had begun to bear fruit were uprooted, and thorny cacti and poisonous hemlocks were planted in their place.

Our German friend told the story of an Iranian family who had to leave their country after the Iranian revolution. Like us, they look at the news almost daily and ask themselves, "Did anything change today? Can we return to our country soon after this order ends?" Each year, their hopes faded, and they were dying out. He advised us to be prepared for a similar fate and to focus on building a new life.

There was some truth in what he said. The regime in Turkey wanted to establish a structure similar to the one in Iran and was implementing the system there. The country was dragged into a climate of fear, and the exploitation of national and religious feelings became the immutable rule of daily politics. A militant law enforcement agency, which controlled every neighborhood under the name of the guard corps, was formed. The constitutional order was destroyed daily, and every word from Erdogan's lips was made more potent than the law and even the Constitution. In this environment, those who dared to speak out were taken to police custody or even imprisoned. Unions and television stations were shut down; journalists and dissidents were arrested.

The country had turned into a lively market on the one hand and a place of plunder on the other, where millions of dollars of veiled funds had been used to cover up the regime's crimes without being held accountable. The National Security Agency, headed by Hakan Fidan, whom Erdogan calls his "secret pot," had turned into a "National Destruction of Humanity." It went on a manhunt, and people were abducted in broad daylight in the middle of the streets. The abducted were tortured for months in torture centers said to be in Ankara, then left in the woods or by the roadside, later to be detained by the police.

After months of torture, the testimonies of these individuals all had similar statements. It was as if they were memorized. Their relatives were asked not to hire a lawyer or raise this issue. When presented by lawyers or their relatives in court, the abductions and torture were dismissed by the court committees. The regime's judiciary cooperated with the structure that abducted and tortured people. It would be delusional to expect the country to change quickly.

It was difficult to accept what happened and watch the country come to this state as a soldier. It was necessary to fight against the regime somehow. Our fighting options were limited in the current circumstances.

I hope millions of people whose brains were polluted by the regime will one day say, "Alas!" A violent struggle against the deceived masses was precisely what the government wanted. But the means of work within democracy and legal rules were utterly exhausted. The only solution would be to explain to the world how dangerous this regime is and how it poses a significant threat to regional and global stability. I decided to write an article that presented facts to reveal these realities.

In July 2017, on the anniversary of that black day, I gathered the documents to support the article. I tried to reveal how the regime is taking the country and its consequences for the EU, the USA, and NATO. I explained in detail what dangers await Turkey, which is moving into a strategic partnership with Russia and Iran. Most people fighting for human rights were trying to explain the tragedy in Turkey and opening Twitter and YouTube accounts. In my opinion, human rights violations are experienced in every part of the world, and this does not occupy an important place on the agenda of democratic and prosperous countries. Focusing only on human rights will not yield results. Our ideas matched with Captain İsmail, who was dismissed after July 15 while he was the Turkish Naval Attaché in Washington, D.C. We believed that dealing with the issue in terms of international relations would bring results. Captain Ismail came to visit us in Virginia from Washington, and we put our heads together and came up with a road map. I would finalize the article, and we would publish it in a prominent newspaper or a university press. In the second step, we would set up a Twitter account and website called Turkey Studies.

We would address Turkey-oriented issues from multiple perspectives and focus on activating decision-makers. Our expectation was not to overthrow the regime with a de facto intervention but to impose sanctions against human rights violations and unlawfulness by the international community and turn its reaction into concrete steps.

If the freedom of the press and expression existed, the truth would come out, and who was guilty would be clear. The regime was using all the means and pressure tools to prevent this. The Parliamentary Investigation Commission, formed to investigate July 15, could not question the leading actors of that night.

Erdogan, the Chief of General Staff, Heads of the Armed Services, the Undersecretary of the National Intelligence Agency, and the Head of Religious Affairs did not bother to show up in person during the investigation hearings. Their written statements were accepted as testimony. It was a great contradiction that the main actors of the most critical and dark night in the history of the Republic would not testify before a commission claiming to try to illuminate the event. They would not answer any questions!

What could a report have completed in this way illuminate?

They knew very well that if these actors were questioned independently, the dirty side of the issue and the inconsistencies and betrayals in their statements would come to light.

Our task was to ask what they could not ask, to say what they could not, and to light to this dirty game. I finished the article in ten days. We were excited. We thought those who read the article would understand the situation, see the facts, and eventually, something would change. That would not be the case at all. We were still waiting for a response from the newspapers we contacted to publish the article, and as the days passed, we better understood our path's difficulty. Since our website was just set up, an article published here could only reach several hundred people.

All the hard work we spent, and our hopes attached to it would be in vain. When the clouds above us were getting dark, my classmate Commander Metin from the Naval War College, who was working on his Ph.D. in Sweden, came to our rescue. He said he could forward the article to his university's editorial board chairman and publish it if the academic board approves it. It was the best news I'd heard in a year. This development was proof of the principle that "if you make an effort and set out with the right intention, God will open doors for you that you never even thought of." We met with Metin almost daily and were excitedly asking if there was a response from the editorial board.

Commander Metin finally gave the good news and said that the article would be published in the university's journal, and the journal would be sent to many vital institutions in Europe. With this article, we can reach decision-makers and policymakers and explain the gravity of the situation.

Finally, Commander Metin sent a photo of the magazine's cover page and the page on which the article was published. With Captain İsmail, we published the article by citing the source on our website. The wife of a colleague living in France said that she could translate the theme into Italian and French. Thus, we were able to expand the audience we could reach. I tried to contribute to getting more readers by sending the article to my colleagues at NATO by e-mail.

As expected, our post on our "Turkey Studies" site reached only a few hundred people, but we decided to continue publishing our new works here to keep on our mission. Every article we wrote, and every post we made was a plea to the owner of divine justice. These were just a drop. We kept our hopes by saying, "The power that gives even a butterfly's wing the power to influence the world will not remain indifferent to our small but sincere steps."

Building a new life abroad was much more complicated than it seemed. Even though I was selling on Amazon, I couldn't make it to the end of the month, and the debts were growing like a snowball daily. I bought a truck of supplies from an auction site which consisted of overstock and customer returns. I started planning to expand my business by renting a warehouse near our house. The materials cost about $6,500, including shipping costs. The original retail prices of the products in the document sent by the company were stated to be $74,000.

Even if I sold the items for a quarter of the price, I believed I would make a substantial profit. Renting a warehouse was just the beginning. The cost of the shelves to store the goods was $2,000. Instead of buying the frames, we decided to purchase the materials I needed from Home Depot and create the shelves ourselves with the help of YouTube.

Working as a family, we built a row of shelves every day. The most beneficial aspect of this process was that Hakan and I spent the whole day together as father and son. We made up for the years we were apart due to long deployments. We managed to finish ten stacks of shelves for $400.

Our warehouse was ready, and we could store the materials we ordered. When the products arrived, our feelings were festive. We opened each pallet with great excitement, and we wanted to see the products as soon as possible, organize them, and place them on the shelves. But we were disappointed with every palette we opened. Eighty percent of the products consisted of returns. We had to pay rent for the warehouse every month, and we gave the last money to so many products with a very low probability of being sold.

Every morning, I posted ads on OfferUp and other digital sales platforms and made only one or two sales per day. Even though I tried not to show it, I was very stressed. Every time I entered the warehouse, a pile of products felt like they started to fall on top of me. I had to change something. Since I couldn't attract customers to the products, I had to take the products to the customers.

One Ramadan morning, we prepared and decided to open a kiosk in a Flea Market. We got up early and rented a place in the market. While Hakan waited at our booth, I made several trips to the car and brought the goods to set up on our kiosk. After four trips back and forth, we filled our cubicle and waited with great hope for customers to come. People were staring at our counter, and the hours were ticking before we could sell anything. It was hot and humid, and because we were fasting, our mouths were dry. I would have sat and cried if I wasn't trying to be strong for my son. But I had to look strong.

At that time, Hatice came with Fatih and Nilgun. The dark clouds above me dissipated with their arrival, and my world was lit up again. Despite everything, we were together, we were connected, we were free, and we had hope. Nothing could be more valuable than this, even if we are abroad or under challenging conditions. I thought, "As long as they are with me and we are healthy, I will try a thousand new jobs, if necessary, but I still will not leave them desperate for care."

We only sold a few products for half the price and moved the goods back to the warehouse. When we returned home, at the iftar table prepared by my wife, I forgot all the gloom of the day and completed the day with gratitude and thanks. Every day new doors are opened, and new fortunes are given. I will chase after my destiny without ever getting tired.

I would never bow to the regime as an aspiring officer and diplomat. This was not only my struggle but also the struggle of many of my brothers-in-arms whose freedoms were stolen. The government had slandered us many times to deceive the public. They spread the slander that we did not deserve our positions. They thought that when we were dismissed from our profession, we would be beggars and fall at their feet and beg.

We had to succeed, stand firm, and start over without needing anyone. If I fed my children with the money I deserved, it didn't matter how big the meals were. That night, I decided to do a job I had been thinking about for a long time. Like many young friends, I would work as a taxi driver and pizza delivery driver. Being a taxi driver was challenging in a city where I was deputy branch head at NATO. I thought about what it would be like to deliver an order to the door of an unqualified and incompetent person sent by the regime or to come across one of them and be their chauffeur. I decided that being a taxi driver, a flea market seller, or a pizza delivery person with my honor would be my most valuable badge on this uniform.

I told my wife I would start driving a taxi the following day. She looked me in the eyes, swallowed her breath, and then tried to encourage me by saying, "I hope it will be for the best."

She had a lot to say; she was sad, but she preferred to keep quiet not to upset me. She made sacrifices throughout her life, raised our children alone, and shouldered the burden of my long deployments by saying, "It's for the best interest of the nation." She supported me in a way worthy of an officer's wife. She could return to Turkey and settle a life with her father and brothers.

That day I left the house as a taxi driver. Hatice was used to saying goodbye to me. She had sent her husband all over the world. I could read by her demeanor that she was proud of me, and she said, "Come home as soon as possible." When I looked in the rear-view mirror, my family again said goodbye as if I was leaving for a deployment.

A few minutes later, my first customers got into the car. They were three sailors, each one around 25-30 years old. They were back from a deployment and were talking about what to do. "Are you a sailor?" I asked hesitantly.

"Yes," he replied, sitting across from me.

"You are fortunate. You are living in a moment that very few, if any, other sailors had the chance before," I said with a smile. They interrupted their conversation and looked at me curiously. Without further ado, I said, "I'm a sailor too. I quit my job as a captain a few months ago, and a captain is driving you right now." There was a profound silence. The young sailors were stunned. Their expectations were a short Uber ride. "How so?" asked the middle one. I could see the surprise in his eyes in the rearview mirror.

I talked about what happened in Turkey and how and under what conditions I left the profession. What I described was too strange to be digested in a drive for only a few minutes. It was like a movie scene. It was my turn to be surprised when the journey ended, and they got out of the car. Three young sailors lined up side by side and greeted me solemnly with a sharp military salute. It was an indescribable feeling. A few hours ago, I was reluctant to be a taxi driver, but now I was greeted by three young sailors who said, "Don't worry, sir, everything will be fine."

I had mixed feelings. An officer dismissed from his profession and declared a traitor in his own country was shown the highest respect in a foreign country. It was as thought-provoking as it was honorable. As I was leaving, I saw in the rearview mirror that they were still saluting me. Tears were already running down my cheeks. I returned home without any other customers. I didn't want anything to distract me from that moment and my feelings.

Time is a tricky concept. The days we say won't pass, pass without us even realizing it, and the days that we say will end as soon as possible would drag along forever. Once again, I saw that time, location, and our experiences were connected.

It was real friends who made life easier. This process taught us that we should question the concepts of kinship and friendship. We learned that those who can stay around us when we are exposed to all kinds of quirks of life are our true friends. Another opportunist who used to call and ask when I was on duty constantly disappeared one by one once I was purged from the Navy. I learned that true intimacy stems not from blood ties but from heart ties.

We became very close with friends who were also discharged from the military. In Virginia, everyone was a comrade to each other, and whoever needed help had someone rushing to his aid. Everyone was also trying to support friends and families deprived of their freedom in Turkey. Friendship in arms had turned into a friendship of fate. What an honor it was to be among these large-hearted people. I often prayed to God, saying, "Thank you for keeping me on the right side." God made those whom he loves loved by his servants as well. Our friendship with our American friends developed daily, and they supported us wholeheartedly. Their friendship relieved our homesickness and gave us fresh air in distant and foreign lands.

Work was the main agenda item for all of us. Even though we lived in a low-rent house, earning at least three to four thousand dollars a month was necessary to cover the expenses. Since Fatih and Nilgun had health problems, doctor's examinations and medications increased the cost. The fact that I had to take a regular job with health insurance and personal benefits instead of an unstable or day-to-day job such as a taxi driver remained in my mind. Due to our legal status, we could not apply to sectors close to our field of education and expertise. Jobs in our profession require a "confidential" level of clearance or at least a Green Card.

One of our young friends, an aviator discharged after coming to the US for his graduate education, started to work as an "operations manager" at Amazon. This development gave us great hope. I was intimidated by the recruitment interview processes and beginning a job in a different industry. I updated my resume to include my twenty years of military experience and graduate and entrepreneurial experience. When I went to Amazon's website to apply for a job, I saw open positions in every state. "How about the idea of going to another state?" I asked my wife. When I asked her, she said, "As long as we have a job, I'm willing to go to Alaska with you."

I applied for operations manager positions in several states. I was eagerly awaiting the result. One of our American friends, Karen, was a career counselor, and she said we could do a couple of mock-up interviews. This was a great idea. Although I had a good resume, I had to know the job interview techniques specific to civilian life and American culture and present my qualifications in the best possible way. We had several mock-up interviews with Karen over the phone and face-to-face. These experiences and the feedback she provided would benefit me in the coming days.

I was gathering information on Amazon, watching Jeff Bezos' YouTube videos, and reading his letters to shareholders. In this exciting process, we had a feverish preparation as a family. Hakan gave me his room and wanted a place to study to support my work and practices. Long after, I got an email from Amazon. They were asking for the appropriate dates for the phone call. I was so excited. It would be my first job application interview experience. I chose a date a few days later. The time passed slowly. I was often testing myself. My wife and children had almost memorized my statements.

The interview day had come. "Let's hope for the best!" I said as I went to the head of the table. I had an interview with an Amazon operations manager named Haley. It took about forty minutes, and before she hung up the phone, she told me they would get back to me in five business days at the latest. The interview went better than I expected. I could answer the questions satisfactorily, managed to overcome my excitement, and spoke in a natural and confident tone. Being able to express oneself in a foreign language was a difficult task. My preparations worked, and I completed the interview without difficulty. I kept repeating the same thing inside of me: Keep putting in the effort; then, many doors will open.

We slept in the same room with my wife and children that evening. We dreamed together. If we get this job, where do we move to, what do we do, and what kind of life awaits us?

Two days later, I learned that I had successfully passed the phone interview at Amazon and had to travel to Seattle, Washington, for the face-to-face interview. Words cannot explain my happiness at that moment. After all the hardships, we needed success like this. This meant passing the first step of the job application and the certification of my experience, education, and skills.

Amazon was one of the largest companies in the world, and I had applied for a management position that could be considered as a senior in the company. We shared this news only with those around us. I still had to complete a face-to-face interview. I thought that if I failed, people would be discouraged, and the days passed quickly.

I bought my plane ticket and packed my suitcase. The meeting was to begin at 7:00 am on Wednesday, October 9, 2017. I had scheduled a connecting flight Tuesday morning from Norfolk to Washington, DC, then to Seattle. I would be there on Tuesday afternoon and spend the evening resting after seeing the building where I would interview.

We all went to Norfolk Airport together. I encountered the first surprise of the day in the waiting room. The Washington DC flight was delayed, and officials needed to know when the plane would take off. I explained the situation to the officials and told them that the flight was vital for me. Although they said, they did their best with a few memorized sentences and were working on getting the plane to take off quickly, the same even after two hours.

It was close to noon, and I was still in Norfolk. I again told the staff to do something urgently; otherwise, I would miss my job interview. They said they could send me via New York, and I could be in Seattle around 9:00 pm local time. I had no other choice. Norfolk was a small airport with no alternative flight plan in sight. I accepted the suggestion.

In the afternoon, passenger admissions started for the New York flight. I said goodbye to my family and got on the plane. After 30 minutes, I encountered another delay. Although the passengers took their places, the New York flight was not taking off. The aircraft had to take off so I could catch the plane to Seattle. Every five minutes, I would ask the cabin crew when we would be leaving, and each time I would get the answer, "In a little while," I was getting very worried.

After a 45-minute delay, the plane finally took off. If everything went as planned, I would have 15 minutes to catch the flight to Seattle. I needed to ensure I was using my time effectively while passengers were getting off or looking for the transfer point. Finally, the plane landed, the doors opened, and I got out of the plane quickly.

To find the gate before the Seattle plane took off, I started running like I was running a hundred meters race. I was running as if someone was chasing me between the curious looks of the people around me. I was sweating when I threw myself on the apron where the Seattle plane was. I handed the boarding pass to the cabin crew. I was so scared, so out of breath, that I couldn't speak. I was stunned when he said that the door was closed and that he could not take passengers. "I had to change my plane just to make it to this flight, and I had to run non-stop for fifteen minutes because of the airline delays. And you are telling me you can't take me on the plane?" I snapped in a rebellious tone.

My anxiety and excitement turned to anger. I could see through the window that the plane had not yet left the apron and had not even started its engines. The official insisted that the boarding process was completed. Another official, who saw my rush and anger, approached us and tried to understand the situation. Repeating similar sentences, he said there was nothing they could do now and that they could not let in or out passengers except for emergencies since the plane door was already closed. He added that he could transfer me to another plane that leaves at midnight. I couldn't believe what had happened.

It was like a force was blocking me. I had no choice but to accept the offer. I could have made the situation worse by getting angry, and I would have missed this opportunity. I sat in a corner, trying to calm down, and waited for the other plane to take off. However, I planned to sleep at the hotel this time, get up early, and make my final preparations.

I waited for the next flight at New York Airport, about three thousand miles from Seattle. The worst part was the nagging question, "Will these disruptions continue?" After a few hours of waiting, the passenger boarding process for the Seattle flight began. This time, unlike before, the plane took off on time.

I was exhausted from the stress and the hustle and bustle I had experienced in the early hours. My eyelids were too heavy to carry. Although my eyes forced me to sleep, my mind was busy and alert, worried I would make it to the interview in time. My only consolation was that there was a three-hour time zone difference between the East Coast and the West Coast.

The plane landed in Seattle around 1:30 am local time. I rented a car from the airport, and after a 20-minute drive, I reached the hotel at around three in the morning. I told the receptionist that I had to get up at 5.30. I went to my room. I had only two hours to sleep and refresh and rest my mind. After setting multiple alarms on the phone at intervals of a few minutes, I put my head on the pillow.

I still couldn't understand what I was going through. I must have fallen asleep as soon as I closed my eyes because after what seemed like a brief moment, I was startled by the phone's sound.

When I heard the receptionist say, "Good morning, it's 5:30," I couldn't believe how two hours had passed, like a few seconds, and the time had come. I got out of bed. As I did before the inspections or similar special days during my military service, I carefully shaved and ironed my clothes again. Breakfast consisting of a strong coffee and a cheese sandwich made me wake up and come to my senses. I was suggesting to myself, "Forget what happened yesterday. Look ahead and focus."

When I arrived at the specified address, I had 15 minutes to spare. Four other people were waiting. As far as I understand, they made a group of people with military careers and invited them to meet simultaneously. We met and wished each other good luck. One of the candidates, Zach, was in his thirties and had served as a nuclear power engineer on an aircraft carrier. Luis retired from the marine. The only non-military candidate was Marcus. He worked at Target stores for many years. The manager who greeted us explained the interview process and said that we were not competing and that each candidate would be evaluated independently. I completed the math test in 15 minutes and was taken to my first interview. The official, who introduced himself as a human resources manager, sympathetically recommended that I be comfortable responding to questions naturally. Like the hot coffee I drank in the morning, this warmed and relaxed me. This intimate introduction took the stress off me and reduced my excitement.

After three different interviews, the interview process was completed. Even though I looked into their eyes and monitored their mouths to see if I could get a clue about the outcome, all three managers said nothing except that they would get back to me in five business days. I gave appropriate answers to the questions and conveyed myself and my qualities naturally and sincerely. Each meeting constituted an additional experience for the next, and when I came to the last interview, I left my excitement behind and answered the questions with the utmost confidence. I consoled myself with the thought that even if the outcome were negative, it would be a great experience.

It was around noon when I got back to the hotel. I called Hatice, told her my interview went well, and returned to the hotel. I had a return flight at midnight. It would be nice to visit Seattle, but I was so mentally and physically tired that I fell into a quiet and peaceful sleep without rushing to get anywhere.

A few days passed, and we were excited to see if we would get a result every time the phone rang. It wasn't easy. I lost my job a year ago, and now I was about to start a career that could be considered equivalent to prestige. The longer the wait, the longer I felt it wouldn't work out. I tried not to show it even though I was worried.

The phone call we were waiting for came precisely five days later. Our daughter Nilgun had therapy at home, and my wife and I were focused on her very carefully. The lady who called said, "Congratulations, you have completed the interviews. Welcome to Amazon!" We felt great joy. We hugged each other with Nilgun and Hatice in our arms.

We even forgot that Nilgun's therapist was at home. She looked at us in surprise, trying to understand what had happened. She was as happy as we were when we shared the news. This news gave hope to our friends and us in a similar situation and trying to establish a new life.

After July 15th, they took everything from us and wanted to crumple us up like rags with one line on a list, equivalent to a death warrant. As one of my commanders said years ago, gold did not lose value by falling into the trash; on the contrary, it is more valuable for those who found it in the trash. The tree of hope, which we cultivated without giving up under the conditions of exile, finally gave its first fruit.

This news was the harbinger of the spring, not only for us but for many other friends in similar positions. After that day, good news began to come from many places. Our friends in exile were achieving successes that can be pointed out one after another, producing projects and receiving job offers from very large institutions and companies. Every good news made us more hopeful and empowered.

While this was the case in exile, the persecution continued in Turkey. The country's most educated and well-equipped people, whose numbers exceeded one hundred thousand and who were labeled as "Decree-Law members," could not get results from the jobs they applied for due to the pressure and fear spread by the regime. Despite all the obstacles, these people do not resort to unlawful ways or means. These people, who had excelled in their white-collar jobs for many decades, would not hesitate to start up in any blue-collar job and make their living. Some of these honorable people were bazaar sellers, and some were peddlers, but they worked any job under any circumstance. Those put behind bars were not giving up their hopes or dreams. Thousands of them applied and graduated from very prestigious colleges when they were in jail, got the highest scores in the exams, graduated with honors, learned several languages, and kept themselves busy with personal development. Because they still believe that one day, the cruelty of the Erdogan regime will end just like any other dictatorship, and they were preparing for these days. They were like diamonds in the making under the heavy pressure of the regime's cruelty. The government was resorting to greater violence and hatred daily. Still, these innocent people behind bars shined brighter, like diamonds formed under high heat and pressure, and illuminated even the darkest dungeons with their light.

As a statesman and soldier in exile, my dream was for our nation to embrace the truth, care for its children, each worth a diamond, and disperse the dark clouds over my country with their light to sail to a brighter future. We still had a long way to go, things to do, and good days to see. My lips were screaming that one sentence stuck in my memory from the first day, "Not yet."

Mehmet DAGCI

The author's life journey began in Yahyali, a small town in Anatolia. He started working at the age of nine due to the separation of his parents and financial conditions. He entered the Turkish Naval Academy in 1992 and served his country and world peace for twenty-four years.

The author, who served as one of the youngest frigate commanders of the Turkish Navy, participated in many international operations within the scope of NATO and the UN. In these duties, he had the opportunity to get to know different geographies and cultures and to work with colleagues from other countries.

He completed his master's degrees in business administration in the US and international relations in Turkey. He studied NATO's strategic transformation needs within the scope of his doctoral education in political science. He represented Turkey at the French Naval Task Force Headquarters and NATO Transformation Command.

Despite his son's health problems, his effort to hold on to life and his joy in life has always been a source of inspiration for the author. The author, who frequently emphasizes that having special children is a privilege despite difficulties, has included many details on this issue in his book.

The author had to say goodbye to his uniform as a Navy Captain as a victim of the witch hunt that started after July 15. He held on to life again with his wife and three children in the US, where he still lives. He continued to list his achievements, from being a taxi driver to a senior management position at Amazon.

Aiming to be the voice of hundreds of thousands of innocent people deprived of their freedom, the author wrote several articles describing the lawlessness and authoritarianism in Turkey. In this book, he wrote about the events that took place in the recent past, through his own life story, from the perspective of a soldier and diplomat.

Printed in Great Britain
by Amazon

23319249R00158